FURPHIES AND WHIZZ-BANGS

ANZAC SLANG FROM THE GREAT WAR

AMANDA LAUGESEN

C.E.W. Bean, Gallipoli

So I have left old Anzac
fond of the place. I have
enjoyable times there in
friends; or going round t
that I ever liked shells
to put up with them as mu
toothache

OXFORD

OXFORD
UNIVERSITY PRESS

Oxford University Press is a department of the University of Oxford.

It furthers the University's objective of excellence in research, scholarship, and education by publishing worldwide. Oxford is a registered trademark of Oxford University Press in the UK and in certain other countries.

Published in Australia by
Oxford University Press
253 Normanby Road, South Melbourne, Victoria 3205, Australia

National Library of Australia Cataloguing-in-Publication data

Laugesen, Amanda, author.
Furphies and whizz-bangs: Anzac slang from the great war / Amanda Laugesen.

9780195597356 (paperback)

English language—Australia—Slang.
Soldiers—Australia—Language. English language—Australia—History.
English language—Social aspects—Australia.

427.994

Edited by Craig MacKenzie
Cover image by Australian War Memorial, POS982·002
Cover design by Kim Ferguson
Text design by Kim Ferguson
Typeset by diacriTech
Proofread by Greg Alford
Printed by Markono Print Media Pte Ltd, Singapore

CONTENTS

HOW TO USE THIS BOOK

A comprehensive word list can be found at the end of the book. This list contains all words that have their own entry (in **bold**), as well as terms mentioned briefly within introductions or entries (in *italics*). Please refer to this list to locate a particular term.

Each chapter covers a particular theme, with specific words discussed in alphabetical entries within each chapter. The headword and its variants are given in **bold**, cross-references to terms with their own entries are in SMALL CAPITAL LETTERS, and slang terms that are mentioned but not given their own entry are in *italics*. Quotations are given to demonstrate usage, as well as to suggest something of the context of a term; full references to all books and manuscript collections can be found in the bibliography at the end of the book. All newspaper sources have been sourced through Trove, using the National Library of Australia's digitised newspaper collections. All soldier and troopship publications mentioned in the text are located in the Australian War Memorial collections in Canberra. Please note that all original punctuation and spelling in quotations have been retained.

A number of dictionaries of Great War slang exist. These are discussed in some detail in the concluding chapter. References are made to these and other dictionaries within individual entries for terms included in this book. In all instances, the bibliography contains the full title and particular edition that was consulted in researching this book. The *Oxford English Dictionary* is referred to in the text as *OED*; the *OED Online* resource has been used, and is available at http://www.oed.com/. This book also makes use of research conducted for both the first and second editions of the *Australian National Dictionary*, and the various databases and collections held at the Australian National Dictionary Centre at the Australian National University in Canberra.

A work such as this relies heavily on lexicographical collection and research undertaken in the past, in several instances by veterans of the Great War. The reader is encouraged to seek out these earlier works, in particular W.H. Downing's *Digger Dialects* (1919; reprinted in 1990 with annotations by J.M. Arthur and W.S. Ramson), A.G. Pretty's *Glossary of Slang and Peculiar Terms used in the A.I.F.* (available online at http://andc.anu.edu.au/australian-words/aif-slang), and John Brophy and Eric Partridge's *Songs and*

Slang of the British Soldier: 1914–1918 (1931). These collections provide veterans' perspectives on the language that are invaluable. Some of the words they record cannot be found elsewhere, and their work stands as a testimony to the war that they experienced and a language that they knew.

ACKNOWLEDGMENTS

This book made use of the resources of the Australian National Dictionary Centre at the Australian National University, Canberra, including material that has been collected for the first and second editions of the *Australian National Dictionary*. It also makes use of the collections of the National Library of Australia (digital and print), and the Australian War Memorial. I would like to thank the staff of both institutions for assistance.

Several people read and commented on the draft, for which I am very grateful. Thanks to Bruce Moore, Damien Browne, Julia Robinson, and Mark Gwynn for their invaluable feedback. Jennifer Oxley and Christina Greer provided assistance with several research and copy-editing tasks.

I would also like to thank France Meyer from the Centre for Arab and Islamic Studies at the Australian National University for her help with queries about etymologies relating to Arabic.

The author and the publisher wish to thank the following copyright holders for reproduction of their material: Australian War Memorial: p. 1 ART19666, p. 16 PB1015, p. 42 H03357, p. 73 ART94726, p. 85 P02282.044, p. 103 E04290, p. 122 E00233, p. 155 E03412, p. 169 P08003.015, p. 196 B01971, p. 215 J00360; p. 230 reproduced by permission of the Australian War Memorial and the Australian Army History Unit; p. 182 reproduced by permission of the Smythe Family, from www.smythe.id.au.

Every effort has been made to trace the original source of copyright material contained in this book. The publisher will be pleased to hear from copyright holders to rectify any errors or omissions.

Introduction

Words from the Big Stoush: Tracing the language of Australian soldiers

The latest Furphy. or The Square Deincurd Ad.

Australia went to war in 1914. The vast majority of soldiers were volunteers with no prior experience of military life. After enlistment, they were initiated into strange and different worlds: the world of the military with its own rituals and habits, the world of war with its excitements and terrors, and the new and sometimes confronting worlds of Egypt, France, England, and other countries where they travelled.

To make sense of these new worlds was at least in part also to begin to comprehend, even create, a new language. Words were a means of coming to terms with their experiences: slang terms as euphemisms for the horrors of the battlefield; old British Army slang that initiated a new soldier into army life; corruptions of French and Arabic in order to communicate with people who spoke little English.

This book explores the words and language of Australian soldiers during the Great War. It is mostly concerned with slang, but there were also new words that came into Standard English during the war with which Australians became familiar. The book defines and explains these words and terms, provides examples of their usage by Australian soldiers and on the home front that can help provide insight into the experiences and attitudes of soldiers and civilians, and it seeks to draw out some of the themes and features of this language to provide insight into the social and cultural worlds of Australian soldiers and civilians.

Language provides a way into the culture created by soldiers. It helps us understand how they reacted to, and made sense of, their experiences. It is revealing of the shared public culture of the army and trenches during the war, as well as the private thoughts of soldiers expressed in their diaries and letters. The use of a slang term can sometimes provide insight into a complex range of emotions and responses to war.

Peter Doyle and Julian Walker in their book *Trench Talk*, published in 2012, argue that 'for the core of the experience, there were no words'. (p. 254) There is some truth to this. However, many soldiers could articulate their experiences, if only obliquely, through their slang, and more broadly through their writing of diaries, letters, and soldier publications. Traces of their voices, feelings, and thoughts can be discovered. This book is an attempt to illuminate some of these traces.

Australian soldiers at war

War was declared on 4 August 1914, and recruiting for the Australian Imperial Force (AIF) began a few days later. The AIF was an army of volunteers. Despite two contentious conscription referendums, compulsory enlistment was never introduced in Australia. By the end of the war, over 400,000 Australian men had enlisted, out of a population of approximately four million people. Eighty per cent of those who enlisted served overseas, and over 58,000 died. The war thus had a deep and lasting impact on Australian society.

The first significant military engagement for Australia was at Gallipoli. The campaign against the forces of the Ottoman Empire was ultimately a military failure. In 1915, soldiers landed on the Gallipoli peninsula on 25 April and were evacuated in December that same year. During that time many soldiers died in battle or of illness as they fought the Ottoman Army. Life on the Gallipoli peninsula, during which most soldiers lived in makeshift trenches, was tedious and dangerous; food and sanitation were poor, leading to health problems. Australians fought heroically in small engagements such as Lone Pine and Quinn's Post, but for much of the time soldiers lived in poorly constructed shelters and trenches and faced ongoing artillery and sniper fire from the enemy.

After the evacuation from Gallipoli, many soldiers were sent to the Western Front, arriving in early 1916. More soldiers enlisted back in Australia, swelling the size of the AIF. Some soldiers remained in the Middle Eastern theatre of war, and the first squadrons of the Australian Flying Corps (AFC) would also serve there. The bulk of the Australian forces, however, served in France and Belgium.

Trench warfare on the Western Front was difficult, dangerous, and frustrating. Attacks formed a relatively small part of a soldier's time in the front lines; soldiers mostly lived in dugouts and experienced regular shelling of their positions. Trench life was unpleasant, especially when the weather was bad, with cold and rain making life particularly difficult for soldiers.

Australians fought with distinction in many engagements on the Western Front, including the Somme, Bullecourt, Bapaume, Ypres, Messines, Polygon Wood, Passchendaele, Villers-Bretonneux, Hazebrouck, and Mont St Quentin. They established a reputation for their prowess in battle, but also a reputation for absenteeism, bad behaviour, and insolence. Casualties were high, particularly in 1917, when over 76,000 Australians were killed, wounded, or went missing on the Western Front.

While fighting and trench life formed part of a soldier's experiences, significant periods of time were spent in the back lines or rest areas, where soldiers might engage in a range of activities from manual labour tasks to route marches. Recreational activities might include sports, gambling (which was against military regulations but engaged in anyway), reading, and enjoying theatrical entertainments. Soldiers also enjoyed periods of leave; for Australian soldiers, leave from the Western Front was often spent in England.

In November 1917, the five divisions of the AIF were grouped into an Australian Corps, and then placed under the command of John Monash in May 1918. Australians participated in a number of important engagements in 1918 that stopped the German advance that had begun early in the year. These engagements included Bullecourt and Mont St Quentin. Australians also participated in important engagements in Palestine that year, and assisted in the capture of Damascus.

In Australia, the war was initially greeted with enthusiasm and many patriotic demonstrations. By 1917, it was evident that Australians were becoming tired of war. Few withdrew their support entirely for the war, however; there remained a sense that it was a duty that had to be met. This shift is not surprising: the realisation that the war would not be over quickly as first imagined, and the reality of high rates of casualties after Gallipoli and the ferocious Western Front battles of 1916 and 1917, challenged the support for war that had been shown in 1914 and 1915. The war also created political divisions in Australia. In particular, the issue of recruitment and conscription was contentious and divisive.

In November 1918, peace was declared. Australian soldiers were brought home relatively quickly through 1918 and 1919, and Australian society was left to recover from the impact of the war and the terrible losses that had been incurred.

Tracing the words

In my 2005 book *Diggerspeak: The Language of Australians at War*, a book that looked at the ways in which wars have shaped and contributed to Australian English, I made the observation that this study could only be a work in progress. This has indeed proven to be the case, and this book aims to more closely explore the language generated during the Great War and how it was used by Australians.

Where can we find the words of Australian soldiers, especially their slang? There are many sources for the language used by soldiers. However, it is important to remember that these sources are mediated by a variety of factors, and we have no real means of directly accessing the original oral culture of soldiers. That oral culture has been lost, but traces of it remain.

One of the most important sources for tracing the language of Australian soldiers of the Great War is the many letters and diaries written by soldiers. In these, we can find something of the voices of individual soldiers as they tried to make sense of, and articulate, their war experiences. These sources are rarely completely authentic in terms of fully capturing the oral culture of the trenches, particularly letters that would be read by family members (especially parents and girlfriends). The often coarse language of the camp and the trenches was rarely conveyed, for example; however, soldiers might include a variety of slang terms, sometimes explaining them for their home audience. Diaries more often capture elements of the language of the trenches, including slang terms soldiers were familiar with and used.

It is worth remembering that letters and diaries should not be considered entirely representative of the true feelings or experiences of soldiers. Soldiers might downplay their feelings of fear, or they might choose not to mention some of their recreational activities. Nevertheless, they are valuable sources in which to find a variety of slang terms and the various neologisms produced during the Great War.

Another important source for tracing the language of soldiers is the various periodicals and newspapers produced by soldiers on troopships, in camps, and while in the lines. These 'trench papers' provide a rich insight into the vernacular culture of soldiers. Soldiers eagerly read such publications, as well as sending them home to family members to read, or to keep for when they returned home from the war.

Soldier publications often engaged directly with the everyday life and travails of soldiers, expressing humour and sentiment, and using the pages of such publications as a forum for venting complaints. These periodicals also helped to shape and deliberately promote a particular image of Australian soldiers that they themselves wished to, and did, put forward. Humour, disregard for authority, and pride in their achievements as fighters were all qualities of the Australian soldier promoted within the pages of many of these publications. These publications should therefore be understood as mediating the experiences and culture of soldiers, and consciously shaping particular aspects of, and ideas within, that culture. They are valuable nonetheless because of their frequent presentation of the distinctive slang of the trenches, and because they provide fascinating insights into the soldier culture which soldiers generated for themselves.

Interestingly, these publications suggest the ways in which slang might be used quite self-consciously by soldiers. Slang was much more likely to be used in particular genre forms: the humorous anecdote, especially one that involved an Australian soldier communicating or dealing with a person who was not Australian; and verse both humorous and sentimental. Slang terms sometimes provided a good rhyme, but soldier-poets perhaps also appreciated the aesthetic value of slang, and the way in which some slang terms could conjure up a whole range of emotions and associations. In these trench publications as a whole, Australian language and slang helped to underpin the conscious creation of an Australian soldier identity, and was thus deployed quite deliberately to assist in this.

Yet another worthwhile place to go hunting for the words used by soldiers, as well as civilians, is in the Australian press of the period. The digitisation of Australian newspapers through the National Library of Australia initiative, Trove, has made the job of finding instances of usage of slang and particular words much easier. What this has also revealed is the extent to which certain words were used in Australia during the war (and after) and their popularity, as well as revealing which words did not gain traction. During the war years, many soldiers' letters home were given to local newspapers to print, thus we not only have access to press reports through these newspapers, but also the voices of soldiers.

The use of many slang terms in the press—either through the publication of soldiers' letters home or through news articles written by correspondents—suggests that many Australian civilians became familiar, if sometimes only in passing, with them. While there may have been a gulf of understanding between the fighting front and the home front, this gulf was partially bridged through this common language and the attempt by those at home to understand something of the world inhabited by soldiers.

Finally, another source for identifying words that soldiers might have used is the various glossaries and dictionaries compiled after the war, several of them by veterans of the conflict. These are discussed in detail in the conclusion to this book. Aside from overseas glossaries, the most significant one for the purposes of tracing Australian soldier slang is W.H. Downing's *Digger Dialects*. Compiling a dictionary of slang used by Australian soldiers in 1919, Downing called the slang he collected 'a by-product of the collective imagination of the A.I.F.' (p. vii) Another important Australian source is the *Glossary of Slang and Peculiar Terms in Use in the A.I.F.* (1921–24) compiled by the chief librarian of the Australian

War Museum (now Australian War Memorial), A.G. Pretty. Although borrowing heavily from Downing, the Glossary contains a number of other useful, and in some cases otherwise unrecorded, terms. Such dictionaries are valuable records and guides to the language of Australian soldiers.

The words that aren't there

Collections of slang compiled during and after the war contain many words that are otherwise not found in the contemporary evidence. Each chapter's introduction includes some of these words for which there is very limited evidence, and which otherwise remain obscure.

Also missing from the printed record are some of the words that were not considered fit to print: these include the profanities that were undoubtedly a significant part of the vocabularies of many soldiers. Allusions to these words can be found, mostly through instances of censored words, often represented by dashes. The use of the word Lvкxuy as a substitute for stronger words can also be found. We thus gain an interesting insight into print culture and censorship of the period. Nevertheless, despite censorship, the language of the soldier was alluded to in various ways. The following anecdote is a good example of how the coarse language of soldiers was presented (and even celebrated) in the press, and connected to the stereotypical larrikin Aussie soldier:

> A returned Australian soldier, who had lost his pay-book and had been informed that no money could be paid him till his papers arrived, called several times at headquarters without success. Then his wrath bubbled over, and he addressed the pay-clerks in historic Australianese. 'You Blanketty blanked cold-blank-footers,' he said, 'the blanky likes of you to keep an asterisk soldier who has blanky well fought on the purple fields of adjectival France out of his pay because you're too blinking lazy to look up your blank blank books.' 'Look heah, my dear fellow,' said a youthful and foppishly dressed 'officah,' 'go away, and don't make such a bally row; I won't have it, d'ye know!' The soldier eyed the slim, scented 'sprig of nobility.' 'And who the blanky so-and-so are you?' he queried. 'I'm the lieutenant in charge of this-ah-section,' replied the scented officer. 'Strike-me-bleeding-pink,' was the soldier's answer, 'and I took you for a blinking war-baby!' (*Cumberland Argus and Fruitgrowers' Advocate*, 27 October 1917, p. 6)

W.H. Downing's *Digger Dialects* includes a number of terms that directly suggest the strong language of the soldiers. He includes, for example, terms such as *blow-to-fook*, *bollocks*, *bullsh*, *f.a.* (for *Fanny Adams*, or *Sweet Fanny Adams*, used as a euphemism for 'fuck all'), and *fooker* (to refer to an English private; it is a play on English pronunciation). A.G. Pretty's *Glossary of AIF Slang* includes expressions such as (*to get one's*) *balls in a knot*, 'to lose one's temper', *bullfodder*, *bull shit*, *f.o.q.*, defined as 'fly off, quickly; fuck off quickly', and *pig arse*. Pretty also includes the entry *blank*, *blanky*, *blankety*, with the definition 'words used as a substitute for foul language'. These two dictionaries provide us with the best evidence of this element of soldiers' language that otherwise is difficult to trace.

The uses of slang

This dictionary is primarily concerned with slang terms, although some Standard English terms are included. Wars, especially the two World Wars, have been very productive of slang. What are the functions of slang? Julie Coleman in her book *The Life of Slang* argues that slang can be used to express or deny emotion and individuality, create humour, identify as part of a group, demarcate hierarchies in a group, and/or express shared attitudes and values. Michael Adams in his *Slang: The People's Poetry* emphasises the social functions and values of slang, adding that slang can nearly always be considered to be 'social critique'. All of these general features of slang applied to the way slang operated within soldier culture during the Great War.

Slang marked a variety of identities for soldiers, demarcating both belonging and exclusions. These boundaries operated in different ways. There was the expression of national identity through the use of distinctive Australianisms and through distinguishing Australian soldiers from others. There was the expression of a masculine identity through, for example, the use of coarse language and humour. Class could be expressed through the deployment of particular slang terms, for example, those that expressed resentment of officers. And, as part of the broader vernacular culture of the soldiers, language assisted in the expression of common resentments, sentiment, and fears shared by all soldiers who experienced the trenches.

Slang thus formed an important part of the coping mechanisms employed by soldiers during the war. Endurance and morale were of paramount importance and while some of this could be fostered by the military authorities—in the provision of various 'comforts', for example—

it also had to be generated by soldiers themselves. Their soldier culture, expressed in a variety of forms, but including language and humour, helped in the creation of a culture that assisted in coping and endurance. Death, killing, the humiliations of military life, the longing for home: all of these could be dealt with and expressed (or elided) through the use of slang. It also helped to give soldiers a sense of agency and empowerment in a situation where they had very little.

Slang also operated to give expression to a range of new experiences and new technologies generated by the war. New technologies needed to be described: for example, weapons or the language of flying. Although some technical terms and jargon developed, as well as a number of acronyms, the war saw a tendency towards the widespread use of nicknames for things such as artillery guns and shells. This perhaps helped to make familiar, even domesticate, items that were alien and fearsome to many.

A fascination with slang

It may be supposed that the slang and distinctive words of soldiers circulated only within the community of soldiers, marking their closed world as separate from the civilian world. However, Australian newspapers had an ongoing fascination with the new words being produced by the war, if only to understand this 'special' world of the trenches and camps. As mentioned above, discussions of language in the Australian press helped to make the world of soldiers more familiar to people at home.

From early on in the war, many articles appeared explaining some of the terms that came into circulation during the war. In 1916, for example, a 'comprehensive dictionary' was provided in the *Bunbury Herald* that gave 'simple explanations for military terms' and instructed readers to 'cut out and keep [the article] for reference'. (8 February, p. 1) A variety of technical terms relating to the war were included, such as *anti-aircraft gun*, *battalion*, *emplacement*, *grenade*, *howitzer*, *mortar*, *redoubt*, *salient*, *shrapnel*, and *trench*. While most of these are familiar to the twenty-first century reader who knows the history of twentieth-century warfare all too well, it should be remembered that many of these terms were less familiar to many readers at the time. In order to understand the many press stories describing battles and other aspects of the war, and to understand the letters they received from home, guides like these became, tragically perhaps, of much use.

A 1917 collection of 'Anzac vocabulary' began with the following commentary:

> I venture to state that if an average Australian averagely slang-acquainted were set down to-night in one of our tents in France and listened to the boys as they talk and joke and chaff he would not understand the greater part of their conversation. It is not the words so much as the manner in which they are used and the significance that attaches to them that would puzzle him. For the war has brought with it a great increase in our vocabulary, and the slang dictionary will have to be re-compiled to be up-to-date. We have been in strange countries, and we have picked up and assimilated to our own use strange words.
> (*Cairns Post*, 26 April, p. 7)

Guides to, and explanations of, Australian soldier slang thus became a regular feature of Australian newspapers throughout the war. Soldier publications, many of which were sent home to family, also often provided short glossaries explaining (sometimes humorously) many of the terms used by soldiers. These glossaries were also sometimes intended to 'initiate' new recruits into the culture of the military.

The war also generated a conversation in the press about the impact of the war in producing slang, and the use of slang more generally. One newspaper piece cited a London newspaper in commenting that there was 'more slang talked to-day, probably, than at any previous time in our history'. (Adelaide *Chronicle*, 27 April 1918, p. 2) Another made the observation that 'Australian soldiers are inventing their own slang. ... We shall need some new dictionaries in our scheme of post-war reconstruction'. (Melbourne *Leader*, 4 May 1918, p. 52) A discussion in a Perth newspaper in 1916, quoting from the British periodical *Saturday Review*, argued that 'in a great national upheaval like the present some words are retiring, while others are being invented or revived to meet the new conditions of life'. Slang was not just 'vulgar argot' but also words particular to a certain profession, and this included the 'profession of all others ... that of national service'. They noted that they just wanted to 'record without praise or blame what the war has brought forward in the way of language'. (Perth *Daily News*, 4 November, p. 6) A lecture by a military chaplain in 1918 on behalf of the charitable organisation, the Australian Comforts Fund, prefaced his talk 'with apologies to the reverend gentlemen present for the slang'. However, he argued, 'the Australian had won for himself the right to use as much slang as he liked'. (*Bendigonian*, 13 June, p. 32) A 1919 commentary on 'service slang' argued that the slang of the services was 'far from being offensive' and was 'both interesting and expressive'. (Perth *Daily News*, 23 January 1919, p. 4)

All of this commentary suggests that the war created a greater acceptance of slang in public discourse and certainly in print, at least for the duration of the war. Indeed soldier slang was often praised for its humour and wit. At the very least, slang was considered acceptable because the soldier had earned the right to use it. The connection of slang to the increasingly revered Anzac helped to change attitudes towards slang—or at least to modify them.

Connections to popular culture

Australian soldiers were avid readers of *The Bulletin* and the verse of Australian poets such as C.J. Dennis, Henry Lawson, and A.B. 'Banjo' Paterson. Their soldier culture drew on a broader popular culture, including a distinctive Australian popular culture as well as a broader Anglo–American popular culture. As discussed earlier, it is worth remembering that slang was often used self-consciously, especially in soldier publications. Within these sorts of publications, it is possible to see how soldier-writers connected to a pre-existing British and Australian popular culture. For example, many soldier publications consciously or unconsciously modelled themselves on the popular Australian periodical *The Bulletin*, and in that publication, slang was often integral to the literary mode employed by writers. Words that may not have been used in any other venue would be found here, often to self-consciously promote a type of Australian nationalism. Slang was often connected to a distinctive Australian culture, and soldiers drew on this connection.

While there was clearly a distinctive vocabulary of the army camp and trenches, derived in part from pre-war British slang, and in part newly created in response to the circumstances of trench warfare and new military technology, there were also connections to a distinctive Australian language (as evidenced in their writing, Australian soldiers were avid users of such Australianisms as *coo-ee*, BONZER, and *dinkum*). Australian soldiers, as discussed below, believed their slang was unique, and that they were particularly heavy and clever users of a distinctive 'slanguage'.

Language however also reflected Australian soldiers' experiences of a transnational popular culture. Soldier publications often included satire and parody of popular culture forms—for example, popular songs. References to theatre and music were sometimes made within their slang: for example, the use of OSCAR ASCHE, the name of a popular actor, as rhyming slang for 'cash', and the name SISTER SUSIE for a female war worker, after a popular song. A.G. Pretty's *Glossary of AIF Slang* includes the otherwise unattested *nat goulds*, 'reinforcements'. Pretty explained: 'So called because they have "landed at last," the name of one of Gould's books.' Gould, author of *Landed at Last* (1899), was perhaps the most popular writer read by soldiers during the war. Australian soldiers thus engaged with a range of popular culture forms before the war and during it, and drew on this national and transnational popular culture in their language.

Speaking Australian

To what extent were there discernible national slangs during the Great War? Certainly, there was a perception current during the war that there was considerable difference between, at the very least, British and Australian soldiers' vocabularies. While it was acknowledged that many slang words and phrases were shared between the Anglophone soldiers, numerous contemporary commentators argued that there were distinctive 'slanguages'.

In 1922, one author argued that many terms 'remained peculiar to the Australians, while the English "Tommies" had a vocabulary of their own'. (Perth *Daily News*, 22 April, p. 11) To prove this point, the author provided a satirical letter purporting to be written by an English veteran of the war, formerly an officer:

Dear Old Thing,—Sorry not to have seen you last Saturday, but had a little stunt on at Hornsey—absolutely a Pukka do; umpteen girls and no end of doings. ... We jazzed till 4 ack emma, and then kipped on the floor. Hope you are in the pink, old Bean, and not feeling too much of an onion at home! ... These old buffers cut no ice with me, and you can put your buttons on Percy that he won't get the wind up. I've been sweating on the top line for a big push up the scale for three months now; and am fed up to the back teeth. Shall grease off and have a dekko aboard if chances are napoo. (Perth *Daily News*, 22 April, p. 11)

This letter was clearly intended to be satirical, but it captured some of the perceptions of British soldier slang: that it was the kind of language stereotypical of the British officer from an upper-class background. Australian slang and the typical Australian were something different.

Was there a distinctive Australian soldier slang? W.H. Downing, compiling his *Digger Dialects* in 1919, believed that there was. He saw the war as having an impact on an already distinctive Australian slang. In the 'iron years' of the war, he argued, Australian slang 'was modified beyond recognition by the assimilation of foreign words, and the formulae of novel or exotic ideas'. He further said that the language of the Australian soldier, captured in his dictionary, 'savours of a new national type, and its characteristics are the same'. (p. vii)

Many humorous anecdotes and pieces were written during and just after the war playing on the notion that Australian soldiers made particular use of slang (fitting with the promotion of an image of them as anti-authoritarian and egalitarian) and were often incomprehensible to anyone except each other. For instance, one item had an Australian soldier meeting King George V, responding to his questions with colloquialisms such as *bonzer*, and ending with the King commenting: 'I'm no snide mug at languages ... but I'd give a pot of dinkum dough if I could speak Australian.' (Perth *Daily News*, 28 January 1919, p. 8)

Certainly, Australian soldier publications helped to forge a distinctive (and self-conscious) Australian identity for Australian soldiers during the war. As much as certain virtues came to be ascribed to the Australian soldier, so too did the use of certain words. Therefore there *was* a distinctive Australian soldier slang, but more importantly there was a distinctive idea that Australians made particular uses of slang and that this was tied to elements of a national character. In reality Australian soldiers also used many slang terms in common with British and other English-speaking soldiers.

Influence on the language

One British soldier mused, nearly a year after the Armistice, 'how many of our war words remain?' In writing about war words, he commented that it hadn't 'been easy for me to recall these phrases. They are not little used. The occasion for them has gone'. (Adelaide *Register*, 6 November 1919, p. 9) While many terms were undoubtedly ephemeral and tied to the particularities of the war, and thus faded quickly, many others had lasting resonance. The Great War had a lasting influence on the English language.

As early as 1919, writers were speculating as to which words would continue to be used. One Australian commentator believed that: ' "Anzac" will never perish. "Camouflage" is a certain stayer. So are "blighty" and "barrage." ' He also identified CUSHY and MOPPED UP as words likely to remain in the vocabulary. (*Western Argus*, 9 December, p. 4) All of these, with the arguable exception of BLIGHTY, have continued to be used (although BLIGHTY is still used in Britain). He also cited NAPOO and STRAFE as likely to retain their popularity; the latter did, the former did not. While it was hard to predict at the time which words would last and which wouldn't, some did and continue to have significance in Standard English and in Australian English.

Numerous terms relating to the war came into Standard English usage. These include words such as TANK and NO MAN'S LAND. Some of these had a lasting influence because of their close association with understandings and popular imagery of the war; these include DUGOUT and OVER THE TOP.

The language of Anzac has undoubtedly had a lasting impact on Australian culture, society, and national discourse. It helped to enshrine the Anzac legend, which has had a continuing, if controversial, impact on Australian society, culture, and identity. Words such as DIGGER and COBBER are often associated with particular Anzac qualities. More generally, some terms that originated or were popularised during the war continue to be used in Australian English. These include terms such as POSSIE, GOOD OIL, KING-HIT, and FURPHY. Our use of these terms is a way in which the heritage and memory of the Great War continues to resonate.

FURTHER READING

Adams, Michael, *Slang: The People's Poetry*, Oxford University Press, New York, 2009.

Beaumont, Joan, *Broken Nation: Australians in the Great War*, Allen and Unwin, Crows Nest, NSW, 2013.

Coleman, Julie, *The Life of Slang*, Oxford University Press, New York, 2012.

Department of Veterans' Affairs, *Royal Australian Navy*, DVA, Canberra, 2010.

Ellis, John, *Eye-deep in Hell: Trench Warfare in World War I*, The Johns Hopkins University Press, Baltimore, 1976.

Fuller, J.G., *Troop Morale and Popular Culture in the British and Dominion Armies 1914–1918*, Clarendon Press, Oxford, 1990.

Gammage, Bill, *The Broken Years: Australian Soldiers in the Great War*, Penguin Books, Ringwood, 1980.

Grey, Jeffrey, *A Military History of Australia*, Third Edition, Cambridge University Press, Melbourne, 2008.

Kent, David, *From Trench and Troopship: The Experience of the Australian Imperial Force 1914–1919*, Hale and Iremonger, Alexandria, NSW, 1999.

Kent, David, 'Troopship Literature: "A Life on the Ocean Wave", 1914–1919' *Journal of the Australian War Memorial*, No. 10 (1987), pp. 3–10.

Laugesen, Amanda, *Boredom is the Enemy: The Intellectual and Imaginative Lives of Australian Soldiers in the Great War and Beyond*, Ashgate, Farnham, 2012.

Laugesen, Amanda, *Diggerspeak: The Language of Australians at War*, Oxford University Press, Melbourne, 2005.

Laugesen, Amanda, ' "Aussie Slanguage": Language and the Australian Soldiers in the Great War', *Journal of the Australian War Memorial*, No. 38 (April 2003).

McKernan, Michael, *Gallipoli: A Short History*, Allen and Unwin, Crows Nest, 2010.

Molkentin, Michael, *Fire in the Sky: The Australian Flying Corps in the First World War*, Allen and Unwin, Crows Nest, 2010.

Seal, Graham, *The Soldiers' Press: Trench Journals in the First World War*, Palgrave Macmillan, Houndmills, 2013.

Stanley, Peter, *Bad Characters: Sex, Crime, Mutiny, Murder, and the Australian Imperial Force*, Pier 9, Millers Point, NSW, 2010.

Watson, Alexander, *Enduring the Great War: Combat, Morale and Collapse in the German and British Armies, 1914–1918*, Cambridge University Press, New York, 2008.

Wilson, Ross J., *Landscapes of the Western Front: Materiality during the Great War*, Routledge, New York, 2012.

He earned his name as *digger*: Australian soldiers

A range of words were used by, and of, Australian soldiers through the Great War. These include those terms that are still most commonly associated with the Australian soldier: DIGGER and ANZAC, as well as ones less familiar today, such as BILLJIM and BILLZAC. They also include a range of terms for the average infantryman shared across English-speaking armies during the war, such as GRAVEL-CRUSHER and SWADDY. They also include names for different contingents of Australian soldiers to enlist, from ORIGINALS to WAR BABIES. This chapter takes a look at a number of these terms.

Many of the terms discussed in this chapter suggest the importance of community and identity for soldiers at war. Soldiers distinguished themselves in a variety of ways: as soldiers (especially as infantrymen), as Australians, and as members of particular groups or services within the AIF. Language reflected and helped to shape these various identities.

One of the first notable features of these terms used to refer to Australian soldiers is that they reflect how Australian soldiers rapidly began to develop a strong sense of their distinctive national identity. One thing that demonstrates this is the rapid adoption and use of the term AUSSIE, used to refer to Australians, used adjectivally to refer to anything Australian, and used to refer to Australia, the country. AUSSIE and ANZAC were words adopted as markers of identity as Australian soldiers came to distinguish themselves from soldiers of other nations. This chapter discusses some of these terms that helped to promote a coherent Australian identity for the soldiers of the AIF.

It is also evident in looking at the contemporary evidence that the 'Anzac legend' was quickly evolving and attaching itself to discussions of AUSSIES, ANZACS, BILLJIMS, and DIGGERS. Australian soldiers were rapidly credited with a range of virtues and qualities, such as being superb fighters, having a disregard for authority and a laconic sense of humour, and being noted for their courage and spirit. The qualities of the soldier were also often linked to the imagined qualities of the Australian bushman. The development of this Anzac legend, which has been powerful in Australian culture and politics over the twentieth and into the twenty-first century, has been credited to C.E.W. Bean, war correspondent during the Great War and official historian of the conflict. While undoubtedly Bean played a central role in the promotion of this image of Australian soldiers, it is also evident that it appealed to many at the time and was promoted in the press and in soldiers' own writings and self-perceptions. This legend proved powerful, despite the reality sometimes being quite different.

One important element of the Anzac legend was to present the Australian soldier as an individual with initiative and resourcefulness: trench warfare and military life allowed few opportunities for individuals to stand out or to demonstrate much by way of initiative. Many of the quotations provided for the terms in this chapter and others reflect many Australian soldiers' desire to assert their individuality and their individual and distinctive qualities in the context of military life and war.

There was also a range of terms used during the war to distinguish groups of Australian soldiers from each other. Most notably, there were those that referred to soldiers who joined at various stages through the war. These terms suggest the ways in which group identity functioned at a more particular level—while Australian soldiers might identify as Aussies when contrasting themselves with soldiers of other nationalities, they also sought to distinguish themselves by their various experiences of war. For example, soldiers who had enlisted and fought at Gallipoli (the originals) sought to distinguish themselves from those who enlisted later in the war.

Other terms capture various occupational roles within the AIF. A babbling brook was a cook, a body-snatcher a stretcher-bearer, and a member of the Medical Corps might be termed a Linseed Lancer. Attitudes towards these characters were generally positive or neutral; a later chapter discusses attitudes towards officers, which could often be more critical. As discussed there, ordinary soldiers sought to distinguish themselves from the brass hats, the staff officers and military authorities who ruled their existence.

Included in this chapter are a number of terms applied to Australian soldiers but which were also used by other armies for their infantrymen. Terms such as beetle-crusher, foot-slogger, and pongo, were familiar and well-used British terms for the infantrymen who carried the weight of being the p.b.i. ('Poor Bloody Infantry'). Here group identity can be seen to be forming in different ways. Soldiers identified as members of the 'poor bloody infantry' in common with those of other national armies. In this sense at least, it was imagined that there was a universal experience of war shared by those who experienced the brunt of the fighting and suffered the various indignities and discomforts of military existence.

Ally Sloper's Cavalry

A term for the Army Service Corps, from the initials *A.S.C.* The A.S.C. were responsible for a variety of services within the military, including transport and supply. Ally Sloper was a popular comic strip character, who appeared in his own comic paper, *Ally Sloper's Half-Holiday*, produced from 1884 to 1916. In these comics, Ally Sloper was presented as a lazy, scheming character. Brophy and Partridge in their *Songs and Slang of the British Soldier: 1914–1918* explain how the term came to be applied to the A.S.C.: 'The A.S.C. were so named by the infantry and artillery because, with their good pay, comfort and comparative safety, they were not considered soldiers at all.' Another variation on Army Service Corps used in the Great War is *Army Safety Corps*, conveying a similar idea.

A 1917 Australian parliamentary debate over preference for returned soldiers saw a politician make the following comments defending those who had served in non-combatant units: 'Mr. Foster said that many of the non-combatant units had suffered heavy casualties. The Army Service Corps, which some people called "**Ally Sloper's Cavalry**," had suffered even more severely than the men in the trenches at Gallipoli. There should be no distinction generally against members of non-combatant corps.' (*Zeehan and Dundas Herald*, 16 August, p. 3)

Anzac

This word was perhaps the most famous of the war, at least in terms of its continuing importance to Australian culture after the war. Initially deriving from, and applying to, the *A*ustralian and *N*ew *Z*ealand *A*rmy *C*orps, **Anzac** came to be used in a variety of ways. **Anzac** has had continuing resonance in both Australian and New Zealand culture.

The first sense of **Anzac** that developed was in direct reference to the Australian and New Zealand Army Corps. As C.E.W. Bean commented in his diary, '**Anzac** has become the sort of code word for the Army Corps.' (Diary, 6 May 1915, p. 33) **Anzac** also was used as an abbreviated form of Anzac Cove (discussed in the later chapter on place names), the place where Australian and New Zealand soldiers first saw battle, and as shorthand for the Gallipoli campaign.

After 1915, **Anzac** quickly came to be used to mean any Australian soldier, or to denote something that was Australian in the context of the military. It was used similarly of New Zealanders. Percy Smythe, an Australian officer, noted in his diary: 'Viv [his brother] got another letter from Mum. They had read about the **Anzacs** at Pozières, but had no idea of our whereabouts. Mum apparently thinks the word "**Anzac**" refers only to those who were at Anzac.' (Diary entry, 9 October 1916, *World War I Diary of Percy Smythe* [online]) As Smythe suggests, the term had rapidly evolved to mean any Australian soldier, whether or not he had served at Gallipoli. For example, in 1917, a short piece in an Australian newspaper declared: 'Reports just received at Cairo from the front state that the **Anzacs** have shown characteristic dash and the greatest gallantry in the most recent fighting in Palestine.' (*Muswellbrook Chronicle*, 31 March, p. 7)

Anzac came to be used in a number of compounds, several of which are mentioned in this book. These include Anzac day, Anzac wafer, and Anzac button. The word **Anzac** came to be protected under Australian law in 1921; this prevents the name from being used inappropriately and provides penalties if the regulation is breached.

Anzac also came to be used adjectivally in reference to something done in a particular manner seen to be redolent of the fighting spirit shown by Australian soldiers at Gallipoli. *Anzac spirit* and *Anzac tradition* are compounds found in Australian English from 1916. This quality could be dubiously claimed, even during the war years: the *Daily News*, a Perth newspaper, noted that **Anzac** virtues were being demonstrated in Perth business houses who were selling navy serge at a cheap price. 'Herein are displayed true **Anzac** qualities—enterprise and sacrifice. Enterprise in buying properly at the right time, and sacrifice in offering the material at such a ridiculously low price.' (8 March 1917, p. 4)

Aussie

Aussie is an abbreviation for 'Australia'. It is also used to mean 'Australian' (as an adjective), and 'an Australian' (as a noun). All these senses of **Aussie** appear for the first time in Australian English during the Great War. The spelling varied, with *Ozzie*, *Ozzy*, and *Aussy* all appearing in print. The term has since become a central term in Australian English. Another notable feature of this term is its use of the '-ie' suffix, a common feature of Australian English.

The popularity of the term with Australian soldiers is clear: **Aussie** referring to 'Australia' and 'an Australian' can be frequently found in their letters and diaries, and in 1918, a popular trench periodical entitled *Aussie: The Australian Soldiers' Magazine*, came into being. Its editor, Phillip Harris, declared in the first number that: 'The journalistic offspring of the Australian soldier should bear an Australian Soldier's name. Hence *Aussie*. To the Australian soldier the name **Aussie** stands for his splendid, sea-girt, sun-kissed Homeland, and his cobbers are always **Aussies**.' (18 January, p. 1)

Aussie referring to Australia appears to be the first sense to develop, being recorded in 1915, and used by Australian soldiers when they first travelled overseas. An Australian nurse noted in 1915: 'I am kept very busy. We are having a farewell dance for the boys going home to "**Aussie**" tomorrow.' (*Experiences of a 'Dinky Di' R.R.C. Nurse*, p. 30)

The adjectival sense of **Aussie** is first recorded in 1916, and became popular thereafter to refer to anything Australian. A letter by a soldier had him thanking the Williamstown Anzac Club for a parcel received: 'I must express my feelings of gratitude to you and all the dear friends in good old Australia, who are working so hard for our comfort ... It is remarkable how an "**Aussy**" parcel is prized.' (*Williamstown Advertiser*, 3 November 1917, p. 3)

Aussie meaning an Australian (and usually 'an Australian soldier' in the first recorded evidence) is first found in print in 1917, although it may well have been in use before then. A 1917 news cable noted: 'The friendship between Australians and New Zealanders is now most noticeable. The forces call each other respectively "**Aussies**" and "Enzeds".' (*Bendigonian*, 20 December, p. 23) The **Aussie** soldier was considered to have special qualities. In an edition of *The Wyreemian*, a troopship periodical, it was noted: 'Fair play is a motto of the "**Aussie**". ... The **Aussie** ... is always cheerful.' (7 November 1918, p. 3)

A less well-attested use of the term during the war was in reference to a wound severe enough to send the wounded person home to Australia. (See entry in Chapter Six.)

babbling brook

Often abbreviated to **babbler**, this is rhyming slang for 'cook'. Both were popular terms used by soldiers to refer to army cooks. **Babbler** is recorded in Australian English from 1904, and originally referred to a cook on a cattle or sheep station. Both **babbling brook** and **babbler** are recorded in various dictionaries of Great War slang compiled just after the end of the war, including W.H. Downing's *Digger Dialects*. The term continued to feature in Australian (and New Zealand) English, with the abbreviation *bab* also recorded after the war. Rhyming slang was a common feature of army slang, dating back in the British Army to well before the Great War. Australian English also makes liberal use of rhyming slang, and therefore it is not surprising to find several Great War Australian soldier slang terms deriving from rhyming slang.

The trench periodical, *The Kookaburra*, included the following instruction to all men: 'We have been asked to state on behalf of the **"babbling brooks"** that all bots, past, present, or future, are hereby warned to steer clear of the cook-house.' (No. 1, 15 June 1918, p. 15) Another periodical, this one a troopship magazine published on the voyage home to Australia, began a story with the line: 'She was a dainty little French Peach and her boy a well-known **Babbler** or Stew King.' (*The Last Ridge*, No. 2, 26 July 1919, p. 6D)

beetle-crusher

A term for an infantry soldier, similar to FOOTSLOGGER or the British term *mud-crusher*. It dates back to the nineteenth century as a British slang term for a boot or a foot.

A former Captain with the Australian Artillery gave a public talk in Perth in 1918 on life in the army. He was recorded as saying: 'The pre-war tradition was for the artilleryman to affect a superiority over the "clod-hopper" or **"beetle-crusher"**, but the latter was now esteemed at his proper value, the artilleryman recognising in the infantryman the means by which alone the objects of the former can be attained.' (Perth *West Australian*, 5 March, p. 5)

Bill Anzac

An Australian soldier. This was a variation on BILLJIM and BILLZAC, and an elaboration of ANZAC meaning an Australian soldier.

A 1916 newspaper article commented: 'The time will surely arrive, when **Bill Anzac**, returning in his thousands, will demand of the Federal Government an account of its stewardship; and none can doubt that the account will be far from satisfactory.' (Brisbane *National Leader*, 29 September, p. 4)

Billjim

A term meaning 'the typical Australian soldier'. It was a transferred use of the Australian English *Billjim*, 'the typical man in the street', first recorded in 1898 and often used in the popular Australian periodical *The Bulletin*. Brophy and Partridge include the term in their *Songs and Slang of the British Soldier: 1914–1918*.

Billjim, as applied to the Great War Australian soldier, was a name popularly used in the Australian press. Up to 1915, it does not appear often, but in 1916 through to 1919 the term is found much more frequently and seems to have been used primarily on the home front. A comment in the Australian press in 1917 was as follows: 'But what about **Billjim**? He will be coming home in thousands and tens of thousands directly. He will want work and land if he is still able to work.' (*Cumberland Argus and Fruitgrowers' Advocate*, 21 March 1917, p. 2) By contrast, soldiers seemed less keen on the term, as this comment from *Aussie: The Australian Soldiers' Magazine* suggests: 'I'm worried about this name **Billjim** that some of the Aussie papers have tacked on to us. I don't like it. Has anyone ever heard a Digger address another as **Billjim**? If a Digger were to say to another: "can you tell me the way to the Battalion lines, **Billjim**"? he'd be almost sure to get a loud ha-ha. The word is certainly not a Digger's word. It doesn't fit.' (October 1918, p. 2)

The term was often associated, like ANZAC and AUSSIE, with particular qualities that Australian soldiers supposedly possessed. An officer, writing for the troopship periodical *The Karoolian*,

commented: 'The "**Billjim's**" serene philosophy or what we may call
the "don't worry attitude"—that partial fatalism of his bush and
"sporty" nature. This it is that enabled him to face and overcome all
odds in the mud of the trenches, in the farm, fowl and pigyard odors
of his billets and in the nerve-wracking pains of his many wounds.'
(Vol. 1, No. 2, April 1919, p. 28)

Billzac

This term is a blend of BILLJIM and ANZAC and was of some limited
popularity during the Great War as a term for an Australian soldier.
The term BILL ANZAC also had some limited use during the war.
Billzac had some currency after the war in two contexts: F.E. Trotter
wrote a book about the war, published in Brisbane in 1923, called
Tales of Billzac: Being Extracts from a Digger's Diary, and the Perth
newspaper *Sunday Times* had a sports correspondent who wrote
under the pseudonym 'Billzac', predominantly through the 1930s.

An article in the *Port Pirie Recorder and North Western Mail* in
1916 provided a romantic description of a typical **Billzac**, which
included in the 'alphabetical' description of his many qualities:
'A lean, lithe, lank, lazy, live, laughter-loving, large-eyed, long-armed,
lantern-jawed, long-necked, loose-limbed, laconic, leg-pulling, lurid
liar.' (2 November, p. 3) The *Kia Ora Coo-ee*, a troop periodical
printed in the Middle East, wrote in September 1918, that DIGGER
was supplanting **Billzac** and BILLJIM: 'This term Digger is a very
universal one in France ... It has supplanted "Billjim" and "**Billzac**" as
generic terms—and even "Cobber," as a name by which you accost
your friends, is quite out of it.' (15 September, p. 8)

Birdie

A nickname for General (later Field Marshal) Sir William *Bird*wood.
It is recorded in A.G. Pretty's *Glossary of AIF Slang* and is well-
attested in the evidence from the period. Birdwood (1865–1951)
was a British Army officer who had served in the Boer War. He was
made commander of the Australian and New Zealand forces in
November 1914. In 1915, he led the Anzac contingent at Gallipoli,

and later oversaw Australian soldiers on the battlefields of the
Western Front. In May 1918 he was promoted to command of the
British Fifth Army. He was generally considered to be popular with
soldiers during and after the war.

A humorous story published in the press in 1916 attests to
Birdie's popularity with Australian soldiers:

> General Sir William Birdwood, it is well known, has a warm
> admiration for the Australian soldier as a fighter, but he does not
> seek to hide the fact that the Anzacs pay little attention to what
> they consider the 'frills' of military observances. ... He was going the
> rounds of the trenches, when he came upon a big Queenslander
> who was on sentry duty, who, beyond a casual stare, took no
> notice of the general. Presently, however, he saw a shell coming,
> and yelled out, 'Duck your — head, **Birdie**!' 'And what did you
> do?' gasped the horrified colonel [to whom Birdwood was telling
> the story]. 'Do?' said General Birdwood, with a twinkle in his eye.
> 'Why, I did as I was told. I ducked my — head!' (*North Western
> Advocate and the Emu Bay Times*, 13 May, p. 2)

The troopship periodical, *The Boonah Budget*, noted that their ship
the HMAT *Boonah* had been visited by Birdwood on 20 April 1919:
' "**Birdie**" in a few WELL CHOSEN WORDS wished us "Goodbye
and Godspeed,"—regretted parting with us and thanked us for the
work done under his Command.' (No. 1, 1 May 1919, p. 3)

body-snatcher

This term was used during the Great War to refer to a stretcher-
bearer. Both W.H. Downing in *Digger Dialects* and A.G. Pretty in the
Glossary of AIF Slang record it as meaning 'a member of a raiding
party'. However, the evidence found in Australian print sources only
attests to the stretcher-bearer sense.

J.L. Beeston noted in his book *Five Months at Anzac* that
stretcher-bearers had been known as **body-snatchers**, but since
Gallipoli, members of the Australian Army Medical Corps could
'hold up their heads with any of the fighting troops'. (quoted in
Brisbane *Queenslander*, 21 April 1917, p. 3)

chocolate soldier

Sometimes abbreviated to **choc**, during the war **chocolate soldier** was a name given to those soldiers who joined the fighting after the Gallipoli campaign. The reference came from George Bernard Shaw's play *Arms and the Man* (first produced in 1894) in which a cowardly soldier is called by one of the other characters in the play 'a very poor soldier; a chocolate cream soldier'. Shaw's play was adapted into a popular comic opera 'The Chocolate Soldier' which was staged to great success in Australia in 1911, and for a number of years following. However, it should be noted that not all the contemporary references to **chocs** were negative, especially once these soldiers had seen military action. W.H. Downing's *Digger Dialects* defines a **choc** as: 'The 8th Brigade ('Tivey's Chocolate Soldiers.') Originally an abusive name; now an honourable appellation.' The 8th Brigade, under the command of Major General Edwin Tivey, fought in numerous important battles on the Western Front, including Fromelles, Bapaume, Bullecourt, and Polygon Wood, and suffered many casualties.

The poet-raconteur Tom Skeyhill included the term in one of his poems:

> Now, when I said to mother,
> 'I've volunteered to fight,'
> She said, 'God bless you, sonny,
> And bring you back all right.'
> But 'e called me a **chocolate soldier**,
> A six-bob-a-day tourist, too. (*Inglewood Advertiser*, 21 December
>   1915, p. 3)

cobber

An Australian English word meaning 'a companion; a friend', and first recorded in 1893. It is also used in New Zealand English. It likely derived from Yiddish *chaber*, 'comrade'. **Cobber** is often used as a mode of address, and was a term popular with Australian soldiers during the war.

A line from a poem in C.E.W. Bean's *The Anzac Book* paid tribute to comrades: 'And my eyes grow bedimmed for the **cobbers** / Who battled and conquered and fell.' (p. 117) An Australian YMCA officer, writing from the Middle East in 1916, described Australian soldiers at the YMCA canteen:

> When the men rush our canteen, as they return from their long drills or marches across the desert, the crowd at the counter is 20 deep, with hundreds of eager hands reaching for the rolls and butter that come all the way from Australia. To get served quickly, the boys call us '**Cobber**,' 'Mate,' 'Top-hole,' and so on. (*Casterton News*, 28 December, p. 6)

Cobber is also found used as a verb (usually in the form **cobber up**) meaning 'to make friends with'. An example of **cobber up** is found in the soldier publication, the *Kia Ora Coo-ee*, in 1918: 'I've **cobbered up** with the bloke on guard here; he yaps a bit of English, so tells me all about you.' (15 June, p. 4)

colonial

As a noun, this was used during the Great War to refer to Australian soldiers, or soldiers of the British Empire collectively. First used of Australian soldiers during the Boer War, this is a specific use of the term *colonial*, 'a person born in Australia of immigrant (usually British) descent'. It continued to be used during the war, often in reference to soldiers of the British Empire (especially Australians and New Zealanders) collectively.

British war correspondent Ashmead Bartlett, reporting on Gallipoli, often used *colonial* to refer to the Anzac troops: 'The position of the **Colonials** was immeasurably improved by the landing of the field guns and several Indian mounted batteries.' (*Quambatook Times*, 12 May 1915, p. 3) Australian soldiers sometimes used the word in reference to themselves: for example, on 27 April 1915, Archie Barwick commented in his diary while at Gallipoli that 'if ever men fought hard, well the **Colonials** did that day'. (*In Great Spirits: The WWI Diary of Archie Barwick*, p. 33) Lance-Corporal C.M.R. Nuttall, writing from a hospital in England after being wounded in France, said: 'They have done all in their power for us wounded **colonials**, and in so doing take it as a pleasure to help us boys so far away from home.' (*Moorabbin News*, 1 September 1917, p. 2)

deep thinker

A soldier who enlisted in the AIF late in the war was sometimes known as a **deep thinker**. The implication is that the person had to 'think deeply' before enlisting. It appears to first have been used by those who served at Gallipoli in reference to those who arrived later, as evidenced in this comment by Australian soldier Roy Whitelaw: 'Tel-el-Keber is to be the new training camp for Australian troops. So when the 50 000 '**deep thinkers**' (as they are known over here) arrive they will have something else to think about for it's nothing but sand, sun and flies near Ismailia.' (Letter, 7 April 1916, *Somewhere in France*, p. 47)

An article in the *Sydney Morning Herald* in 1916 noted the distinctions between the different contingents of Australian soldiers: ORIGINALS, DINKUMS, **deep thinkers**, and WAR BABIES. It said:

> Consequent upon the transfer of Anzac troops back to Egypt, the men met a new race of Australians, who explained they would have enlisted earlier had they realised earlier that things were so serious. The Anzac troops treated them in a condescending way and christened them '**Deep Thinkers**' on the ground that they had thought very deeply before donning khaki. Still another band came to hand, however, and these the Anzac men dubbed 'War Babies.' In France, however, 'Originals,' 'Dinkums,' '**Deep Thinkers**' and 'War Babies' are on a level footing, or will be before long, and there is no doubt that the first engagement they all share will obliterate petty differences and distinctions. (7 June, p. 7)

digger

An Australian soldier. First used during the Great War, this name came to be used of Australian soldiers fighting in later conflicts, and became a central term relating to Australian understandings of

Australian participation in war. During the war, it was also used by, and in reference to, New Zealand soldiers. **Digger** was sometimes abbreviated to *dig*.

The etymology of **digger** is disputed. Several theories have been posited. *Digger* was used in Australian English from the 1850s to refer to miners, and was often used as a term of address. *Aussie: The Australian Soldiers' Magazine* argued in 1918 that the term was much used on the goldfields of Western Australia and 'came to France when the sandgropers gave up digging on the goldfields of WA and carried on with it on the battlefields of France and Flanders'. (February, p. 2) As this quotation suggests, Australian soldiers often were literal 'diggers', put to work digging trenches and doing other manual labour, and hence were referred to as **diggers**.

That **digger** came from Australian soldiers' ability to dig was a popularly accepted etymology during the war, and clearly also linked to the earlier Australian English use of the term to refer to miners. Another contribution to *Aussie* in March 1918 included the following comment from a soldier: 'What makes you refer to **Digger** as the "new word"? Why, my old father and grandfather were "Diggers", and they got the hundred percent golden stuff, too. Aussie, engaged in less profitable digging in this shell-shocked land, has merely revived the word.' (p. 3)

Another possible origin (or reinforcement of the term) relates to New Zealand English. A.G. Pretty's *Glossary of AIF Slang* claims that **digger** was first used by the New Zealand Expeditionary Force, from where it was picked up and used by Australian soldiers. Evidence from a 1917 New Zealand troopship publication supports this possibility, arguing that 'the New Zealander is the "**Digger**" as the Australian is the "Ossie" '. (*Digger*, 41st Reinforcement at Sea) This **digger**, according to the *Dictionary of New Zealand English*, evolved from the New Zealand English *gumdigger*, 'one whose occupation is retrieving and selling fossil kauri gum'.

A 1918 article discussed the genesis of the name, acknowledging that 'the origin of the expression is vague'. It argued that in 1914 Australian soldiers were referred to as TOMMY CORNSTALKS, after

Gallipoli they were BILL ANZACS, and then just ANZACS. The author continues:

> About the time of the first Pozières attacks [1916], it is said, a high British officer passed a body of men at work with pick and shovel, and asked, 'Where did you soldiers come from?' The spontaneous chorus came back to him with many smiles, 'We're not soldiers; we're diggers!' From then the name seems to have stuck. Men began to address each other familiarly as '**Digger**'; it was always a happy substitute for any name.

However, the author continues by speculating that another possible origin came from the mining fields where ' "Digger" came easiest to the lips' and came with the men to the battlefields, first used of the Mining Corps, and then all soldiers. He concludes: 'For all time the Australian soldiers will probably be known as a "**Digger**," though he will not know why.' (Sydney *Labor News*, 12 October, p. 11)

The evolution of BILLJIM to **digger** is captured in this quotation from a troopship periodical reflecting on the war experience:'[Billjim] soon absorbed into the vastness of the never-ending monotony, of toil, blood, thunder and mud—then he earned his name of "**Digger**".' (*Homeward Bound*, p. 23) However **digger** evolved, it is clear that by the end of the war it was a popular term used of and by Australian soldiers.

The Australian **digger** was believed to possess many special qualities, as suggested in this quotation from a post-war assessment of the Australian soldier:

> No more original figure than the Australian soldier has appeared in the war. The '**Digger**,' as he is affectionately called, is as unique as the 'Poilu.' Hard to manage in camp, he improved in morale as he neared the firing line. He was fearlessly himself. He behaved in the Strand as he would have done on a Saturday night in the streets of Wagga Wagga. Defiance of convention was his one pose ... But there was no body of men who so triumphantly satisfied the supreme test of discipline, the test of being ready in the field just when they were required, and of moving under fire to whatever point they were asked to occupy. (*Yarragon, Trafalgar and Moe Settlement News*, 10 July 1919, p. 7)

Similar sentiments were expressed more pithily in verse in a troopship publication, the *Saxon Sentinel*, with the following lines: '**Digger**, the resolute, reliable, true, / The fighter who saw the bloomin' war through.' (No. 1, 7 January 1919, p. 5)

dinkum

A term (usually found as **the Dinkums**) for a soldier of the AIF's Second Division. The Second Division of the AIF was formed in Egypt in July 1915 and sent to Gallipoli to fight. After the evacuation, they were sent to France, where they distinguished themselves fighting on the Western Front in battles at Pozières and Mont St Quentin. Casualties for the Second Division were high, with over 8000 soldiers killed in action, and many more wounded. *Dinkum* is an Australian English word meaning 'genuine, true'; see also DINKUM DIGGER.

Sergeant John H. Falconer, one of the **Dinkums**, in 1916 when writing about his Gallipoli experience, described the first advance of his men towards the fighting lines: 'Some sights were pitiful to witness, but in answer to our excited questions, as to how things were going, they [soldiers just having seen action] gave cheery and confident replies. On various occasions we replied, to them as new soldiers would, that as soon as we arrived on the scene Johnny Turk would hook it. These replies helped the 2nd Division earn the name of "**The Dinkums**".' (*On Active Service* [online]) C.E.W. Bean wrote in 1917 that 'the "**Dinkums**" became a title for men to be intensely proud of. Men who were through the first fortnight at Pozières need never be ashamed to compare their experiences with those of any soldier in the world, for it is the literal truth that there has never in history been a harder battle fought.' (*Letters from France*, p. 226)

dinkum digger

A combination of *dinkum*, an Australian English word meaning 'genuine, true', and DIGGER, 'an Australian soldier'. **Dinkum digger** was a term that was used to imply the archetypal Australian soldier and his alleged qualities, such as independence, disregard for military authority and discipline, mateship, and a laconic sense of humour. It first appears in 1918, and thus may have been popularised by the Dinkum Digger Concert Party, active in 1918 in providing theatrical entertainments to soldiers, but clearly alluded to the particular qualities being attached to Australian soldiers.

An early recorded use of **dinkum digger** commented on soldiers returning home to Australia: 'We got a few Anzacs home on furlough and now the whirligig of war leaves them with an early prospect of civilian life. Some have been such "**dinkum diggers**" rambling the earth's surface they won't care to settle down.' (*Port Macquarie News and Hastings River Advocate*, 30 November 1918, p. 6) Another writer praised the unique qualities of the **dinkum digger**: 'He is a species of comparatively recent origin and is noted chiefly for his unrivalled impudence, his cool, calculating scorn of everybody and all things, and his inordinate passion for expressive, nay, strong language.' (*Urana Independent and Clear Hills Standard*, 19 September 1919, p. 3)

eggs-a-cook

This term referred to, or was used to describe, the AIF's Third Division. The call *eggs-a-cook* was a frequent cry of Arab street sellers in Egypt. Fraser and Gibbons in *Soldier and Sailor Words and Phrases* argue that the Third Division adopted it for themselves because of their self-perception of being 'hard-shelled', but it is more likely that it was a reference to the Third Division's colour patch (see also F.M. Cutlack's explanation below), as it was only ever applied to the Third Division. Formed in 1916, the Third Division saw considerable action on the Western Front through 1917 and 1918.

F.M. Cutlack, one of the Australian official war correspondents in France, wrote in 1919:

> General Monash's name will always be closely associated—and deservedly so—with the efficiency of the Third or **Eggs-a-Cook** Division, as it was universally known amongst other Australian Divisions in France. The name sprang from its recumbent egg-shaped shoulder patches, but there was also a subtle gibe in it. The

Third Division included many officers of Gallipoli experience—
that was General Monash's careful foresight: but on the whole it
was a formation brand new to war, and did not appear in France
until the war was two years old. They were the latest comers as
complete units of the AIF. They were deemed to know nothing of
Cairo and Egypt, where the native boys hawked oranges and other
wares with a quaint jargon, and where the eating houses posted up
notices like 'Eggs-a-cook, eggs-a-bread'. (*Sydney Morning Herald*,
27 December, p. 8)

A.G. Pretty's *Glossary of AIF Slang* also records *eggs-a-fried*, and
defines it as a name given to the 4th Division Pioneer Battalion
'who wore a circular white patch with a smaller circular patch
superimposed'. While not recorded elsewhere, the term *eggs-a-fried*
clearly derived from the colour patch.

foot-slogger

This was a term for an infantryman. Dating back to the nineteenth
century, during the Great War it was used by and of all the English-
speaking armies, including Australian soldiers. See also the similar
terms BEETLE-CRUSHER and GRAVEL-CRUSHER.

Gunner Arnold Storer, writing from France in 1916, said of the
infantry who were doing so much fighting:

The infantry have stood the brunt of it, and gallantly have they done
so. When one sees the withering shell fire that is systematically
poured along the front line, where, as is often the case here, there
is not even the suggestion of a trench to take cover in, but merely a
succession of shellholes, one cannot but feel admiration for every
'**foot-slogger**' whose duty demands him there. (Adelaide *Register*,
18 October, p. 8)

gravel-crusher

A term for an infantryman, similar to BEETLE-CRUSHER and FOOT-
SLOGGER. This was a slang term that dated back to the nineteenth
century, and it gained some popularity during the Great War. Route

marching was sometimes known as GRAVEL-CRUSHING. (See entry in Chapter Two.)

A soldier (and former journalist) writing from Gallipoli commented: 'The Australians have had some unique and pretty desperate fighting in Gallipoli, and our fellows did themselves proud. Some of the Light Horse used to refer to us rather contemptuously in Egypt as "**gravel crushers**". But we got our own back when we saw them struggling up the precipitous hills.' (*The Farmer and Settler*, 25 June 1915, p. 1)

Holy Joe

This term for a priest or religious minister pre-dated the war (going back to the nineteenth century), and was more commonly and originally nautical slang. It was used by soldiers during the Great War as a name for an army chaplain.

Chaplain-Major Mackenzie, winner of the Military Cross, was described in the Sydney *Sunday Times* in 1918 as also being known as '**Holy Joe**', 'Salvation Joe', 'Old Mac', and 'Padre Mac'. (28 April, p. 9)

Hughesilier

A.G. Pretty's *Glossary of AIF Slang* defines **Hughesilier** as follows: 'Name applied to men compulsorily placed in camp for so-called home defence purposes after the failure of the 1916 conscription referendum for service overseas in Australia. The idea being that once in camp, [a] number of the men would volunteer for the A.I.F. The scheme was only partially successful.' It is a humorous play on *fusilier*, a name given to soldiers of particular regiments who were originally armed with fusils (a light musket), and Billy *Hughes* (1862–1952), the Prime Minister who introduced and campaigned for two conscription referendums in Australia. The scheme referred to was an unpopular scheme introduced briefly in 1916 by Hughes' government to try to get more men into the army. While there is some evidence for the term, it is not particularly well-attested and was fairly ephemeral.

In November 1916, the Lismore *Northern Star* noted: 'During the week men from the called-up camps volunteered freely for the AIF. It is said that many "**Hughesiliers**" presented themselves with the object of being rejected so that they could be released from camp.' (13 November, p. 4)

Linseed Lancer

A slang term for a member of the Royal Army Medical Corps, also applied to a member of the Australian Army Medical Corps, during the Great War. It pre-dated the war as army slang. *Linseed* or flaxseed was used for medicinal purposes, such as in poultices used to treat boils, and linseed oil was sometimes given as a treatment for constipation.

A summary of J.L. Beeston's book *Five Months at Anzac* quoted the following:

> The stretcher-bearers were a fine body of men. Prior to this campaign the Army Medical Corps was always looked upon as a soft job. In peace time we had to submit to all sorts of flippant remarks, and were called **Linseed Lancers**, Body-snatchers, and other cheery and jovial names; but, thanks to Abdul and the cordiality of his reception, the A.A.M.C. can hold up their heads with any of the fighting troops. (Brisbane *Queenslander*, 21 April 1917, p. 3)

marmalade

A term for a new recruit that was popular with Australian soldiers. Most sources suggest that it derived from the marmalade or jam a new recruit received; marmalade and jam were staples in military provisions. An AIF recruit, still based in the NSW Liverpool camp, wrote:

> We were very merry, and called back 'Good-bye Girls', 'Good-bye Mother', etc. A special train soon conveyed us to Liverpool where, as we marched into camp, we were greeted with '**Marmalades**! Marmalades!!' This is the name given to new recruits just entering camp. I think the name originated from the amount of jam we receive. (*Northern Times*, 11 September 1915, p. 6)

original

The first contingent of soldiers who enlisted and fought in the war were sometimes known as the **originals** (see the *Sydney Morning Herald* quotation at DEEP THINKER). The term is first recorded in 1916.

A 1919 notice in the 'Personals' column of the Broken Hill newspaper *Barrier Miner* recorded that Private R. Rapley had just arrived back in Broken Hill. It said of him: 'Private Rapley was among the earliest to enlist in Broken Hill, and was one of the "**originals**". After a spell on Gallipoli he was returned home on sick leave in 1916, but on recovering again joined his comrades in arms, this time in France.' (10 July, p. 2)

P.B.I.

This is an abbreviation for *poor bloody infantry* and was commonly used during the Great War. It was a term used to describe soldiers in the infantry. According to the *OED*, it is first recorded in 1916. It reflected the hard slog typically endured by the infantry.

An article in the Lismore newspaper *Northern Star* described a show put on for the soldiers and recorded one of the performers' comments: ' "Dud day for the R.F.C. again. What a pity there's no dud days for the **P.B.I.**"—**P.B.I.** being "poor blooming"—or, well, blessed—"infantry" '. (8 April 1918, p. 8)

pongo

An infantryman was sometimes known as a **pongo**. Originally nautical slang, during the Great War it was commonly used in the British and Australian military forces to refer to a soldier in the infantry. Its origin is uncertain, although the *OED* suggests a possible transfer from *pongo* meaning an African ape or an orang-utan. By the 1940s, it was being used in Australian English to refer to an Englishman, especially a British soldier.

A 1915 newspaper report on life in the Australian military camps recorded the following observation on the soldiers' lexicon:

A soldier's vocabulary is, perhaps, unique. He has multitudinous terms that cannot be found in a standard dictionary. Here are a few:—The private soldier is a 'bird'; the infantryman a '**pongo**'; the field officer is a 'brass hat'; the man that is not enthusiastic in his desire to meet the enemy has 'cold feet'. (Hobart *Mercury*, 18 March, p. 5)

A 1919 troopship periodical recorded the following verse:

The bugle blew for dinner,
And the **Pongoes** on the floor
All gathered round the table,
Till they numbered near a score. (*The Khyberian*, April-May, p. 29)

ragtime army

A term applied to, and used to describe, the AIF, implying that they were disorderly. The term *ragtime infantry* is used in the popular soldiers' song of the Great War, 'Fred Karno's Army'. *Ragtime* is a style of African-American syncopated music that was then fashionable.

Private S.E. Ferres wrote home from Egypt in 1915: 'We call ourselves the "**Ragtime Army**," no doubt we look it when we arrive back at camp in the evening after a long day's march. We have a little verse about the "Ragtime Army" it is sung to the tune of Tipperary.' (*Forster Mirror and South Gippsland Shire Advocate*, 18 March, p. 3) Another Australian soldier, Private Stephens, wrote home on a postcard, 'Looking around me here, I have come to the conclusion that "Australia's **rag-time army**" has done well.' (*The Farmer and Settler*, 13 July 1915, p. 2)

rainbow

A term applied to the last of the reinforcements to join the AIF. It derived from the notion that these soldiers only arrived after the war's end, as suggested in this comment from 'A Soldier' in Palestine: 'It is going to be very weary, this time of waiting [to go home]. But all must be patient, from the "Dinkums" to the "**Rainbows**". "**Rainbows**," by the way, is the nickname of the last reinforcements to arrive. "After the storm they cometh," d'you see?' (Orange *Leader*, 5 March 1919,

p. 1) The troopship periodical *The Sardine* commented in verse on them: 'That our late 'Roos have been called the **Rainbows**; / Well, goodness knows what to call the "Won't-goes".' (August 1919, p. 2)

reinstoushment

An Australian English term for a soldier sent in as a reinforcement. It is a play on the words *reinforcement* and STOUSH.

A poem printed in the troopship periodical *Homing* at the end of the war included the lines:

> When a front trench went sky-'igh,
> Yer could 'ear the cusses cry—
> **Reinstoushments**! Quick!' ([c. 1918], p. 23)

A humorous story recounted in the Perth *Sunday Times* in July 1919 told of a subaltern's encounter with General 'Pompey' Elliott:

> A reinforcement subaltern, reporting to brigade headquarters, asked of a stoutish man sitting in shirt sleeves at a table: 'Where's the staff captain?' 'In the next room' was the curt answer. The **'reinstoushment'** was horrified: 'Don't they teach you any better manners in the brigade? Stand up when you speak to an officer!' The shirt-sleeved one stood to attention and the subaltern passed in to the staff-captain. (20 July, p. 11)

The shirt-sleeved man was, of course, General Elliott.

six bob a day tourist

This was a term for an Australian soldier, first recorded in 1915. It makes reference to the (relatively generous) rate of pay, six shillings a day, given to them. It was decided that the Australian soldier's rate of pay would match the wage of an average worker; this resulted in Australians being the best-paid soldiers of the war. See also TOURIST.

Private Fred Must, from Broken Hill, wrote home to his mother in 1915 after being wounded at Gallipoli: 'The Tommies will do anything for an Australian or New Zealander now. They have found out that the **"six bob a day tourist"** has plenty of grit.' (*Barrier Miner*, 11 July, p. 2) Of a soldier, the troopship periodical *The Wyreemian* commented: 'In August 1914, he joined a little party that was forming in Aussie under the name of "The **Six-Bob-a-Day Tourists**". He broke rules and committed every sin on the programme (except the unpardonable one of being found out).' (7 November 1918, p. 4)

swaddy

An infantryman. It is first recorded in British English slang in 1812, and continued to be used well into the twentieth century (although it has now been superseded by *squaddie* in British English). The *OED* suggests an origin for **swaddy** in *swad*, 'a country bumpkin; a loutish or clownish fellow'. It occasionally appears during the Great War in relation to Australian soldiers.

A 1916 account from a soldier in Cairo has him commenting: 'To the average Australian **swaddy** who has but a fleeting, superficial knowledge of the city and its environs, the Cairo of to-day does not muchly differ from the Cairo of a year ago.' (*Geraldton Guardian*, 13 January, p. 1)

Tommy Cornstalk

A name given to an Australian soldier; Australian soldiers collectively. It combines the British term for a soldier, TOMMY, from *Tommy* Atkins, a term for an ordinary British soldier, with *cornstalk*, an Australian English word for 'a native-born Australian' (in reference to their perceived tallness) dating from the early nineteenth century. **Tommy Cornstalk** was the primary term used to refer to Australian soldiers who fought in the Boer War, and continued to be used in reference to Australian soldiers through the Great War. Other terms superseded it during the war, particularly ANZAC and DIGGER, but it had some popularity in the Australian (and British) press right through the war years. Soldiers were less likely to use it of themselves.

A 1915 notice in an Australian newspaper called for the donation of sandbags for the trenches at Gallipoli: 'according to Sergeant Johnson, a returned hero, a shipload of sandbags would be the most practicable and acceptable gift that could arrive at

Gallipoli, for without the sandbags **Tommy Cornstalk** has small chance of partaking of any Christmas cheer with a degree of comfort.' (*Bairnsdale Advertiser and Tambo and Omeo Chronicle*, 13 October, p. 3)

Tommy Kangaroo

A term for an Australian soldier; Australian soldiers collectively. It combines the popular term for a British soldier, Tommy, from *Tommy Atkins*, a term for an ordinary British soldier, with the Australian animal, *kangaroo*. There were various names for Australian soldiers used in the British and Australian press during the war, this one being more popular in 1915 and 1916, after which names such as Anzac and digger became more common. It can be compared to Tommy Cornstalk.

A letter to the editor in the *Kalgoorlie Miner* argued: 'It is a long way to Berlin, and many large breweries litter the way, and I am sure that Tommy Atkins and our own brave "devil-may-care" **Tommy Kangaroo** will do their duty, when the time comes, and suck these breweries as dry as the arguments of our letter-writing cold-tea cranks.' (28 April, p. 2)

tourist

A term for an Australian soldier serving overseas. More commonly, such a soldier was referred to in full as a six bob a day tourist. In some instances, it appears to be used specifically of the first contingent of soldiers to enlist and serve in the AIF.

Major Dixon Hearder, an officer from Western Australia, addressing a conscription debate, said in 1917: 'when the first batch of volunteers left Australia they were told amongst other things that they were Cook's six-bob-a-day tourists. What had those **tourists** done? ... The glorious deed of the 125,000 who left Australia during the first 18 months of war had made the name of Australia immortal.' (*Castlemaine Mail*, 7 December, p. 2)

There was some use of **tourist** to specifically mean a member of the first contingent of Australian soldiers to serve overseas, who were also known as the ORIGINALS. The term was also used by, and of, New Zealanders. New Zealand reporter Malcolm Ross wrote of the Anzac soldiers: 'The first contingent became known as the **Tourists.** They were out to see a bit of the world.' (*Launceston Examiner*, 17 August 1916, p. 3) Sergeant Lawrence also commented in his diary on the **tourists** and DINKUMS: 'Yesterday on the heels of the 2nd Australian Division who by the way spread the report in Egypt that they are the "Dinkum Australians" and the 1st division are merely **tourists** and that *they* are *the men* who will show them.' (Diary entry, 16 September 1915, *Gallipoli Diary of Sergeant Lawrence of the Australian Engineers*, p. 88)

war baby

This term was used during the Great War to refer to a very young (and usually inexperienced) soldier. Australian soldiers used it to refer to soldiers who joined later in the war, many of whom had only just reached an age when they could enlist. See the quotation from June 1916 in the *Sydney Morning Herald* at DEEP THINKER for a sense that the **war babies** were a later group of soldiers to enlist.

Australian soldier Bert Smythe wrote in a letter home: 'They have all the under 19 youngsters—"**war babies**" we call them, doing permanent duties, guards etc. Jolly smart guards they make too.' (Letter, 17 February 1917, *Letters from Bert Smythe* [online]) *War baby* was a term also used of babies born outside of marriage and fathered by soldiers during the war, an issue that was of concern and discussed by the press and governments during and just after the war, including in Australia.

Things are well up to putty here: Life in the army

One of the areas that generated a range of new words and slang terms during the Great War was the everyday life, routines, and realities of being in the military. For Australian soldiers, life in the army was a new and different experience to civilian life. It was inevitable that they would encounter, adopt, and begin to create a new vocabulary. Some of these terms relating to military life were old British Army slang terms first encountered by Australians as they served alongside the British army; others were generated by the exceptional circumstances of the Great War. All terms spoke eloquently of a very different sort of life to civilian existence.

This chapter examines some of the terms related to military life during the war. Some suggest the mundaneness and discomfort of military service and reactions to it, such as GRAVEL-CRUSHING and the phrase

UP TO PUTTY. Others speak of the everyday humiliations of army life, such as SHORT ARM PARADE or CHAT. Soldiers' desires to escape military life are also captured in the vocabulary: they often went AWL or on FRENCH LEAVE.

Food terms feature strongly in this vocabulary of military life. Unsurprisingly, food and drink were major pre-occupations of soldiers. At Gallipoli, Australian soldiers endured a poor diet due to the limited supplies available to them. At the Western Front, the quality of the food varied considerably depending on where they were. Food and alcohol could also offer solace and comfort to men. Other terms reflected other aspects of life and the attempt to find some enjoyment: soldiers played gambling games such as TWO-UP or CROWN AND ANCHOR, they frequented ESTAMINETS, and they enjoyed their GASPERS.

Too much indulgence could lead to soldiers getting CRIMED and sent to the CLINK. Australian soldiers were notorious for getting into trouble and ignoring military regulations. Drunkenness, absenteeism, and a variety of other problems challenged commanders of the AIF through the war. Venereal disease was experienced in particularly high rates in the AIF.

A range of terms in this chapter are not distinctively Australian, although they were used frequently by Australian soldiers. As Australians entered the world of the army, they came to know a number of terms that were from the British army, many in circulation before the war and some coming from the British experience in India. These include words such as ROOTY or BURGOO. Language thus helped to initiate Australian soldiers into a broader military apparatus and culture.

But the Great War also generated new terms reflecting various aspects of military life, some of which were distinctively Australian. The best known of these are those that applied to information and rumours: these include terms still used in Australian English—FURPHY, GOOD OIL, and DINKUM OIL. This reflected the fact that reliable information was one of the most desired but least available things for soldiers.

Military life undoubtedly generated many more terms than can be traced in the written evidence. W.H. Downing's *Digger Dialects* includes a range of terms that provide insights into military life, but are not to be found in any other sources. They most likely existed, but were either not widespread, or for some reason never found their way into the printed record in any extensive way in this period. Some of them are worth mentioning here, because they add to our picture of how language can tell us something about the realities of the war. Some of these words and expressions include: *Anzac stew*, defined by Downing as 'the food upon

which Birdwood's army made a world-wide reputation. It consists of an
urn of hot water and one bacon rind'; *branding-paddock*, 'parade-ground';
camel-dung, 'an Egyptian cigarette'; *concrete macaroon*, 'an army biscuit';
and *Menin Road meat extract*, 'bully beef; beef tea'. Downing added in his
definition for the last one: 'So-called from the number of dead horses
and mules on the Menin-road (Ypres sector).'

abdominal crash

This term was used both figuratively, in the same way as GUTSER, to
mean 'a failure; a disappointment', and more literally, to mean 'a
crash; a fall'. A.G. Pretty's *Glossary of AIF Slang* notes it as 'a polite
adaptation' of GUTSER, 'a failure'. Brophy and Partridge record it
in *Songs and Slang of the British Soldier: 1914–1918* as meaning
'an aeroplane smash; also, any nasty fall'. The term was used by
Australian soldiers, and was sometimes abbreviated to *abdominal*;
it is not particularly well-attested, suggesting it was not as popular
as GUTSER.

In 1918, one Australian soldier wrote a letter to the editor of the
Richmond Guardian in which he talked about some people he was
referring to 'com[ing] what we over here term an **abdominal crash**,
or, plainer, "a gutzer" '. (17 August, p. 3) The troopship periodical,
The Last Ridge, included the following report of doings on the ship:
'Last night Scotty got Letemoff to tie up one end of his sleeping bag,
but as soon as he climbed in, came an **abdominal crash** on the deck.'
(No. 2, 26 July 1919, p. 8)

adrift

To be absent without leave (see AWL) was to be **adrift**. This slang
term has its origins in nautical use. Many soldiers went on periods of
absence without official permission in the course of the Great War.

An Australian soldier wrote home from England in May 1918
to report: 'Some 7000 blokes are reported to be **adrift** in the Old
Country—come on leave, scoot to Ireland or some other place,

and are hard to locate. Ireland gives safe shelter to these beauties, and altogether she is playing the game pretty low down in war matters.' (*Richmond River Herald and Northern Districts Advertiser*, 3 May, p. 2)

Anzac button

This term is recorded in W.H. Downing's *Digger Dialects* and is defined by him as 'a nail used in place of a trouser button'. A reviewer of Downing's book wrote in 1920 that he thought the **Anzac button** was 'beyond question the invention of a bushman far away from home'. (Perth *Western Mail*, 22 January, p. 35) Patsy Adam-Smith recorded in her book *Anzacs* (published in 1979) that: 'Stretcher bearer Jim McPhee of the 3rd Division Field Ambulance told me "... We had some silly sayings. An **Anzac Button** was a nail in place of a trouser button." ' However, the term is not well attested during the war years, and there is no direct written evidence of the term from that period.

Another sense of ANZAC BUTTON is recorded in Australian English, and referred to buttons that were bought as a means of fund-raising for returning veterans. (See entry in Chapter Ten.)

Anzac wafer

A biscuit given as part of army rations. It was a popular term used by Australian and New Zealand soldiers in France. In the Great War, AIF rations were based on those of the British Army (4000 calories). Basic foods given to soldiers included preserved meat and biscuits, complemented by items such as bacon, cheese, bread, jam, onions, and potatoes. Because the food was unchanging and often unappetising, a number of slang terms developed that reflected soldiers' disenchantment with what was given them to eat. Another term used by Australian soldiers to refer to an army biscuit was FORTY-NINER.

In a 1918 newspaper account of an Anzac's experiences entitled 'Through the Battle', the soldier noted: 'Then we had a feed—our first for 18 hours. Biscuits as hard as steel—"**Anzac wafers**"—we call 'em—and bully beef.' (Adelaide *Register*, 22 June, p. 8) In the January 1919 edition of the soldier publication *Aussie: The Australian Soldiers' Magazine*, an Australian soldier, Corporal C.W. Lane, told his story of 'giving Fritz the slip', that is, escaping from behind German lines. He writes of travelling through the night as a prisoner of the Germans, finding a cellar to stay in, and after the captives had 'searched every crevice for anything we could find', Lane's companion found 'a piece of **Anzac wafer** about a square inch, and gave me half of it'. (p. 7)

AWL

Applied to a soldier classified as being *A*bsent *W*ithout *L*eave, the initialism **AWL** later became more commonly the acronym **AWOL**. **AWL** was a standard military abbreviation used by the British and Australian armies during the Great War, although there are some recorded instances of **AWOL** also being used. 'Absent without leave' dates to the nineteenth century as an official British army designation for a soldier who abandons his duty without permission. Australian soldiers were more often charged with absenteeism than desertion.

In 1917, Australian soldier Jim McConnell wrote in his diary while in France: 'About one third of our boys still **A.W.O.L.** (absent without leave).' (Letter, 2 November, *Letters from the Front*, p. 69) In 1918, *Aussie: The Australian Soldiers' Magazine* included in their 'Aussie Dictionary' as the definition for **AWL**: 'An expensive form of amusement entailing loss to the Commonwealth and extra work for one's pals.' (15 January, p. 10) The military authorities regarded a soldier's going on leave without permission with somewhat less humour. A notice posted in 1919 after the Armistice, but before many soldiers were repatriated, declared under the heading '"**A.W.L.**" Overseas' that: 'all soldiers absent without leave after August 15 will forfeit free passages, war gratuity, and any subsequent privileges.' (Perth *Daily News*, 1 August, p. 6)

banjo

This was a term for a shovel, deriving from its shape, and is an Australian English word dating to just before the war (first recorded in 1913). It was a term used by Australian soldiers, a number of whom became quite familiar with having to 'swing the **banjo**' in digging trenches and undertaking other manual labour tasks. It also appears in New Zealand English, and was used by New Zealand soldiers. **Banjos** are often mentioned in accounts from the war, suggesting the realities of such work as part of army life.

Edward Lay, while serving in Egypt, noted in his diary: 'A day on the **banjo** filling in trenches out on the desert—beginning to think that our time is getting short in Egypt.' (18 March 1915, *Edward Lay's First World War Diary*, p. 33) W.J. Harvey, an Australian reporter, wrote a piece on life for Australian soldiers at the Western Front. He commented:

> The Australian has distinguished himself not only as a fighter, but also as a worker. With the shovel or any other implement he is a veritable champion. Even men who have not been used to swinging the '**banjo**' (as the boys call the shovel) have shifted tons and tons of earth in different places and on different jobs. The shovel, indeed, has done almost as much as the gun in this war. Our boys have shovelled so much earth over here that they declare they have made one part of France lower than the other. (*Bendigonian*, 15 March 1917, p. 25)

Stretcher-bearer William Slater wrote in his diary in the same month of 1917: 'As we got back early in the morning from Houplines we didn't go on to our job until after dinner. We "swing the **banjo**" again.' (Diary entry, 28 March 1917, *War Diaries of William Slater*, p. 23)

beachogram

A term for a rumour. It is a modification of *telegram*. Like FURPHY and LATRINE WIRELESS, this term suggests the importance attached to accurate information during the war, something many soldiers felt was hard to come by. **Beachogram**, unlike FURPHY, was a short-lived term used at Gallipoli, and probably made reference to the Anzac soldiers' position on the beaches.

J.L. Beeston, who served at Gallipoli, wrote in 1916: 'The other type of donkey generally indulged in what were known as Furfys or **Beachograms**. Furfy originated in Broadmeadows, Victoria; the second title was born in the Peninsula. The least breath of rumour ran from mouth to mouth in the most astonishing way.' (*Five Months at Anzac*, p. 34.)

bint

A term for a girl or woman. It comes from the Arabic *bint*, 'daughter', and came into English in the late nineteenth century through the British presence in Egypt. It was commonly used by British soldiers in Egypt and the Middle East during the war, and was picked up by Australian soldiers who spent time there. It was originally used in reference to Egyptian women, but also might be used more generally to refer to any woman, especially later in the war.

An article in an Australian newspaper in 1918 that examined some slang words of the war commented: ' "Chats" will remain slang, of course. So will **"bint"**, meaning a young woman. It deserves mention only because of a crisp definition supplied by a youthful Aussie of inquiring mind, who said that in his observation a **bint** was a "small dark tart".' (*Koroit Sentinel and Tower Hill Advocate*, 7 December, p. 3) The soldier periodical *Kia Ora Coo-ee* wrote in a list of comments to their correspondents: 'Our Secretary, whose bint in Sydney goes by the same name, took a liking to your M.S., and during our absence from the office posted it to her.' (April 1918, p. 15)

bivvy

A term for a temporary shelter for soldiers or a small tent. It is an abbreviation of *bivouac*, 'a temporary encampment of troops in the field'. This was a word often used by Australian and New Zealand soldiers during the war, with much of the early evidence for this term appearing in Australian and New Zealand sources.

An Australian soldier at the Western Front described life in the trenches: 'After much wading through the ooze, we reach the support-trenches, where we find those we are to relieve awaiting our coming. If we are appointed for duties in this trench we turn to the "**bivvies**" allotted to us and take off our packs.' (*Cobram Courier*, 30 November 1916, p. 7) The troopship periodical *The Boomerang* included the following verse written after the end of the war:

> A year ago I sat inside my **bivvy**,
> Cursing about my miserable lot,
> Wishing that I were once again a civvy
> Roaring about the things I hadn't got. (20 May 1919)

blanky

A euphemism for strong language and profanities, often in place of words such as *bloody*. In the press, an oath or profanation might be replaced by the word **blanky** or a —. This practice dates back to the middle of the nineteenth century in print. During the war **blanky** often appeared in humorous stories about Australian soldiers, which often served to illustrate their casualness and contempt for authority without reproducing the profanity directly.

C.E.W. Bean, writing about Gallipoli in the press, told the following story of an Australian soldier on the Peninsula:

A senior officer was going through the trenches, when a shell lobbed ahead of him. He heard sounds of objuration, and came upon a man who was expressing his opinion of 'the **blank blank blanks**. Why the **blank** can't they keep their **blanky blanky** shells to their **blanky** selves, the **blanky, blanky, blanks**, &c.?' 'You seem annoyed,' said the officer. 'Yes, the **blanky blanks**. So would you be if the **blanky** swine put a **blanky** shell into your tea which—I beg your pardon, sir,' he said hastily. 'I didn't see it was you; but the beggars blew the dirt of the parapet into my tea.' (Adelaide *Advertiser*, 17 August 1915, p. 9)

bonzer

A word used to describe something or someone surpassingly good. It can be used as a noun, adjective, or adverb. **Bonzer** is an Australian English term dating to the early twentieth century, and possibly influenced by the French *bon*, 'good'. Variants such as *boshter* and *bosker* were also popular in Australia in the early twentieth century, but during the Great War, one of the most popular words used by soldiers to describe a variety of things and experiences was **bonzer**.

Many soldiers used the term in their letters and diaries. Private Dick Daw, a soldier from South Australia, wrote home to his aunt and cousin in 1917 to say: 'They are nearly all West Australians in our party, and "**bonzer**" fellows. I had a lad from there as a mate, but he got killed, worse luck; he was one of the best mates I've ever had.' (*Kalgoorlie Miner*, 24 January, p. 3). Another Australian soldier wrote from Egypt to thank the Omeo Plains Red Cross Society for their comforts parcels, saying 'The parcel was a "**bonza**". ... It is really wonderful the work our Australian people have done for us boys.' (*Omeo Standard and Mining Gazette*, 16 March 1917, p. 2) In 1918, *Aussie: The Australian Soldiers' Magazine* included the following humorous item:

> Polite Frenchman: '*Bon soir, monsieur!*'
> Aussie (misunderstanding): '**Bonza** war, be blowed! It's the worst blanky war I've ever been to.' (No. 3, March, p. 11)

boozer

This slang term for 'a place to buy and drink alcohol' can be found in British English from the late nineteenth century. However, by the time of the Great War, it appeared to have become a word predominantly used by Australians and New Zealanders. In the context of the culture of soldiers, **boozers** (more commonly referred to as ESTAMINETS during the war) had their attractions, and the term can be found used by Australian soldiers during the war, reflecting their regular haunting of such establishments.

Archie Barwick, an Australian serving on the Western Front, wrote in his diary in 1917 of a visit to an ESTAMINET: 'The little "**boozer**" is chock full of Tommies & Australians, & beer, wine, mullager & grenadine are circulating freely & opening all their mouths.' (Diary entry, 16 October, *In Great Spirits: The WWI Diary of Archie Barwick*, p. 267) An account by an Australian prisoner of war records: 'Here we were handed over to the Prussian Guard, and marched for some distance to a village near Beaumont, passing through several villages en route. The guard halted us at every "**boozer**" we passed and regaled themselves with beer and wine, but did not allow us to have even a drink of water.' (*Chronicle and North Coast Advertiser*, 9 May 1919, p. 7)

bull ring

A name for 'a training ground notorious for the severity of the drill required', originating in the Great War. It alludes to the bull-fighting or bull-baiting ring, with the idea being that the inhumane treatment of bulls was transferred to the soldiers undergoing training.

The most notorious of these **bull rings** was the British base at Étaples in France, renowned for its severe discipline. Bert Smythe, an Australian soldier in France, wrote in his diary: 'Learn to my disgust that I've to go throu the "**Bull ring**". Came off guard this arvo about 4.30 p.m. Got to go to the **Bull ring** tmw.' (Diary entry, 16 March 1917, *Letters from Bert Smythe* [online])

bully

An abbreviated form of *bully-beef*, 'a type of pickled or tinned beef'. *Bully-beef* comes from the French *boeuf boulli*, 'boiled beef'. **Bully** made up a substantial part of a soldier's diet.

The soldier periodical, *Honk*, recorded in an alphabet: 'B is for **Bully** and Biscuits we chew, because it is months since we tasted a stew.' (1915, p. 3) C.E.W. Bean's *The Anzac Book* included a contribution that told the story of a character named 'Wallaby Joe': 'No matter how circuitous the maze of trenches, he could find his way with ease. He could turn out all sorts of dishes from his daily rations of flour, bacon, jam, and of course the inevitable "**bully**" and biscuits.' (p. 60)

burgoo

A term for porridge or stew. It derives from *burghul*, an Arabic word for a type of cooked, parched, and crushed wheat, which ultimately derives from the Turkish *bulgur*. It was originally a nautical term used in the eighteenth century for a type of porridge eaten on ships.

While the word was known to Australians and New Zealanders before the war, it was often used within the context of the institution of the military and reflected the kind of institutional fare soldiers had to eat. During the war, it became a familiar term for many. Gunner Leslie Hanley wrote home to his father from the Western Front: 'The life is not quite so bad as it is painted. We do all-right. We have "**burgoo**" in bed of a morning; taking it in turns to get up and make it. Of a night before we turn in, we have coffee with the rum issue in it.' (*Upper Murray and Mitta Herald*, 22 March 1917, p. 2) A poem entitled 'Farewell to the Cooks' and written for the troopship periodical *The Khyberian* in 1919, produced during the soldiers' return home, included the following verse:

> From spuds not peeled and meat so scarce.
> From **burgoo** burnt, and bacon worse;
> You gave the sergeants tasty pie,
> But left poor diggers there to die. (April-May, p. 12)

chat

This term for a louse, a type of parasitic insect that plagued soldiers during the war, was frequently used by Australian soldiers. The word had a long history, first being recorded in 1690 as British underworld slang and then recorded in later canting dictionaries. However, it does not appear to have been widely used until the Great War when all the English-speaking soldiers used the word as they all underwent the common experience of being infested with lice. Lice were a plague in the trenches, and aside from being the source of great discomfort, were dangerous to soldiers insofar as they carried TRENCH FEVER.

Chat was also used as a verb (and in the noun form **chatting**) to refer to the activity of trying to rid oneself of the parasites. Brophy and Partridge provide a colourful description of the activity in *Songs and Slang of the British Soldier: 1914–1918*:

> As time went on, **chatting** became part of normal routine during quiet and rest periods; indeed, it was almost a social occasion, and in huts or dug-outs during the winter, and outdoors if there was summer sunshine, rows of men could often be seen with their shirts or trousers or tunics laid over their knees, cracking lice and jokes together. What has become of all the millions of these parasites since the War is an unsolved problem.

Gunner W.J. Duffell, an Australian soldier, wrote home to his mother in 1916 asking, 'Next parcel, please don't forget some life buoy & Mortien for it is almost impossible to keep free from **chats** as we call them.' (Letter, 1916, *Soldier Boy: The Letters of Gunner W.J. Duffell 1915–18*) Another soldier, Jim Osborn, wrote in his diary: 'The "**chats**" do not discriminate on the battlefield and from the highest to the lowest all suffer from the "**chat**".' (Diary entry, 15 January 1916, *War Diaries of Sergeant Jim Osborn*, p. 48)

clink

A military prison or a guardroom. It dates back to the sixteenth century with reference to 'gaol', and from 1880 in reference to military imprisonment. During the Great War, the term was popularly used by soldiers in reference to being put under detention by military police.

In 1916, a report about a military training camp in Bendigo, Victoria, quoted their commanding officer, Colonel McVea, on the men under his command: 'They are a splendid lot of men, the best I have ever had under my command. ... I have not yet found it necessary to put one of them in the military gaol or "the **clink**", as they call it.' (*Bendigo Advertiser*, 3 November, p. 8)

crime

This military term, used as a verb, means 'to be charged with a **crime** or offence'. It dates back to 1570, but from the end of the nineteenth century it was used primarily in a military context. It was frequently used during the Great War to refer to the charging of soldiers with various offences.

The term was used by Australian soldiers during the war, as this quotation demonstrates: 'While our Battalion was being inspected, Col. Elliott caught a chap named Brown chewing. So he told Major Hart to "**crime**" him".' (Diary entry, 15 January 1916, *War Diaries of Sergeant Jim Osborn*, p. 48) A soldier's offences were usually recorded on a *crime sheet*.

Crown and Anchor

A type of gambling game played with dice that was popular in the British Army. The game was also played by Australian soldiers. It dates back to the eighteenth century, and originated in the Royal Navy. The dice used in the game have faces with a crown, anchor, and the four card-suits; players place bets on a board or cloth with the same symbols. Gambling was against military regulations, but many soldiers played both **Crown and Anchor** and the Australian gambling game TWO-UP.

A 1919 article on troopship diversions commented: 'For the soldier finding his money going too quickly at two-up is the game of **crown and anchor**—a game that would induce even the Kaiser to have another go.' (*Port Pirie Recorder*, 8 April, p. 4)

dinkum oil

The term **dinkum oil** is a product of the Australian experience of the Great War. It had two senses which refer to two understandings of information during the war: the first was 'accurate information'; the second was 'inaccurate information; a rumour'. *Dinkum* is originally an English dialect term that became a central term in Australian English meaning 'genuine, reliable, true'. It is used adjectivally to describe something or someone who had these qualities. *Oil* is used figuratively in Australian English meaning 'information', from the idea that oil is a substance essential to the running of a machine.

The first printed evidence to appear in newspaper records for the 'accurate' sense of information during the war dates from 1915. Corporal George A. Leyshon, a young soldier from Victoria, who would soon die from his wounds at Gallipoli, wrote home to his mother on 12 April. He recounted General Sir Ian Hamilton inspecting the soldiers and telling Leyshon's C.O. that they would soon head off into combat: he gave the Colonel 'what we slangly call the "**dinkum oil**" '. (Melbourne *Argus*, 19 May 1915, p. 7) *The Kookaburra*, a soldier periodical published in Egypt and France, wrote in 1916: 'The sound of the Despatch-Rider's Motor made our hearts go pit a pat. Did he bring the "**Dinkum Oil**"?' (26 July 1916, p. 5) This sense of **dinkum oil** is also recorded in New Zealand English in this period. However, it should be noted that even when **dinkum oil** could be understood to mean 'accurate information', there was often a touch of irony in the tone.

Diary evidence records one of the first uses of **dinkum oil** referring to a rumour or piece of unreliable evidence. Albert E. Coates, another Victorian soldier, wrote: 'We have no word as to when we are likely to leave or where we are bound for. There are a lot of "Furphy's" or "**dinkum oil**" (as rumours are called) about, but we cannot believe them.' (Diary entry, 21 February 1915, *The Volunteer*, p. 47) This sense of **dinkum oil** was sometimes just shortened to **dinkum**, as in this example from the 1916 *Anzac Book*: 'I was on the beach one day when a friend met me and asked if I had heard the latest **dinkum**.' (p. 56)

The term gave its name to a trench periodical, *Dinkum Oil*, which was produced at Gallipoli in 1915. The decision to give it this title reflected the way such periodicals were considered to provide useful and reliable information to soldiers—C.E.W. Bean who helped to establish the magazine initially intended to call it *Furfies Gazette*, with the idea that such a publication would dispel rumours and provide accurate information to the men. In 1917, Frederick

J. Mills (as 'The Twinkler') produced another publication with a similar title: *Dinkum Oil: Original Australian Wit and Humour*, a collection of stories by Australian soldiers that was very popular and sold thousands of copies. This publication no doubt helped to popularise the term back home in Australia, but also had many soldier-readers.

The two senses of, and the frequent references to, **dinkum oil** recorded during the war reflect the importance of information for the average soldier who was not usually given much information about what was happening in the broader context of the war. Unsurprisingly, there are many such terms for information or rumours that date from the war, not least FURPHY and GOOD OIL, but also including less well-known terms such as BEACHOGRAM and LATRINE WIRELESS.

dixie

This term was used for two types of utensils used in the army during the Great War. The first sense of **dixie** was for a large pot, usually used for cooking, and was a British Army term that dated back to the nineteenth century. The *OED* suggests that it was first used in 1879 in the form *dechsie*, an Urdu word meaning 'copper pot'. The second sense refers to a small container for food or drink used by an individual, and is considered to be an Australian English term.

In 1915, Australian soldier Roy Whitelaw who was on a troopship heading overseas wrote in a letter home of his descriptions of life on board: 'The corporal selects two men each day to act as mess orderlies. At every meal these men have to fall in with a dish and **dixi** each, march up the steps to the deck and another flight to the cookhouse where, after waiting their turn and filling their dishes they come down the best way they can. If they slip (which they often do) we go without our tea.' (Letter, 31 October, *Somewhere in France*, p. 6) An article in a 1918 edition of the Adelaide *Register* told the 'Tale of a "**Dixie**" ' written by an Australian sergeant, concluding with the observation: 'Ask a soldier which of his many accoutrements—bar his rifle, gas helmet, etc.—are most necessary, and the "**dixie**" will always stand out.' (30 December)

flag-wagger

A name given to a member of the army signals corps; a signaller in the army.

Lieutenant A.A. Milne commented in a piece published in the Hobart *Mercury*: 'A signaller wears two crossed flags on his left arm; as a "**flag-wagger**" he is known. But this does not mean communication in the field is carried on simply by waving a flag. ... On the contrary, signalling in this war has become a very elaborate matter indeed.' (29 October 1918, p. 6)

flea-bag

A term for a soldier's sleeping-bag or bedroll. It derives from the idea that such bedding attracts a variety of bugs, including fleas.

An Australian serving on the Western Front wrote: 'Under the concussion of those two incessant howitzers, the ceiling and plaster of two walls had collapsed, enveloping us all. ... We dug out our "nap" from under the debris, crawled back into the "**flea bags**", and slept on to Reveille.' (*Broadmeadows Camp Sentry*, 3 August 1917, p. 2)

flybog

A term for jam or treacle that derives from the belief that jam and treacle attracts, and traps, flies. This Australian English word was first used in the context of the Great War by Australian soldiers.

Like terms such as ANZAC WAFER, the use of a word such as **flybog** by soldiers was a commentary on the food that they were given. The *Port Pirie Recorder* quoted a humorous story with an Australian soldier saying: 'Back in the waggon lines we get butter, rooty, rice, an' **flybog**, and if yer get **flybog** yer don't get butter, an' if the cook don't win a game, well, yer go dead stiff for a feed!' (8 May 1918, p. 4) After the war, the term continued to be used in Australia, and was particularly taken up and used by Australian writer 'Bill Bowyang'.

forty-niner

This term for an army biscuit is first recorded in the context of
the Boer War. While not recorded in any of the collections or
dictionaries of Great War slang, it had some currency in the
vocabulary of Australian soldiers, and can be found in accounts by
Australian soldiers from the period of the war. Another word used
by Australian soldiers for an army biscuit is ANZAC WAFER.

J.L. Beeston who served at Gallipoli wrote: 'One particular kind
of biscuit, known as the **"forty-niners"**, had forty-nine holes in it,
was believed to take forty-nine years to bake, and needed forty-nine
chews to a bite.' (*Five Months at Anzac*, p. 19)

French leave

'To take **French leave**' dated back to the seventeenth century, and
refers to departing unnoticed or without permission. In military
contexts the expression was used to mean desertion or going absent
without leave (see AWL).

Private R.J. Harris wrote home to recount his experiences after
the evacuation of Gallipoli: 'Last night, when on board the ship, I,
with others, took **French leave** and got over the side of the ship to
take a look at Alexandria. ... As we were short of money we could
not have a good time.' (*Evelyn Observer and Bourke East Record*,
28 April 1916, p. 3)

furphy

Sometimes abbreviated to **furph**, this word means a rumour
or false report, and is one of the words from the Great War that
continues to be used in Australian English. It originated with the
name of the firm J. *Furphy* and Sons, who manufactured water
carts in Shepparton, Victoria, which were used to supply water to
the military training camp at Broadmeadows, Victoria, where many
soldiers who enlisted were first sent. Soldiers who gathered around
the water carts would swap stories and rumours, many of which
had no basis in fact, hence the name **furphy**. It is likely that the

term was first used in the Broadmeadows army training camp, but it clearly was often used at Gallipoli, which is the context for much of the first evidence. The carts were often placed near latrines for the purposes of washing, and this was where soldiers gathered and rumours spread. A person who was fond of spreading rumours was sometimes known as a *furphy-king* or *furphy-monger*. Similar terms to **furphy** are BEACHOGRAM and LATRINE WIRELESS. Less well-attested variants include *furphigram* and *wash-house wireless*.

Both **furph** and **furphy** are first recorded in 1915 in a wartime context. John L. Treloar wrote in his diary in February 1915: 'Today's **furphy**, for never a day goes by without at least one being created, was about lights being prohibited in camp on account of the possibility of German airship raid. Some of the troops do not suffer from lack of imagination.' (*An Anzac Diary*, p. 83) C.E.W. Bean, who was a war correspondent at Gallipoli, wrote in his diary in June of the same year: 'The place has been full of spy rumours these last few days ... Blamey has asked me if I can get out a '**Furfies** Gazette', with these **furfies** [rumours] so exaggerated as to laugh them out of court.' (*Bean's Gallipoli: The Diaries of Australia's Official War Correspondent*, p. 158) A joking piece in the *Colac Herald* later in 1915 explained to those at home: 'A "**furph**" is something "heard from good authority"—generally relating to our future movements.' (15 November, p. 4)

gasper

A term for a cigarette, first used during the Great War. The *OED* records that a **gasper** was usually a cheap or inferior cigarette. Brophy and Partridge in *Songs and Slang of the British Soldier: 1914–1918* argue that **gasper** was used 'almost exclusively by officers'. Cigarettes provided one of the few pleasures for soldiers when in the trenches.

A contributor to the soldier periodical the *Kia Ora Coo-ee* wrote the following small item on the various cigarettes smoked by soldiers:

> I've been making a study of issue fags, or '**gaspers**' as they are vulgarly termed, and I would be glad if somebody would enlighten me on a certain point, which has puzzled me a lot. Who named

the different brands? They are good names, we must admit: 'Red
Hussar', 'Flag', 'Ruby Queen', 'Oro', 'Three Sisters', 'Lucana',
'Rough Rider', 'Kitchener', 'Trumpeter', 'Tabs', 'Brittania', etc. Yes,
I'd like to know who christened them, so that I might take off my
hat to him and offer a 'Ruby Queen.' (15 October, p. 5)

gaspirator

During the Great War, a gas mask was sometimes known as a
gaspirator. The word is a jocular play on *respirator*, a Standard
English word for a gas mask.

A description of an Australian soldier described him appearing
with his 'tin hat at a steep angle over his right eyebrow, **gaspirator**
at the "alert"—it was hard to recognise in him the race-day "Dag"
who, in pre-war days, used to swing the bag on country courses
back South in the Land o' Sun.' (*Port Pirie Recorder*, 8 May
1918, p. 4)

good oil

Good oil was a term used during the Great War to refer to reliable
information. *Oil* in Australian English is used figuratively, and is
based on the idea of oil being essential to the running of a machine.
Good oil is first recorded in a wartime context in 1916, and went
on to be a popular term in Australian English. Like DINKUM OIL,
FURPHY, and other such terms, **good oil** indicated many soldiers'
pre-occupation with obtaining information as to what was going
on, and their concern with the reliability of that information.
A similar term, recorded in W.H. Downing's *Digger Dialects* and
A.G. Pretty's *Glossary of AIF Slang* is *good guts*, defined simply as
'information'.

A reporter in July 1916 wrote about a visit made by Australian
Prime Minister Billy Hughes to the Australian soldiers in France.
He noted:

> The boys had expected a short address from the Prime Minister,
> but their wish was not gratified: there was no speechmaking. They
> had hoped, they said, that 'Billy' would give them the '**good oil**'

(something reliable and informative) about the war—not about the trenches and guns; they know all that—but about the probable duration, When will they get to Berlin? They want to know. (*Riverina Herald*, 26 July, p. 2)

gravel-crushing

A term for the route marching undertaken by infantrymen. Infantrymen were therefore sometimes known as GRAVEL-CRUSHERS. (See entry in Chapter One.)

'Trooper Bluegum' (Oliver Hogue) wrote about the Australian experience in Gallipoli, noting how some of the Light Horsemen had to give up their horses. He quoted Colonel Ryrie: 'My brigade are mostly bushmen, and they never expected to go **gravel-crushing**, but, if necessary, the whole brigade will start to-morrow on foot, even if we have to tramp the whole way from Constantinople to Berlin.' (*Western Star and Roma Advertiser*, 12 June 1915, p. 4)

gutser

Often used in the phrase come a **gutser**, to take a heavy fall, and figuratively to experience a disappointment or a failure, this was popular with Australian and New Zealand soldiers during the Great War. While it likely pre-dated the war, the war years popularised it, and it continued to be used in Australian and New Zealand English after the war. The variant spelling **gutzer** is also recorded.

A 1922 article on 'Diggers' English' observed that **gutser** was a word particularly associated with the AIF. The author contended that the word was well-known to schoolboys before the war, and that 'when the Ack-I.-F. was created and "diggers" were brought into being, there was a handy term all ready for use, which could be applied easily to anything unsuccessful, any failure or disappointment.' (Perth *Daily News*, 22 April, p. 11) The same author argued that the term was 'never far from the tongue of the "Digger" or those in any long association with him'.

An article on Australian soldiers from 1918 discussed the use of the phrase: 'He [an Australian soldier] can "come a **gutser**" for his pay when his pay-book is overdrawn, for his dinner when he is late, for his girl when she does not meet him, for a drink if he finds the canteen shut.' (*Gordon, Egerton and Ballan Advertiser*, 23 August, p. 5) Private W.H.A. Miller serving on the Western Front wrote home to say: 'They lost very heavily, and during the day Fritz counter-attacked three times, but without result. He "came a **gutser**" was the way we put it.' (*Forbes Advocate*, 22 January 1918, p. 2)

The variant *abdominal* (see also ABDOMINAL CRASH) is recorded in W.H. Downing's *Digger Dialects* and A.G. Pretty's *Glossary of AIF Slang*. Another variant is *come a thud*.

iron rations

A term for emergency rations, given to soldiers in case they were cut off from supplies. The term was used in military slang for some time before the war and dated back to the middle of the nineteenth century. It probably derives from the hard army biscuits (dry rations) soldiers were given. Another use of IRON RATIONS during the war referred to a heavy shelling. (See entry in Chapter Eight.)

Corporal Hampden Woods wrote home in a letter reproduced in a Victorian newspaper:

> If you were at any base railway station when a draft of men was going up the line you would notice, attached to each man's haversack, a little white calico bag. These bags however, do not contain wool or knitting needles, but a tin of compressed meat 'bully beef' and six army biscuits, more familiarly known as Anzac wafers. The official name given in these is '**iron rations**,' but soldier call them by other terms. ... The idea of '**iron rations**' is that should a soldier be completely cut off from supplies in general and his company 'quarter-bloke' in particular, he will always have sufficient food for one day at least. (*Colac Herald*, 14 December 1917, p. 2)

In his diary, Australian soldier Michael James Egan wrote: 'Got our issue of **iron rations** etc. By Jove we'll be loaded this time but have to take a good stock of grub and ammunition as the heads think we may lose connection with headquarters for a time.' (Diary entry, 23 September 1917, *WWI Diary of Michael James Egan*, p. 36)

kangaroo feather

This was a term for the emu feather plume worn on the hat of a member of the Australian Light Horse during the Great War. It is first recorded in the context of some of the Australian colonial mounted infantry units sent to South Africa during the Boer War, and appears again from 1915 with reference to the Australian Light Horse. W.H. Downing's *Digger Dialects* also notes the term as meaning 'a tall tale' or 'an impossible thing', from the idea that a '**kangaroo feather**' is a fanciful thing, but there is little printed evidence to support this sense.

One comment in the Australian press was as follows: 'One of the Tommies wrote home that it is easy to pick out Australians here, as they wear **kangaroo feathers** in their hats, and speak English nearly as good as the Indians.' (*North Western Advocate and the Emu Bay Times*, 26 February 1916, p. 7)

kibosh

To 'put the **kibosh** on' is a British slang expression dating back to the nineteenth century, and means 'finished off; put an end to'. It is probably originally London underworld slang that may have come from Yiddish. It became popular during the Great War, thanks to a song called 'Belgium Put the **Kibosh** on the Kaiser'. The variant spelling **kybosh** was also often used.

An Australian poem, written by poet–raconteur Tom Skeyhill in 1915 and addressed to his 'cold-footed cobbers', included the verse:

So I'm pullin' off me colors
And I'm slingin' my Webb away,
I'm layin' down me rifle
I don't care what they say,
If 'e can shirk 'is duty,
And won't come out an' drill,
Well, two can play the same game,
Then in comes Kaiser Bill,
I'm not afraid of bullets,
I'd 'ave died without a groan;

But 'e's put the **kybosh** on it,
Me Brother Wot Stayed at 'Ome. (*Geraldton Guardian*, 25 January
    1916, p. 1)

latrine wireless

Occasionally abbreviated to **latrine**, this was a term used during the
war to mean 'a rumour', and derived from the notion of the latrine
area as a source of rumour or gossip. (See also FURPHY.) The variant
latrine rumour was used in American and British services' speech.
Brophy and Partridge's gloss on *latrine rumour* in their *Songs and
Slang of the British Soldier: 1914–1918* is as follows:

> *Latrine Rumour*—Wild and unsubstantial stories and prophecies.
> They usually took one of the following forms: (1) Rumours about
> German strategic and tactical plans, new weapons and traps;
> (2) Changes of High Command, new theatres of war, Napoleonic
> schemes of victory; (3) Secret doings by one or other of the Allies
> which would relieve the pressure on the British front; (4) Spy and
> treason stories; (5) Auguries of a life of comparative ease and
> luxury in the near future. ... Such rumours became associated with
> latrines because these shanties were practically the only places
> (except the grave) in which a private soldier could be comparatively
> secure from the eye and voice of authority. Consequently men
> sat there for long periods, reading newspapers, gossiping and
> exercising their imagination and credulity.

Brophy and Partridge also record other similar terms, such as
cookhouse rumour, ration-dump yarn, and *transport rumour.* A variant
recorded in an Australian troopship periodical is *wash-house
wireless*: 'The latest *wash-house wireless* is that Spain had declared
war on England. The calamity came about owing to Spaniards
shoving up the price of onions.' (*The Log of the Lunatic Ship*, No. 3,
1916, p. 2)

Sergeant G.W. Brownhill, writing in the *Forbes Advocate*, noted:
'Rumors—**latrine wireless**, we call them—fill the air about the
chances of returning to Australia but anyway I am sure to get away
sooner or later within the next month or two.' (28 September 1917,
p. 7) The Australian soldier magazine *The 'Two Blues'* suggested that

the term was superseded by FURPHY at some point during the war: 'In our Australian camps all we now call "Furphies" were called "**Latrine Wireless** messages" and later "**Latrines**".' (December 1918, p. 3)

mungaree

Mungaree, meaning food, was current in British slang from around the middle of the nineteenth century, and came from Italian *mangiare*, 'to eat'. During the Great War soldiers made frequent use of the term to describe military food. Australian and New Zealand soldiers also used the abbreviated forms **munga** and **munger**.

Private Arthur Pickford, serving with the Australian Light Horse in Palestine, wrote in a letter home to his brother: 'We got plenty of Jacko's **munger** (food), but best of all was his raisins, in sack bags— the best I ever ate. I filled my haversack with them.' (*Clunes Guardian and Gazette*, 19 February 1918, p. 2) The soldier periodical the *Kia Ora Coo-ee* told a story in which a soldier called Jim came up with a tin of sausages. 'We hadn't stopped a mail for weeks', wrote the author of the story, 'so the **mungaree** didn't reach him in a parcel; Jim just got it—and no questions asked. It was damn good, too.' (April 1918, p. 20)

oil

A term for information or news, usually found in the combinations DINKUM OIL and GOOD OIL. *Oil* is used figuratively in Australian English to mean 'information', and it derives from the idea that **oil** is a substance essential to the running of a machine.

The soldier periodical *Kia Ora Coo-ee* commented: 'As soon as we get "the **oil**" about the paper famine, we began to collect boxes, packing cases, and stray bits of timber—anything that one could write on.' (15 October, p. 18)

Oscar Asche

Rhyming slang for 'cash', this term was often abbreviated to **oscar**. Both are Australian English terms first used around the time of the

Great War and were popular with Australian soldiers. *Oscar Asche* was a well-known Australian actor (1871–1936).

Ça Ne Fait Rien, the publication of the 6th Battalion, assured its readers that they 'will get value for their **Oscar** by buying a copy'. (October 1917, p. 1) Another periodical, *The Sardine*, observed: 'Two Diggers, short of **Oscar Asche**, and with 14 days' leave, decided to take advantage of the Y.M.C.A.' (No. 6, August 1919, p. 7)

Paris leave

During the Great War, this was leave granted for a soldier to travel to, and stay in, Paris, which was a particularly desirable location for leave near the end of the war.

A soldier noted the following in his diary: 'Everything as usual. I am convinced I spent my best holiday in Paris and hope to take **Paris leave** in lieu of Blighty leave.' (Diary entry, 25 July 1918, *An Anzac's Diary*, p. 77) A poem in *Aussie: The Australian Soldiers' Magazine* included the following lines:

> And, straightwire, Digger, you'll've naught to grieve,
> Whether Lance-Private, Serg't or Sub.,
> If you spend the whole o' your **Paris Leave**
> 'In the Sun' at th' Army Leave Club. (8 March 1918, p. 10)

rooty

A British Army term for bread that came from Hindi *roti*, and as a slang term dates back to 1846. It was picked up and used by Australian soldiers during the Great War. Although usually applied to bread, it could be applied to food more generally.

Australian Gunner Roy Dean, wrote home while on leave in England in 1916 to say: 'It's funny to hear some of the boys talking of their billets—some in hotels, some in business houses, and others in private homes. Some consider it a shame to walk on the carpets with their boots on, and a slip is sometimes made at the table, as when asking for bread they forget and call it "**Rooty**".' (Orange *Leader*, 11 February, p. 8)

short arm parade

A medical inspection of the penis in order to detect venereal disease. Such inspections were a common feature of military life during the Great War. Brophy and Partridge in *Songs and Slang of the British Soldier: 1914–1918* write that this was '[a]nother example of the degrading slavery to which the necessities of war compelled decent, reticent men to submit'.

Australian soldiers had somewhat mixed responses to such inspections, as might be expected. Percy Smythe observed in his diary, '[a]fter dinner we had a **"short arm" parade**, but I don't think any venereal was found in the company.' (Diary entry, 19 March 1916, *World War I Diary of Percy Smythe* [online]) John Ridley had a stronger reaction to the inspection: 'In afternoon had muster of **short arm parade** in West Australian deck. A disgusting parade which brings out all the impurity of this race. Such parades make one disgusted with the whole.' (Diary entry, 11 October 1915, *Born to Be a Soldier: War Diary of Lieutenant John G. Ridley*, p. 3)

signalese

During the Great War, army signallers employed a special code in communications, often dubbed '**signalese**'. A system of pronunciation was used for clarity and to prevent misunderstandings. This alphabet was used by soldiers in a variety of ways to form new words. The alphabet used by signallers included the following: A = Ack; B = Beer; D = Don; M = Emma; P = Pip; S = Esses; T = Toc; U = Uncle; V = Vic; Z = Zebra. This particular phonetic alphabet was changed by the British War Office in 1921, but a variety of phonetic alphabets continued to be used in military communications. A number of terms derived from this alphabet were quickly brought into soldiers' vernacular during the war. Most of those found in the written evidence tend to be fairly standard military terms that would have been used by signallers in communications, and from there passed on into use by the broader soldier population.

Two of the most well-attested terms are *ack emma*, 'a.m.', and *pip emma*, 'p.m.' In communications, *ack* + *emma* was used to refer to *a.m.* or *ante meridian*, 'morning', and *pip* + *emma* to refer to *p.m.* or *post meridian*, 'afternoon; evening'. A newspaper article in the Orange *Leader* noted that in 1918 the British Army at home and abroad was moving to a 24-hour clock so as to 'minimise the possibility of a 12 hour error in any specified time by the omission or misreading of a.m. or p.m.—the "*ack emma*" or "*pip emma*" of the army signallers'. (31 December, p. 3) The terms moved into more general use by soldiers, as the following quotation from a soldier periodical suggests: 'At eight *ack emma*, Monday, we "partied", [left where they were, from the French *parti*] and that day we did not go by air, but through it.' (*The Kookaburra*, No. 1, France, 15 June 1918, p. 11)

Other elements of army and trench life led to the development of **signalese** terms. These include *o pip* for 'observation post', and *emma gee* for 'machine gun'. The soldier publication *The Rising Sun* commented of the Australian soldier: 'How we marched and billeted, marched and "bivvied" and toiled on till at length he came within sound of the big doors banging, and of the little birds whistling at night from the crackling "*Emma Gees*"—and then he fought the mud, and fought his disgust and his fears, and perhaps he hopped over and fought the Hun.' (8 January 1917) An anecdote reproduced from *The Bulletin* in the Australian newspaper, the *Cobargo Chronicle*, went as follows:

One of the dinkum doers announced that he 'wasn't goin' ter carry no rifle' and before leaving the billet he planted his gun between the stone floor and the mattress. When the parade fell in he successfully hid himself between his mates, and all went well until the first 'Slo-Parms' was given. At once he was spotted from the sergt-major's *O Pip*. The martinet looked him up and down. 'Haven't you got your rifle with you?' he roared. 'Well, to tell you the Gorstruth,' says the hard doer, 'I have got it with me; but it's in me pocketbook.' (4 May 1918, p. 4)

Y Emma is another such term. 'Y.M.' was a common abbreviation used during the war for the YMCA. The YMCA provided huts, tents, and other spaces that offered soldiers a space for reading, writing and enjoying various entertainments, as well as dispensing coffee, tea, and other comforts. The term is well attested in the Australian evidence. 'A Soldier's Story' recorded in the *Port Fairy Gazette* in January 1918 had a soldier writing home: '[W]hen I left the place I'd made up my mind that the Y.M. is good enough for me. From that moment I cut out the Estaminets, and now spend all my spare evenings in the *Y. Emma*, the only bit of home we chaps in France ever get.' (21 January, p. 2)

Few specifically Australian **signalese** terms developed during the Great War, but one that can be found in the printed record is *ack-eye-fuff*. This was **signalese** for A.I.F., the Australian Imperial Force, the name given to Australia's fighting force in the Great War. *I* had no phonetic rendering, and so was represented with *eye*, and *fuff* was a humorous elaboration on *f*. The soldier periodical *Ça Ne Fait Rien* included the following commentary on Sergeant 'Bootmaker' Wilson: 'By making special boots for "diggers" with bad feet and expert treatment for corns and ingrowing toenails Sergt. Wilson has rendered many a march easy. He has done his work better than any other snob in the *Ack-eye-fuff*.' (21 February 1919)

In addition to these terms that can be traced in the Australian evidence, war dictionaries, such as W.H. Downing's *Digger Dialects* and Brophy and Partridge's *Songs and Slang of the British Soldier: 1914–1918*, record several terms for which no other written evidence can be found in the Australian sources. Some of these terms include: *beer esses*, 'B.S.', 'bull shit' (A.G. Pretty's *Glossary of AIF Slang* defines this as 'flattery, kidstakes'); *emma-emma-esses*, 'M.M.S.', 'Men May Smoke', referring to a smoke break (this term appears in notices announcing veterans' reunions in Australia in 1919, although not otherwise attested); *esses-emma*, 'S.M.', Sergeant-Major; and *tock emma*, 'T.M.', a trench mortar.

slanguage

A term for slangy speech. It was used around the period of the Great War, including in discussions of slang developed by Australian soldiers.

Australian soldiers themselves saw their **slanguage** as something that distinguished them. In *Aussie: The Australian Soldiers' Magazine*, editor Phillip Harris wrote in the second number of the periodical:

> Others don't like our **slanguage**. But *Aussie* would remind these friendly critics that there is a lot of slang in the talk of our Army. And whatever defects our Aussie vernacular may have, it certainly has the virtue of being expressive. *Aussie* merely aims at being a dinkum Aussie—and a dinkum Aussie uses the language of the Aussie. He doesn't want to be a literary stylist. And, after all, the slang of to-day is the language of to-morrow. The history of the Aussie Army is being given by the Official War Correspondents. *Aussie* wants to give its spirit—and that can be done only by allowing you to say the things you want to say in your own language and your own way. (No. 2, February 1918, p. 1)

A reporter commented on Australian soldiers in Egypt through 1915: 'One cannot help but smiling when he thinks of the many shocks in store for some of the British tourists when they visit Egypt in future years, for the street ragamuffins have mastered all of the choice epithets of the Australian back blocker. But maybe by that time Bernard Shaw will have tutored the British pleasure seeking public into a passable knowledge of the intricacies of the great Australian **slanguage**.' (*Geraldton Guardian*, 13 January 1916, p. 1)

spook

A term for an army signaller, especially a wireless operator. Its origins are unclear although probably deriving from the use of *spook* meaning a ghost or apparition (a use that dates back to the nineteenth century).

An Australian soldier from Lismore wrote home from France: 'I am back on the gun again having applied for a transfer from "**spook**" (battery scout 2nd signaller) to gunner, and been successful. Have had plenty of shooting: in fact, too much.' (Lismore *Northern Star*, 20 September 1916, p. 5)

two-up

A gambling game in which two coins are tossed in the air and bets are laid on whether they both will fall heads or tails uppermost. Two-up dates back to the middle of the nineteenth century and was a popular game with Australian soldiers during the Great War. It became closely associated with ANZACS in Australian culture subsequently. The game is now only played in Australia on ANZAC DAY or in certain casinos. Soldiers enjoyed gambling and many frequently participated in such activities, although gambling was against military regulations. Another popular gambling game, particularly identified with British soldiers, was CROWN AND ANCHOR.

Archie Barwick, fighting on the Western Front, wrote in his diary: 'At the present time "two up" is very popular among the boys—they play it every opportunity they get. Some of them win large sums of money & many others go broke, but it is no use trying to put gambling down in the Army for they will always find some way or other to gamble & two up is I think about the fairest.' (Diary entry, 12 October 1916, *In Great Spirits: The WWI Diary of Archie Barwick*, p. 179) In 1919 an inquiry was held into the way soldiers were treated on one of the ships returning them to Australia. Testimony was heard, and it was reported:

> The witness said 'two up' was the favourite pastime of the Australian soldiers, and he had seen officers join in the game in France, but never in England or on board ship. He had seen acres of schools in Egypt. He knew gambling was unlawful in military as well as civil life, but many petty offences in the army were overlooked. He had seen men playing 'two up' five minutes before going over the top, and perhaps they were saying a prayer at the same time. (Adelaide *Chronicle*, 25 January, p. 11)

Various two-up terms were in use during the war. Making an opportune bet was known as *coming in on the grouter*; the *mick* was a coin's tail, and *mick* was also used as a verb referring to a spin of the coins so that the tail landed uppermost; to toss the coins in the air was the *spin*, and the player who tossed the coins was the *spinner*.

up to putty

The phrase **up to putty** is used to indicate that something is 'no good; worthless; ineffectual'. It is a variant on phrases such as *not up to snuff*, with *putty* suggesting something soft and malleable. The phrase pre-dated the war by some years in Australian English, but became popularly used (and found much more in print) through the war years as it was liberally used by some soldiers as a particularly apt expression for life in the military and at war. It is sometimes abbreviated to *up to* or *upter*. The latter is recorded in W.H. Downing's *Digger Dialects*.

Lance Corporal Lamb, writing home to his mother in Australia, said: 'When we going [sic] into the trenches; talk about exciting. Fritz was sending across gas shells in hundreds, and we had to don our gas helmets. It was **up to putty**, groping along in the dark with our helmets on.' (*Mullumbimby Star*, 16 August 1917, p. 2) Another Australian soldier, Corporal Frank Hanley, writing from France told his parents: 'Things are well **up to "putty"** here. Rations, eh! 17 men to a loaf of bread.' (*Port Fairy Gazette*, 6 June 1918, p. 3)

*If the Kiwi King
you're after*: Military
hierarchy, bureaucracy,
and other sources of
complaint

CHAPTER

3

A number of slang terms used by Australian soldiers were those that
referred to and described things soldiers disliked. Unsurprisingly,
soldier culture allowed for the expression of many of the petty and
less petty complaints and resentments of the average soldier towards
military hierarchy and authority. Some of the targets of their greatest
disdain included officers—BRASS HATS, military bureaucracy and official
information—EYEWASH, and the military police, who were given names
such as RED CAP or JACK. This chapter examines some of these terms.

Australian soldiers during the Great War became renowned for their
contempt for authority and for challenging the restrictions of military life.
Many soldiers saw being in the army as a job, and challenged it in ways
they would a job whose conditions they resented. For example, officers
had to earn an ordinary soldier's respect, rather than automatically be
accorded it. Unsurprisingly, these sorts of attitudes frequently clashed
with the traditions and rules of the military.

Australian soldiers were particularly contemptuous of British
authorities. Compared to British soldiers, they were more likely to
challenge the rules and traditions of the army, often to British officers'
disapproval. For the most part, Australian military leadership overlooked
many of the Australian soldiers' infractions. Historian Peter Stanley notes
that while the only official difference between Australian and British
military authority was that Australian soldiers could not be executed as

a punishment for serious crimes, the 'unspoken rules' that applied to them were 'quite different'.

Australian soldiers' attitudes to authority, whether contemptuous or humorous, are captured in Australian terms such as ROSELLA or KIWI KING for an officer, QUARTER-BLOKE for the Quarter-master, and MOTHER'S PET for a military policeman. Along with British soldiers, they made use of other terms such as BRASS HAT for an officer, RED CAP for a military policeman, and BUMF for official paperwork.

Australian soldiers also expressed their contempt (as well as occasional jealousy) of those who either had not enlisted or who managed to get out of front-line or arduous duties in the military through their language. Popular terms in use during the Great War include LEADSWINGER and DUG-OUT KING.

There are also a number of colourful terms recorded in W.H. Downing's *Digger Dialects* that are not recorded elsewhere, but which further capture some of the attitudes of soldiers towards characters for whom they had no great affection. Some of these are listed below, with Downing's original definitions:

> *Anti-Christ on tin wheels (or crutches)*—'a pompous or self-sufficient person'.
> *bludge on the flag*—'to fail to justify one's existence as a soldier'.
> *Brasso King*—'an officer who insists that his men should polish the brass-work on their equipment and uniforms'.
> *broken-doll*—'an inefficient staff-officer returned to his unit'. [Probably from the popular song 'A Broken Doll' (1916)]
> *bumbrusher*—'an officer's servant'.
> *hairy-belly*—'a sycophant'.
> *war lord*—'an officious or pompous officer'.

Clearly captured in this list of terms from Downing is the average soldiers' dislike of sycophants and officers who behaved in a way that took advantage of their rank.

∞

battle police

During the Great War, military policemen on duty behind the lines of an attack, stationed there to make sure all soldiers went into the line, were known as **battle police**. Front-line troops often expressed their dislike of these men.

British war correspondent Philip Gibbs wrote about Australian soldiers fighting at Messines Ridge. He describes their actions, as they mined under German lines:

> When a young officer jammed down the lever, the ground billowed out and the noise of the explosion was prolonged by a mighty cheer. The men couldn't help it. They had been ordered to keep the strictest silence, even to the **battle police** on duty, but when the mines lifted the miners realised that their long work had been a glorious success, and they couldn't restrain from jubilation. Anyhow, the Huns were past hearing their cheers. (*Zeehan and Dundas Herald*, 12 June 1917, p. 3)

brass hat

A British Army slang term for a high-ranking staff officer, and used by Australian soldiers during the Great War. The term derives from the gold braid on the hat of a senior officer. It first appears in the printed record in Rudyard Kipling's writings of the late nineteenth century. Terms such as these originated from enlisted soldiers' attitudes towards higher military authorities and staff officers who were often regarded with resentment, contempt, or mockery. **Brass hat** was one of the more popular terms used by average soldiers to refer to an officer who was not situated in the front lines.

A letter to the editor from someone in Perth in 1918 commented: 'In these Australian days Jack is as good as his master—sometimes better—and I am of the honest opinion that better feeling would prevail if some modification were brought about. For instance, what good is done by compelling a wounded "Billjim" (often on crutches) to salute a "**brass hat**" (an officer whose dugout is in London) when struggling down the Strand.' (Hobart *Mercury*, 29 January, p. 6)

bumf

Short for *bumfodder*, this was a term in popular use with the English-speaking armies to refer to official forms, paperwork and other bureaucracy. Due to its 'crudeness', it is difficult to find written evidence for it, however, it is well attested in slang dictionaries from the period immediately following the war.

A.G. Pretty's *Glossary of AIF Slang* defines **bumf** as: 'That portion of the enormous mass of Official correspondence which was used for a more undignified purpose than originally intended. Later applied more generally to correspondence and literature of little value.'

cushy

This is an Anglo-Indian word meaning 'comfortable, easy'. It derives from the Hindi *khūsh*, 'pleasant'. While probably picked up by the British Army in India, it became popular during the Great War and passed into general usage thereafter.

A 1915 newspaper article commented: 'Probably there is no word derived, or adapted, from the Hindustani so much in use among regulars, reserves, Kitchener's army, or Territorials as "cooshi" or "kooshi" which is always rendered as "**cushy**", to signify that one is nicely comfortable, or that a task is easy to perform.' (*North-Western Advocate and the Emu Bay Times*, 20 November, p. 1) By 1918, the term was common, as in this example: 'Captain Ornstien, in wishing the guest Godspeed and a safe return, said Corporal Owens had been at the front before, and had been wounded, but he had elected to go again. He was going into the railway unit, and although some might think that a pretty "**cushy**" job, he could tell them that it was not.' (*Maryborough and Dunolly Advertiser*, 16 October, p. 2) Brophy and Partridge in *Songs and Slang of the British Soldier: 1914–1918* comment with irony from the point of view of the ordinary soldier: 'Other people were always getting **cushy** jobs.'

dingbat

An Australian slang term for an army batman (an officer's servant). *Dingbat* is recorded in Australian English in the sense of 'a simpleton, a fool' from the turn of the twentieth century; the standard term *batman*, used of an officer's personal servant, likely influenced the wartime sense.

A poem printed in the *Kapunda Herald*, entitled 'The Dingbat', included the following verse:

> He's not a bally Batman, he's a
> **Dingbat** now, you know,
> We do not call him Orderly or Servant
> Near the foe—
> And he shines well 'mid polish
> Tins in heaps. (31 May 1918, p. 4)

dog's leg

A lance-corporal's chevron or stripe. It is an army term that pre-dates the war, probably going back to the late nineteenth century. It is recorded in both W.H. Downing's *Digger Dialects* and A.G. Pretty's *Glossary of AIF Slang*, although it is not well-attested in Australian print sources from the war years. The quotation below pre-dates the war, but suggests that Australian soldiers would have been familiar with it.

A 1912 newspaper article on army slang noted that: 'The "**dog's leg**" is the lance-corporal's chevron or stripe, which, worn on the arm, denotes his rank. Possibly the term is in some way connected not only with the shape of the stripe but with the nature of the duties which the lance-corporal is called upon to perform.' (Adelaide *Advertiser*, 6 November 1912, p. 18)

dug-out king

This term was used during the war to refer to someone deemed to be cowardly—that is, they preferred to stay in a DUGOUT rather than fight. **Dug-out king** was first used by Australian soldiers at Gallipoli and it remained a popular term in use through the war years. Brophy and Partridge in *Songs and Slang of the British Soldier: 1914–1918* record the term, defining it as a '[f]amiliar way of referring to an officer or NCO who took advantage of his rank and office to remain in his dug-out as long as possible. Some of this genus never showed their heads above ground from the moment of entering a trench till it was time to leave.' They note the variant **dug-out warrior**, which can also be found in the Australian press during the war.

A reporter serving with Australian Army Medical Corps at Gallipoli wrote: '[A]nybody about whom the men are in doubt has a nick-name. "So-and-so, the **dug-out king**," aptly describes a man who spends what is considered an unfair amount of time under cover.' (Melbourne *Argus*, 6 October 1915, p. 7) One general was referred to as 'principal **dug-out warrior**'. (Perth *Sunday Times*, 8 April 1917, p. 24) Brophy and Partridge also record the term *dug-out disease* meaning a '[c]hronic fear of death and danger, which kept those, whose rank permitted any choice, safe in their dug-outs'.

eyewash

This term for official deceit, or 'something done for effect rather than practical purpose', was familiar to all English-speaking soldiers. It reflected the general distrust of official pronouncements and authority that soldiers experienced during the Great War. It dates back to the late nineteenth century, and appears to have been first used by British officers in India, but it achieved widespread popularity during the war. It is a transferred use of *eyewash*, 'a wash or lotion for the eye', and relates to the idea that **eyewash** might literally obscure vision, as official deceit might obscure truth.

The *Dubbo Liberal and Macquarie Advocate*, reporting on the war in 1917 noted that: 'This army has learned how things should be done, and we Australians, who have been rather apt to think that the R.A.M.C. sacrificed medical efficiency for red tape and **eye-wash**, are filled with admiration for their thoroughness.' (29 June, p. 3)

hummer

This slang word for 'a scrounger, a cadger' is first recorded in Australian English in a military context in 1916. It probably comes from *hum*, 'a cadger', also found as a verb, 'to cadge'. Both are Australian English terms first recorded in 1913, and probably derive from *humbug*, 'to impose upon, hoax, delude'.

Aussie: The Australian Soldiers' Magazine wrote in October 1918 that '[t]here is no such thing as stealing in the Army. There are no thieves. The only thing that the Army produces are "**Hummers**" and "**Pinchers**". The Army is great on borrowing.' (p. 15)

jack

A military policeman might be known as a **jack**. As a slang term for a policeman, it dates to the late nineteenth century, and is a form of the name *John*, often used as a generic proper name.

An article by a Queensland soldier on the words and phrases of the Australian soldier noted that: 'The military police have earned the title of the "**Jacks**".' (*Gippsland Times*, 27 May 1918, p. 3)

kiwi

A **kiwi** was a soldier (often an officer) with highly polished accoutrements. The term comes from the popular brand of boot polish, *Kiwi*, and is first recorded as an Australian English term in 1916. During the war, it was often used to refer to those who were located far from the front line in military office jobs. Terms such as **Kiwi Brigade** and **Kiwi King** were used by soldiers, deriving from this sense of **kiwi**.

A 1917 newspaper article referred to the staff at Horseferry Road (AIF Headquarters in London) as 'the "**Kiwi Brigade**", in the language of the trenches, in apt allusion to the general polish of their outfits'. (*Warwick Examiner and Times*, 13 October, p. 1) The soldier periodical, *The Kookaburra*, included a poem with the verse:

> If the **Kiwi King** you're after, he ain't a cause for laughter,
> You can pick him by his swank and haughty bark.
> He's a guy who drives a quill in the office with a will,
> He's a Non. Com. in the Ammunition Park. (Vol. 1, France, April
>   1917, p. 4)

lance-jack

A standard British military slang term for a lance-corporal. It pre-dates the Great War. It was certainly used by Australian soldiers during the war, and was used in Australia as early as 1911 in the context of the Citizen Military Forces. A lance-corporal was the lowest non-commissioned officer in the army.

The troopship periodical *The Sardine* included the following lines in a poem about life after the war:

> I wonder if the Captains will sling orders at a mob?
> I wonder if **Lance Jacks** will toss pennies for a bob?
> I wonder if I'll come a thud when looking for a job?
> I wonder! (No. 6, August 1919, p. 8)

leadswinger

A popular slang term, used in both the Navy and Army before the Great War to mean 'a loafer; a malingerer'. It derives from the phrase SWINGING THE LEAD, meaning 'to idle; to malinger'. Swinging the lead was a task undertaken in the Navy and involved taking soundings with a lump of lead to ascertain the depth of water— it was considered to be an easy task, and hence preferred by the lazy. Brophy and Partridge in *Songs and Slang of the British Soldier: 1914–1918* add to their definition for **leadswinger** the following comment: 'Often used affectionately and with the faintest suggestion of reproach.'

Many jokes and anecdotes about military life mentioned the **leadswinger**. Cecil L. Hartt, in his 1918 book, *Diggerettes: Digger Jokes and Stories*, wrote: 'The battalion dag thought he was genuinely crook and fell in on sick parade. The M.O., a man of notoriety among **leadswingers**, had a look at the dag and commented cuttingly on his robust appearance.' (p. 23) A 1919 newspaper anecdote went as follows:

> It was at the 'bull-ring' at Etaples, the AIF First Division Base in France, where the new drafts had a final hardening process of training. The 'sick, lame and lazy' had fallen out, and there paraded before an unsympathetic M.O. the champion malingerer of the battalion. 'It's my feet, sir,' moaned the **lead-swinger**. 'They are all right when we are running, but as soon as we 'alts they 'urt something cruel.' 'Well, my lad,' replied the quack, 'when the company halts you go on marking time. That's easy, isn't it.'

'The M.O. here is a fair swine,' remarked the tale-teller as he got his full pack ready to join his platoon. (Burnie *Advocate*, 12 July, p.7)

mother's pet

A term for a military policeman, deriving from the standard abbreviation, *M.P.* It is recorded in Downing's *Digger Dialects* and A.G. Pretty's *Glossary of AIF Slang*, but it is not particularly well-attested in the written evidence.

A humorous item in the Australian press made reference to **mother's pet**:

> Garge: 'I see you've got M.P. on your sleeve. Be you a member of Parliament, then?'
> Military Policeman (sarcastically): 'No, I'm **mother's pet**.' (*Cobram Courier*, 31 October 1918, p. 3)

quarter-bloke

A military slang term for the Quartermaster or Quartermaster Sergeant (also sometimes referred to as the *Q.M.*), the officer responsible for providing soldiers with clothing and/or rations. It first appeared during the Great War, and was used by both British and Australian soldiers.

John Gideon wrote home to his mother: 'I have been Acting Quarter Master now for some time and it is one of the best jobs a chap can get here. I have great fun with the boys, especially when there is a rush on; and the clothing business is funny. They call me the little **quarter bloke**.' (*Essendon Gazette and Keilor, Bulla and Broadmeadows Reporter*, 31 October 1918, p. 1) The troopship periodical *The Last Ridge* included the story:

> At the close of a day of great fatigue, he who was called Digger walked by the wayside and talked unto himself, saying, 'My strides look more distressed and crieth unto me to be laid at rest with their forefathers. I will return unto one—even a very great one—named Quarter Master Sergeant, known to the multitude as the "**Quarter Bloke**", and will say unto him "Quarter, thou mighty one of the clothes chest, cast thine eyes upon my strides

and thou wilt see they are nigh unto destruction." ' (No. 2, 26 July 1919, p. 9)

red cap

A term for a military policeman, so called because of the red band on their military caps. It was used by British and Australian soldiers during the Great War.

This account from an Australian serving in the military police in Cairo in 1916 describes attitudes towards the **red caps**:

> We are what is called **'redcaps'**, owing to the red hat band we used to wear. And a most hated and despised lot we are too. Hated because we are policemen. ... Military police and others who hold soft jobs at headquarters and other places far from the firing line, are credited with being cold-footed. (*Richmond River Herald and Northern Districts Advertiser*, 18 July 1916, p. 2)

roar up

This term, meaning 'to reprimand severely; to berate', is an Australian English term first recorded in 1916. After the war, it came into general use in Australian English.

In 1916, a newspaper article about Australian officers described officer training: 'His instructor is a rough man with a rough vocabulary, embracing the whole Australian language in its most varied and lurid forms. ... He has to bear it in silence. Better to be "**roared up**" than ignored. It shows his instructor is taking an interest in him.' (*Sydney Morning Herald*, 12 February, p. 7) A 1918 newspaper article noted of the Australian soldiers: 'The men do not mind being "**roared up**" as long as it is done in a straightforward sort of way.' (Rockhampton *Capricornian*, 17 August, p. 42)

rosella

This was an Australian English term referring to a staff officer. It is a transferred use of the name of a type of brightly-coloured Australian parrot, and makes reference to the colourful red and yellow insignia of a staff officer.

Aussie: The Australian Soldiers' Magazine included the following comment on a staff officer: 'A certain **Rosella** in the Aussie Army is known as Old Bloodlust, partly on account of him viewing the war as a personal quarrel between himself and the whole Hun Army, and partly on account of always regarding a soldier proceeding in a direction other than towards the Front Line as squibbing it.' (January 1919, p. 11)

stellenbosched

To be **stellenbosched** was to be moved to a position or role of limited consequence. Officers were sometimes **stellenbosched**. The term was a British Army term, dating to the Boer War, and deriving from the town of *Stellenbosch* in the Western Cape, South Africa.

While senior officers were sometimes **stellenbosched** as a result of incompetence, the term might also refer to any officer being moved to a job where they had little to do. An article in the Perth *Sunday Times* noted that Jim Throssell, winner of the Victoria Cross at Gallipoli, had been 'one of those who were for some months "**stellenbosched**" in Egypt'. (11 June 1916, p. 10)

swinging the lead

This term refers to malingering, loafing, or evading duty. Someone who **swung the lead** was known as a LEADSWINGER. Brophy and Partridge in *Songs and Slang of the British Soldier: 1914–1918* note that to be successful in **swinging the lead** was 'a great source of pride with some soldiers'. A variant was *swinging the hammer*. Yet another similar term recorded in contemporary collections of war and services slang is *dodging the column*, which Brophy and Partridge define as: 'The art and science of avoiding unpleasant and especially dangerous duties.'

Bert Orchard, serving on the Western Front, wrote in his diary in 1916: 'Very wet & cold, had a spell nursing my knee. "**Swinging the lead**" in military language.' (Diary entry, 5 September, *Diary of an Anzac: The Front Line Diaries and Stories of Albert Arthur 'Bert' Orchard*, p. 108) An Australian sergeant, working in England, wrote home to say: 'I trust my work here is of some importance. I would certainly resent being accused of "**swinging the lead**". My lengthy stay here has not been through any action of mine.' (*Wyalong Advocate and Mining, Agricultural and Pastoral Gazette*, 26 September 1917, p. 2)

work the nut

This expression means 'scheming, malingering'. A soldier who did this was sometimes referred to as a *nut-worker*. It derives from the slang sense of *nut* referring to one's brains or intelligence.

A 1916 article by a returned soldier included a commentary on the state of discipline in the AIF:

> I do not even suggest that the greater number of these men have been '**working the nut**'—the soldier's expressive colloquialism for malingering—but, granting that each and every case of illness is a genuine one, there is a clear indication that there must be a screw loose somewhere, and the looseness of the mechanism will be probably found to have its origin in looseness of judgment in the selection of the right stamp of men on enlistment. (Perth *Sunday Times*, 16 July, p. 3)

Alley at the toot:
Languages

A number of words in the Great War soldier's vocabulary were borrowings from, or corruptions of, languages heard while overseas. For Australian soldiers, the primary languages spoken by people they encountered while serving abroad were Arabic and French, and therefore unsurprisingly it is from these two languages that we find a number of Great War slang terms being taken. Some of these words had already entered the British Army's vocabulary and were transferred from there to the Australians; others were Australian soldiers' own peculiar twists on French and Arabic words.

Many of the quotations in this chapter suggest something of the difficulties soldiers experienced when conversing with people who spoke a different language. This miscommunication often became the basis for humorous anecdotes, jokes, and stories in soldier periodicals. In some cases, Australian soldiers' apparent linguistic 'abilities' were celebrated as indicative of their distinctive qualities, as in this short piece printed in a troopship periodical, which was headed 'Adaptability of the Aussie':

> Esperanto is not in it. Dinkie dye, the buckshee lingo that the digger is railroading tout suite to Aussie is some class, believe me, although some would say it is pas bon. A promenade of the mess decks is all that is necessary to convince one that the Australian has concocted a universal language, probably the most cosmopolitan language the world over, which all soldiers compree. They have grasped the surface meaning of various languages, and the combination of the old Gyppo, French and Belgian, interspersed with well-known Cockney, American and Australian sayings, tends to make their thoughts original, humorous and expressive. The Australian adaptability is responsible for this. Some have even grasped a little of the Italian, Russian and German jargon, so that future linguistic aspirants in Australia, and the novelist will require to air his knowledge of languages with caution. (*The Last Ridge*, No. 2, At Sea, 26 July 1919, p. 5)

The evidence of soldiers' understandings (or lack of comprehension) of foreign languages and foreign cultures sometimes comes through where one finds examples of Australians using corrupted foreign words. Serving overseas involved a considerable culture shock, as well as opportunities for cultural interactions. Attitudes towards the local inhabitants of places they visited or served are often evident: racism is often present in their commentary on Egyptians, for example.

The languages from which Australians borrowed most of their words were Arabic and French. Australian soldiers, who served in Egypt and the Middle East, borrowed a number of words from Arabic, such as AIWA, SAEEDA, and IMSHI. These words reflected the desire to communicate with (or in some cases, give orders to) Egyptians and other locals.

Slang words taken from French tended to be either a rendering of pronunciations of French words, for example, COMPREE, or were Anglicisations of French words or, more commonly, phrases, such as SANFAIRYANN and NAPOO. Again, the adoption of these terms by soldiers is reflective of the desire for some basic communication with the civilians they encountered, even if that communication was often limited to buying drinks in an ESTAMINET or chatting up a French girl.

Many soldier periodicals included a variety of humorous glossaries that related to the adaptation and corruption of French words by soldiers. In these glossaries, the definitions related to the actual meaning, but were usually interpreted in some humorous way. A good example of such a glossary is the following written for a soldier periodical:

French English Vocabulary

Arranged by an eminent professor of languages, chiefly bad language.

ALLEY, TOOT SWEET: In regimental parlance "at the double". In the language of the Anzac "spring off your tail you Roo".

COMMONG TALLEY VOO: Thought by some bush-whackers to mean "common tallow candles".

EN CORE: When eating an apple and come to the core, you use this expression. The language of France is so easy if you have brains—Anzacs kid themselves that they have cornered the brain market.

FINNEY: Sounds rather fishy, but you find it a handy word when you have searched your issue pockets for sous and find nix.

TRAY BONG: Not as supposed by some blokes to be a bonbon costing a tray. It's the expression you use when consuming strawberries and cream at the front—in your dreams.

ZIG ZAG: Bitten by an estaminet dog. Also the name of a cigarette paper which looks that way the morning after the night before. (*The Kookaburra*, Vol. 2, July 1917, p. 5)

The mutilating of French was often regarded as a sign of the humour and wit of Australian soldiers, and indicative of their basic irreverence. A 1922 article on the language of the diggers commented on the (otherwise not well-attested) *come a tallez plonk* used much in the way of 'come a GUTSER', and which was described as both 'ingenious' and a mark of their 'gay disrespect' for the French language. (Perth *Daily News*, 22 April, p. 11)

Several terms in addition to those discussed in this chapter can be found in contemporary commentaries on war slang and Anzac vocabularies, including W.H. Downing's *Digger Dialects*, but appear not to be widely attested in the Australian written evidence otherwise. These include *atcha*, 'alright', a general British Army term derived from

Hindi *accha*, 'good' (it is mentioned briefly in the Australian press during the war years as soldier slang, but there is little other evidence that Australian soldiers used it); *gas-gong*, 'boy', from the French *garçon*, *mazonk* (or *mademoiszonk*), from the French *mademoiselle*, 'Miss', and *mercy blow through*, 'thank you', from the French *merci beaucoup*.

Another aspect of language during the war, not reflected in this book, concerns the home front in Australia. This was the changing of German names, for example, towns with German names, German street names, and German products, to something more acceptably English; those with German family names also sometimes changed their name. This had an impact not just on the Australian population and landscape, but also affected Australian English. In South Australia, for example, the pastry known as a *Berliner* became the more patriotic *Kitchener bun*.

Foreign languages contributed to soldier slang and, rather ephemerally, to Australian culture, in a variety of ways. An exploration of the words and their use provides fascinating insights into the cross-cultural encounters of Australian soldiers during the Great War.

☙❧

aiwa

Also often represented with the spellings *ewah* and *iwah*, this was a term taken from Egyptian Arabic and used to express agreement. The Arabic term is *aywah*, 'yes, indeed', a colloquial form of *na'am*, 'yes', which may be short for the expression *ay wa-llāh*, 'yes, by God'.

The *Kia Ora Coo-ee* in an article 'Arabic Made Easy' provided for their readers a guide to some of the more popular Arabic words in use. It explained: 'One of the most familiar and simplest Arabic words is **aiwa**, which means "yes". It is easy to pronounce, as it has not any of the letters, guttural or coming from deep down in the throat, which distinguish the Arabic language.' (15 October 1918, p. 13)

alley at the toot

From the French *allez tout de suite*, 'go immediately'. As with many other terms borrowed from the French, this represented an Anglicisation and corruption of the original French, although keeping the original meaning.

F.M. Cutlack, a war correspondent, recorded an Australian soldier saying of a battle: 'An extremely warm corner was a haystack which gave excellent cover to some machine guns. At this point our casualties were heaviest, but the position was soon stormed, and the Boches '**alleyed at the toot**.' (*Swan Hill Guardian*, 29 July 1918, p. 4)

après la guerre

A popular phrase with the soldiers, adopted straight from French, and meaning 'after the war'. Brophy and Partridge in *Songs and Slang of the British Soldier: 1914–1918* explain the significance of the phrase for soldiers:

> The fact that this phrase was so soon caught from the French is a sure indication of how much the thought and wish for peace was in everybody's mind. ... [The phrase] carried two connotations for the soldier: It was used jokingly for indefinite and remote future ... And, secondly, the phrase was a depository of secret sentiment, of longing for survival and for the return of decency, quiet and beauty.

For the most part, many of the Australian examples of the use of this phrase suggest a more literal use of the term to simply refer to the time after war's end.

Lieutenant Geoffrey Drake-Brockman, a West Australian and engineer, wrote to the Civil Service Association from France to say: 'Perhaps some day, **après la guerre**, the West will see me again.' (Perth *West Australian*, 27 December 1916, p. 5) An Australian artilleryman from Hobart, writing home to his parents in 1918, commented: 'In spite of being told that Tassy [Tasmania] has been found drifting in the Atlantic, or has been capsized, we still hold out hopes of finding her where we left her when we return, "**après la guerre**".' (Hobart *Mercury*, 19 September, p. 5)

baksheesh

This is a term meaning 'free of charge; something for nothing'. It was brought into general English through the Anglo-Indian Army from Hindi (although originally of Persian origin). It meant 'a tip; gratuity', and was sometimes used in this sense. In the Great War it was also used in adjectival form, with a variety of spellings, with the suggestion that something was 'free of charge'. The term was picked up and used by English-speaking soldiers, including Australians and New Zealanders, who served or passed through Egypt and the Middle East. It came to be often rendered as **buckshee.**

William Dawkins, serving in Egypt in 1915, wrote in a letter home to his mother:

> We had some funny experiences among the natives. As we were trotting along one of the bunds (canal banks) we overtook an old gentleman riding a donkey in the usual fashion without reins. As we approached, the donkey bolted and as I passed, the old boy was white with fear and gradually working to the rear of his mount. At Cutler's approach, hidden by helmet and field boots the old boy absolutely collapsed and lay stretched out on the roadway. We were going back to see him but as the whole countryside was turning out and as we thought the ancient gentleman was only wanting some '**backsheesh**' we galloped off. (*From Duntroon to the Dardanelles*, p. 111)

In December 1915, Bert Orchard noted in his diary: 'A water pipe burst & we scored a few gallons of **"backsheesh"** water for our own use.' (Diary entry, 1 December, *Diary of an Anzac: The Front Line Diaries and Stories of Albert Arthur 'Bert' Orchard*, p. 80)

A 1918 Australian newspaper article described the various uses of the term by soldiers:

> '**Buckshee**' means 'something for nothing.' If, after the 'gippo' has been rationed out, a little of the stew is left in the Dixie, you will hear the sergeant shout out, 'Who wants a **buckshee** bit?' The lucky fellow who lights up a cigarette when cigarettes are very few and far between will be greeted on all sides by the cry, 'Got a **buckshee**, mate?' Like all words that your soldier-man favours, it is made to serve a variety of purposes. A **buckshee** man is a man too many when a fatigue has been numbered off. If he is lucky he may be told to stay behind; but more often than not he is given a **buckshee** shovel and told to carry on. (Launceston *Examiner*, 26 October, p. 5)

A troopship periodical, *Homeward Bound*, noted of **buckshee**:
' "[B]uck-shee" being an Australian rendering of the Egyptian word
"bak-sheesh", meaning "Give alms".' (1918, p. 45)

barrak

A term used to make a camel sit, derived from Arabic *barraka*,
'to make (the camel) kneel down'. This was a word of somewhat
limited currency but known to soldiers of the Imperial Camel Corps,
who named their unit publication *Barrak*. The Imperial Camel
Corps (ICC) was formed in January 1916 and fought in numerous
engagements against the Turkish army through 1916 to 1918.

A story from the soldier periodical *The Cacolet* in September
1917 recounted a soldier being ordered by an officer to: ' "**Barrak**
him, can't you!" was snapped at me again. Then the Sergeant
softened and showed how the deed should be done.' Also in 1917,
an Australian newspaper column noted:

> The last mail from Egypt brought a copy of the Camel Corps
> review, 'Barrak', from a soldier boy. On the cover, which is of course,
> true blue, is a camel, No. 3843, just ready for the desert, while a
> member of the corps, dressed in shorts and putties, is evidently
> trying to speed his going. His way, '**Barrak** you —', suggests that
> words have failed him. (Newcastle *Northern Times*, 20 October
> 1917, p. 4)

bukra

From the Arabic word *bukratan*, 'tomorrow'. It is included in W.H.
Downing's *Digger Dialects*. It was first adopted by British soldiers in
the Middle East in the late nineteenth century, and was used during
the Great War.

There is not much evidence to suggest that this term was used
widely by Australian soldiers serving in the Middle East, but a letter,
reprinted in 1916, from an Australian soldier, Private M. Davis,
records how a staff officer he knew had received a letter from a man
named Abdou Mohammed asking for money. Davis commented
of the request: 'Whether Abdou eventually received his "charges"

I don't know. He would probably get it "**bukra** mish mish" which, translated, means "in the sweet by and bye".' (*Maryborough and Dunolly Advertiser*, 9 June 1916, p. 4) The proper Arabic expression is *bukra fī-l-mishmish*, 'tomorrow in the apricot season' implying 'wishful thinking'.

clefty

This term was used by soldiers to mean 'to steal'. It may derive from the Arabic verb *kalifa*, 'to become brownish-red in the face'. In Turkey and some Arabic countries, a brownish-red face is considered to express shame, particularly when referring to someone who lies or steals. Another possible origin is in Greek, where *klephtys* means 'a thief'. The term was used by Australian soldiers serving in the Middle East.

A 1918 *Kia Ora Coo-ee* article, reprinted in the Australian press, recorded: 'When you start to sort your gear up, and throw last week's water out of your bucket, you discover that the iron rations for your horse have been "**cleftied**".' (15 June, p. 8) In 1919, an article on Anzac slang noted: 'Sometimes you'll hear him [the Australian soldier] complain that someone has **cleftied** (stolen) something.' (Perth *Sunday Times*, 9 March, p. 7)

compree

This is an Anglicisation of the French *compris*, meaning 'understood? is that clear?' Brophy and Partridge in *Songs and Slang of the British Soldier: 1914–1918* note this word as being 'in constant use' during the Great War. A recorded variant was *compray*.

An Australian newspaper commentary from 1917 stated: 'After the war many French phrases will be brought back by home-coming soldiers, and their constant use in everyday life will no doubt add words to the British dictionary. Unquestionably, the expression most likely to be adopted is "**Compree**," spelt in French Compris, and meaning, "Do you understand"?' (*Kalgoorlie Miner* 24 October, p. 2) Australian soldier Corporal Hector Brewer, writing in 1916 describing Republic Day in France, said: 'All the way from the station to the Caserne Pepeniere Barracks the street on either side was packed with people shouting "Vive la Englise!" "Vive la Canadie!" "Vive la Australie!" and a lot of other things which we didn't **compree**.' (Perth *Sunday Times*, 12 November, p. 14)

disaster

A term for a *piaster*, a unit of currency used in Egypt and Turkey during the period of the Great War. The word is partly a rhyme and partly a play on the coin's low value. It was a term used by Australian and New Zealand soldiers serving in the Middle East.

Australian soldier, Sergeant Colin Joyner, wrote home from Egypt in 1915: 'We have forgotten about English money. It was funny at first seeing the men puzzling over the different Egyptian piaster (or "**disaster**", as they call them) pieces.' (Adelaide *Register*, 17 March 1915, p. 7)

estaminet

This French word for a place where alcoholic drinks are served was brought into English during the nineteenth century, and widely used by soldiers during the war. **Estaminets** were, according to Brophy and Partridge in *Songs and Slang of the British Soldier: 1914–1918*, not really pubs or cafés; instead they were 'essentially small, and belong only to villages and very minor towns'. Further, they argued that a typical **estaminet** must have 'a low roof, an open iron stove and a fug'; **estaminets** 'furnished the jolliest and most heart-warming experience the private soldier met with'. The term was well-known to soldiers serving in France. See also BOOZER, a term used by Australian and New Zealand soldiers.

Private Jim McConnell wrote in his diary: 'There is also a couple of "**estaminets**", what we call hotels, in this village. I was very disappointed when I tasted the wine. It was absolutely rotten.' (23 December 1917, *Letters from the Front*, p. 88) In a letter home to his father, Australian soldier Fred Biggs wrote: 'The beer here is not too good. Every house in the villages and country on our line of march is an **estaminet** (inn), where they make their own beer.' (*Brisbane Courier*, 13 June 1916, p. 7)

feloosh

Also sometimes spelt **filoosh**, this term was used during the war to refer to money. In Egypt and other Arab countries, the plural *fulūs* means 'money'. This term was in general use by soldiers stationed and serving in the Middle East.

An Australian woman recorded receiving a postcard from a soldier who thanked her and her fundraising committee for the items sent to the soldiers: 'At the time we got them we were mafish **filoosh** (no money), so you have the pleasure of saying you have saved three lives.' (*Melton Express*, 22 April 1916, p. 2) Another soldier writing about Cairo, commented: 'To the man without "**feloosh**" the city, the camps upon the desert sands, and all the surroundings combine to make a veritable purgatory.' (Adelaide *Register*, 30 December 1915, p. 6)

fini

An Anglicisation of the French *finis*, 'finish'. This term is recorded with various spellings.

An article on words that came from French into soldiers' English was published in the *Anzac Bulletin* and reproduced in the *Healesville and Yarra Glen Guardian*. It noted: 'A latecomer is informed by the cooks that dinner is "**fini**" or "napoo".' (20 July 1918, p. 2) The troopship periodical *The Khyberian* included a poem with the lines: 'Then fatigues will be "**finee**," and route marching done. / And the chats all napoo, like ould Jerry the Hun'. (April–May 1919, p. 34)

hod

This term came from the Arabic noun *hawd*, 'a water basin; a reservoir'. It was a word used by Australian soldiers serving in Egypt and the Middle East during the war.

George Auchterlonie, an Australian Lighthorseman with the 8th Light Horse Regiment, recorded in his diary in 1916: 'Went on & dismounted under a ridge, but decided it was too warm so beat a hurried retreat. Went to a "**hod**" after water but it was very salt & he (horse), wouldn't drink altho without 24 hrs, wouldn't eat either & it is nearly knocked up.' (*Dad's War Stuff: The Diaries*, p. 15)

igri

An exclamation used to urge a person to hurry up. It derives from Arabic *ijri*, 'hurry', the imperative form of the verb *jarā*, 'to run, hurry, rush'. In colloquial Egyptian Arabic, 'j' is pronounced 'g'. A.G. Pretty's *Glossary of AIF Slang* records the variant spelling **igaree**. Pretty also records the phrase *igaree at the toot*, 'run away quickly from' (the French *à tout de suite* becoming *at the toot*). This phrase is interesting in its blend of Arabic and French corruptions, although given that French was spoken in Egypt, it was not necessarily a term that developed with the soldiers who moved from Egypt to the Western Front.

C.E.W. Bean wrote in June 1915 in a report back to Australia from Gallipoli that was widely reprinted in the Australian press:

> The war cry of the Australian as he went up the hills the first morning consisted of snatches of Arabic slang and profanity. 'Imshi Ya'la, you beggars,' which is 'Get on', or '**Igri**', which you shout at your cabdriver when you want him to hurry. It was 'Imshi Yalla' and '**Igri**' all up the hills that day, and the Turks imshi yallered and **igrid** for all they were worth. The Turks **igrid** too fast, and our men seldom had a chance of trying a bayonet on them. (Adelaide *Advertiser*, 17 August 1915, p. 9)

A 1917 commentary on 'Anzac vocabulary' noted the development of the (otherwise not attested) phrase *at the ig*, meaning 'at the double'. (*Cairns Post*, 26 April, p. 7)

imshi

This was a term meaning 'go away' and derived from the Arabic *imshi*, 'go away', the imperative form of the verb *mashā*, 'to walk, go, move along'. The longer form **imshi yalla** was also used by soldiers; yalla was a contraction of *Yā Allāh*. **Imshi yalla** means 'come on; let's go; hurry up'.

Along with IGRI, **imshi** and **imshi yalla** can be found reported in the Australian press as being used by Australian soldiers in Gallipoli. In particular, it was reported as the Australian soldiers' 'war cry', illustrated in this quotation from a June 1915 newspaper article (which probably made reference to Bean's account of the fighting):

> Our men had to act on many occasions on their own initiative, as their officers suffered severely. They just charged right ahead, yelling, '**Imshi**, you beggars,' and stuck everything that came in their path. '**Imshi**' is an Arabic word they learnt in Cairo, which means go to the devil. (*Forbes Advocate*, 11 June 1915, p. 2)

isma

An exclamation, 'What's up?' or 'I say!' It derives from Arabic *isma'*, 'listen'.

Australian soldier, Private Edward Sexton, wrote an account of his experiences in Egypt: 'The tram stops. What the deuce is wrong! A babel of voices, in which the conductor joins, "**Isma, isma**"? (What's up?) Only ran into a mule who thought he had more right to the track than the tram.' (*Daylesford Advocate, Yandoit, Glenlyon and Eganstown Chronicle*, 11 July 1916, p. 4)

mafeesh

A term adopted from Arabic, used by soldiers to mean 'finished; done with'. It comes from the Arabic *māfīsh*, a colloquial form of *māfīhi shay'*, literally 'there is not a thing in it'. It was used by English-speaking soldiers based in Egypt and the Middle East. Brophy and Partridge in *Songs and Slang of the British Soldier: 1914–1918* compare the use of **mafeesh** to the way NAPOO was used in France.

A 1916 newspaper article on Anzac slang recorded: 'Imshi is Gippy for clear off or get away, and **mafeesh**, which is borrowed from the same tongue, means nothing.' (*Camperdown Chronicle*, 4 May, p. 6) Charles Francis Laseron, a writer and sergeant in the

AIF, wrote: ' "**Mafeesh**" means literally "finish," and when said with a shrug of the shoulders is very expressive, whether used to say that a certain commodity has run out, or even to denote that someone has departed this life for ever.' (*From Australia to the Dardanelles*, p. 50)

A 1917 commentary on 'Anzac vocabulary' made a similar point to Brophy and Partridge, although claiming **mafeesh** as particular to the Australians: ' "**Mafeesh**" is another word that will live. It occupies the same place with as "fine" (French, fini finished) does for Tommy Atkins.' (*Cairns Post*, 26 April, p. 7) The term is, however, more broadly attested, including being used by New Zealand soldiers.

magnoon

This term means 'psychologically disturbed; eccentric'. It derived from the Arabic *majnūn*, which in turn derives from the Arabic verb *junna*, 'to become possessed, insane'. The 'j' is pronounced 'g' in colloquial Egyptian Arabic, hence the corruption to **magnoon**. It may have pre-dated the war, as there is some evidence to suggest it may have been used at the time of the siege of Khartoum and the British in the Sudan. However, most of the evidence suggests it was only first used widely during the Great War, and was used primarily by Australian soldiers.

Private A.C. Harris, writing home from Palestine about the work of the Imperial Camel Corps, and describing the camels said:

> I have never yet met an Australian or English soldier who really liked his camel. ... We just tolerate our camels—ugly, ungainly, smellful creatures; but a desert campaign would be pretty hopeless without them. ... Sometimes they go '**magnoon**' (mad), and even then will single out their tormentor. If he is slow getting away, then it means patch work for doctors and nurses in the most up-to-date military hospital. (*Koroit Sentinel and Tower Hill Advocate*, 13 October 1917, p. 2)

maleesh

An exclamation used by soldiers to indicate dismissal, 'never mind; forget it'. It comes from the colloquial Arabic *mā' alayhi shay'*, abbreviated as *mā' alīsh*, meaning 'there is nothing in it' or 'do not worry about it; never mind'. Like MAGNOON, this term was possibly first used in the late nineteenth century in the context of the British involvement in the Sudan. During the Great War, it became popular with Australians and New Zealanders serving in the Middle East.

A 1916 account of Egypt by an Australian included the following comment on the Egyptians encountered: 'The natives know what is in store for them when they are taken into custody, and they howl at the top of their voices while being marched off. They are the biggest liars imaginable, and when detected do not show the slightest shame or annoyance. "**Maleesh**"—"Never mind"—they say.' (*Port Pirie Recorder and North Western Mail*, 4 July, p. 1)

napoo

This term was used by soldiers during the Great War to mean 'finished, gone', and is a corruption of the French *il n'y en a plus*, 'there's no more'. Early glossaries of Great War slang suggest that the term was first heard by soldiers when the keepers of the French ESTAMINETS replied to their requests for drinks. Brophy and Partridge in *Songs and Slang of the British Soldier: 1914–1918* add to their definition of **napoo**: '[T]he word came to be used for all the destructions, obliterations and disappointments of war.'

William Slater, a stretcher-bearer, noted in his diary in September 1917 when getting a health rating after being wounded that 'unless I'm a C Class [unable to return to duty] man my chances are **napoo**'. (Diary entry, 15 September 1917, *War Diaries of William Slater*, p. 51) Lance-Corporal Norman V. Wallace, writing from France in December 1918, wrote: 'Fritz, as usual, is responsible for all this marching, as he has blown the railways to atoms in parts, and hasn't left a bridge or embankment. If all the curses that are called upon his head should take effect I think he would be "**napoo**" by now.' (Adelaide *Advertiser*, 4 March 1919, p. 6)

point blank

A term for white wine. It is an alteration of the French *vin blanc*, 'white wine'. A.G. Pretty's *Glossary of AIF Slang* suggests: 'The term is used on the Rifle Range as the name of a poisonous white paste that is applied to the foresight of the rifle to aid sighting. Its adaption as a name for *vin blanc* was brought about partly by the similarity in the spelling of the second word and also partly because of the harsh effect it frequently had on Australians who drank of it too freely.' Other related terms deriving from *vin blanc* include *plink-plonk* and *plinkety-plonk*, from which the Australian English term *plonk*, 'wine', derives.

Australian soldier Bob Dow wrote home to Horsham in 1918: 'More than once an arm has been placed on my shoulder, my hand has been firmly grasped, and I've heard: "Ah, Australie! Bon camarade, Australie!" Perhaps the "vin blank" (or "**point blank**", as the boys call it) has been introduced.' (*Horsham Times*, 15 October, p. 5)

saeeda

This was used by soldiers as a greeting and farewell. A variety of spellings appears in print, including *sieeda* and *sayeeda*. In Arabic, the expression *fursa sa'īda*, literally 'happy opportunity', is commonly used in saying goodbye to someone, as in 'it was nice to meet you'.

Charles Francis Laseron commented: ' "**Si-eeda**," to give it its phonetic spelling, meaning "good day," has later become remarkably corrupted, being even used as a noun, natives of any sort being called by the troops "Si-eedas".' (*From Australia to the Dardanelles*, pp. 49–50) 'Trooper Bluegum', writing in an account of the desert war in 1917, said: 'After the great transformation had been effected the Anzacs, who went to Abbasia as Light Horsemen, emerged as full-blown Cameliers. Perched on the hump of their huge, ungainly mounts, and with five days' water and tucker aboard, they bade a cheerful **Saeeda** to the nurses in the adjacent hospitals, and in a long, shambling, but very picturesque column, moved out into the wilderness.' (*Sydney Morning Herald*, 16 May, p. 7)

san fairy ann

This is an Anglicisation of the French *ça ne fait rien*, 'it does not matter'. This was a popular expression with English-speaking soldiers. Other corruptions of the French expression include *san mary ann* and *sandbag mary ann*. W.H. Downing in *Digger Dialects* records the variant *san ferry ann*. Brophy and Partridge in *Songs and Slang of the British Soldier: 1914–1918* provide a cynical gloss for the term:

> As the intelligence of the soldier penetrated year after year the infinite layers of bluff and pretentiousness with which military tradition enwrapped the conduct of the War, so his cynicism increased, became habitual. Men ceased to show initiative, not so much because they were dispirited by war, but because they realized that the stupidity of authority was impregnable. Neither virtue, courage nor skill were demonstrably of any avail to protect a man from the quite impersonal violence of shells or bullets, from the malignance of a biased superior or from unnecessary and dangerous duties carried out by order from above. Naturally he adopted a fatalism comparable to that of the Moslem murmuring his enervating 'Maalish'—It does not matter. Let a Quartermaster make an income from surreptitiously vended food and clothing, let a Divisional General order a hopeless raid in order to win a CMG for himself, let Johnny Cold Feet wangle a cushy job at the Base, let anything happen, the only appropriate comment was— *San Fairy Ann*.

An Australian soldier wrote home a comment on some trench language he had read in the newspaper: ' "**Sanfairyann**" means not the same as "Napoo," but it does not matter, or no matter, in plain Australian.' (*Cairns Post*, 29 August 1918, p. 4) The term was also recorded in a 1919 Australian newspaper article on 'Digger Yabber', the language of the trenches: '[W]ords in the hands of an artist flourish and spread like the green bay tree ... "Ca n'fait rien" (it can't be helped), which sounded to him like "**san fairy ann**" became "san Mary Ann".' (Perth *Sunday Times*, 9 March, p. 7)

stanna

A term used by soldiers to mean 'stop; wait'. It derives from the Arabic verb *ista'nā*, 'to wait'.

Sergeant Sydney Scott sent home a poem to his sister, Maud, in Australia, which contained a variety of terms taken from Arabic. He explained to Maud: 'You may not understand some of the words. A "waddy" is a dry creek; "fanaties," ten-gallon cans which are put on each side of the camels to carry water; "**stanna**" is to stop, and "barrack" is to make the camel lie down; "magnoon" is when the camels go mad.' A few of the lines in the poem he sent to her went as follows: 'You may "**stanna**", you may "barrack", you may any blanky thing; / But you can't slip in a dugout when you've camels on a string.' (*Kapunda Herald*, 12 October, 1917, p. 2)

toot sweet

This is an Anglicisation of French *tout de suite*, 'quickly, immediately'. It was a popular term used by soldiers serving in France, and was applied to all kinds of situations.

The *Dandenong Advertiser and Cranbourne, Berwick and Oakleigh Advocate* reproduced a section of an article from the *English Weekly* in August 1918 that included the comment:

> The Australian soldiers in France are inventing their own slang, in addition to adopting the usual Americanisms which we are all using nowadays. They call their country 'Aussie', and pronounce it 'Ozzy.' They call their pals 'cobber'—'a cobber of mine' means 'a pal of mine.' A man who has had a good time on leave reports that he has had a 'bosker' time, while those who have been in France have anglicised 'tout suite' into '**tootsweet**', and will often add 'the tooter sweeter.' We shall add some new dictionaries in our scheme of post-war reconstruction. (22 August, p. 3)

Jim McConnell, serving in France, wrote in his diary in 1918: 'I was sitting writing letters when I heard a shell coming. I rushed **"toot sweet"** down into our cellar and heard a crash right behind me as the building next door was hit and a lump of timber flew through the window next to where I had just been sitting.' (*Letters from the Front*, April, p. 155)

Fritz was napoo: Enemies and friends

A variety of names were applied by Australian soldiers to both their enemies and their friends and allies during the Great War. Nicknames, pejorative and otherwise, for other national armies and especially enemy armies, are a common feature of war slang, and there were a number of such terms in circulation during the Great War.

Attitudes to the British varied, despite considerable loyalty to the British Empire and the popular view that Britain was 'home' for many Australians. The experience of visiting Britain and serving alongside (and sometimes under the command of) the British could for many Australian soldiers foster a sense of Australian nationalism. British soldiers were viewed with both affection and a certain amount of derision, but the relationship was an important one. Archie Barwick commented in his diary: 'It's very seldom you will hear a Tommy say anything bad of an

Australian, or our boys of the Tommies, with the exception of a few who are being taught a much needed lesson.' (Diary entry, 3 August 1916, *In Great Spirits: The WWI Diary of Archie Barwick*, p. 138) Several terms were used by Australians to refer to British soldiers, including CHOOM, TOMMY, WOODBINE, and POMMY. Other 'friends' included the American soldiers, who were variously known as SAMMIES, YANKS, and DOUGHBOYS. The French were sometimes called FROGGIES, and Egyptians were nearly always known as GYPPOS. The New Zealanders, fellow ANZACS, were often referred to as ENZEDS, and occasionally MAORILANDERS.

Revealed in press and soldier accounts of the war are the various prejudices and stereotypes applied by Australian soldiers to the many different ethnicities they encountered. This is unsurprising, given the ways in which racial attitudes operated in the period, but often makes for uncomfortable reading for a modern audience. Attitudes towards Egyptians, for example, were often openly racist and derogatory, and can be considered alongside the ways in which soldiers communicated with local people in places like Egypt, discussed in the previous chapter.

The enemies that Australians fought, notably the Germans and the Ottoman Army, were given the greatest range of nicknames. Germans (soldiers or the people generally) might be known as FRITZ, HUN, HOCH, ALLEMAND, or JERRY. Turkish soldiers (the Ottoman Army was in fact made up of soldiers from a range of ethnic backgrounds) were often called ABDUL, JACKO, or JOHNNY TURK. Some terms were also used in close association with certain nationalities. Examples of this are the terms FRIGHTFULNESS and KULTUR, used in relation to the qualities of the Germans, and promoted in the propaganda of the period.

Some terms are included in W.H. Downing's *Digger Dialects* that are not found elsewhere. These include *bowie-knife army* for the American Expeditionary Force, and *cark sucker* for an American soldier (playing on a supposedly American pronunciation of *cock sucker*). The latter is an example of one very unlikely to find its way into print otherwise.

The terms in this chapter, and the quotations that illustrate them, further reflect the experiences Australian soldiers had during the war as they travelled abroad, and encountered new countries and new cultures. While this language reflects their racism and the stereotyped attitudes promoted in the popular press and official propaganda of the period, it also demonstrates the diverse encounters that Australians had with other people and cultures.

Abdul

A name given to a Turkish soldier; Turkish soldiers collectively. It was a use of a stereotypical name given to Turkish and Arabic people by the British. Soldiers had several names for the Turkish enemy they fought at Gallipoli and in the Middle East, including **Abdul** and Johnny Turk. **Abdul** was commonly used throughout the Great War by soldiers and in the Australian media.

Mentions of **Abdul** appear in many soldiers' accounts of the war. In an account of his experience of combat at Gallipoli, Australian soldier Bert Smythe wrote: 'They were short of both bombs & ammunition, but were sticking it out, cursing & swearing, as I believe, only Australians can, as **Abdul** threw bomb after bomb into the trench & ripped the sandbags to pieces with their machine guns as they traversed them back & forward along the parapet.' (Bert Smythe, 'Four Days at Anzac', August 1915, *Letters from Bert Smythe* [online]) Although the term was stereotypical, in that it made use of a common Turkish or Arabic name, the evidence suggests that Australian soldiers often expressed admiration for their Turkish enemy, as demonstrated in this excerpt from a poem included in *The Anzac Book*:

> So though your name be black as ink
> For murder and rapine,
> Carried out in happy concert
> With your Christians from the Rhine,
> *Life* will judge you, Mr. **Abdul**,
> By the test which *we* can—
> That with all your breath, in life, in death,
> You've played the gentleman. (p. 59)

Allemand

A term for a German, especially a German soldier; Germans collectively. It comes from the French for the German language, *Allemand* (see also Brophy and Partridge's etymological speculation quoted at BOCHE). The variant *Alleyman* is also recorded by Brophy and Partridge, and W.H. Downing in *Digger Dialects*.

While perhaps used more by British soldiers, some Australian soldiers picked up the term **Allemand** for a German soldier, as evidenced by the following quotation from a 1916 letter home by Private George Hood, a former schoolteacher from Billimari:

> Well, I must now conclude this rather crude epistle and take my turn on sentry go to keep an eye on 'Mr. **Allemand**' per medium of the periscope. We rarely ever see him, for like us, he prefers to keep his head well down, or otherwise he will soon lose the number of his mess. The war ends with any man who dares to put his head six inches above the parapet. We have already lost a few in this way, and so has '**Allemand**'. (*Canowindra Star and Eugowra News*, 14 July 1916, p. 2)

The troopship journal *The Boomerang* included in their 1919 Christmas edition the following lines of verse: 'Cold as an Esquimaux, silent and grim / Cold as the hate of the **Allemand**'s hymn.'

Boche

This was a term used to refer to a German, a German soldier, or Germans collectively (usually as 'the **Boche**'), and was popular during the Great War. It is a French word, possibly from the French *caboche* meaning 'head', but having a slang sense in French meaning 'rascal' or 'a bad lot'. Its usage by the French to refer to German soldiers may date to the Franco-Prussian War of 1870–71; Brophy and Partridge in their *Songs and Slang of the British Soldier: 1914–1918* present a possible etymology, writing that: 'The Germans, having among the French a reputation for obstinacy and perhaps as "bad lots," from *Allemands* became *Alboches*. About 1900 *Alboche* was shortened to *Boche* as a generic name for Germans.' During the Great War, the name was picked up and used by British and other English-speaking troops.

The Australian press speculated on the origin of Boche during the war. One correspondent noted in 1916: 'The word "**Boches**" is applied by the French to the Germans and is frequently used by ourselves, though many of us do not know its origin.' (*Bairnsdale Advertiser and Tambo and Omeo Chronicle*, 23 September, p. 3) The term **Boche** can be found frequently in the British and Australian press during the war, usually with pejorative overtones. The following excerpt from a 1916 newspaper article is a good example of this:

> That baffling word, '**boche**', which we have hitherto recognised as French argot for blockhead, is given a lofty lineage by a 'Lancet' ethnology. When you gaze upon the square, forbidding face of Von Hindenburg you meet the clue. Here is a typical representation of that type of head known as short or brachycephalic, and the squareness leads to 'block' head, and thence to '**boche**'. Not to original sin, but to original brachycephaly, therefore, does the modern German owe his term of contempt. Primitive peasant women 'marry the type of man voted handsome by their fellows. A fleshy-necked, short-headed type has probably always set Gretchen adoring'—and so we have an intolerable multitude of Von Hindenburgs. (*Chronicle and North Coast Advertiser*, 20 April, p. 6)

Reverend H. Linton, a chaplain from Broken Hill and Wilcannia who was stationed in France, wrote home: 'We then went outside and tried to find a quiet place to sit down and talk, and learn something about my work, but the **Boche** sent over about 200 shells, and gave us no peace.' (Broken Hill *Barrier Miner*, 10 January 1918, p. 2)

camouflaged Aussie

Camouflaged Aussie is recorded in W.H. Downing's *Digger Dialects* and A.G. Pretty's *Glossary of AIF Slang* as meaning 'an Englishman serving with the AIF'. A closely related term appearing in the press during the war is **camouflage Woodbine**, referring to a soldier who had enlisted in the AIF but had only been in Australia a short time before enlisting. Fraser and Gibbons in *Soldier and Sailor Words and Phrases* note the word CAMOUFLAGE coming into vogue during the war years 'as an expression implying any deception'. WOODBINE was more generally used by Australian soldiers as a term for a British soldier.

A 1918 article by Gunner David Worrall (formerly a journalist) supplied some humorous stories of life at the front, one concerning a **camouflage Woodbine**: 'The two cockies were having an argument. Both had been in Aussie only six months before they had enlisted. And the pot called to the kettle: "Garn, yer ain't an Aussie, yer only a **camouflage Woodbine**".' (Orange *Leader*, 28 August 1918, p. 1) In 1919, in an article about a welcome home celebration for the returning soldiers, there was a reference to an Irishman, Sergeant Mulvaney, calling himself a '**camouflaged Aussie**'. (*Horsham Times*, 30 September, p. 6)

choom

An Australian and New Zealand soldier slang term for an English soldier, and based on a humorous British dialect pronunciation of *chum*. British soldiers often referred to each other (and other soldiers) as 'chum', which Brophy and Partridge note in their *Songs and Slang of the British Soldier: 1914–1918* as more popular than either 'mate' or 'pal'; to the Australians, British soldiers became identified with their pronunciation of it as **choom**. After the end of the war, **choom** was used in Australian English more generally to mean someone from England.

C.E.W. Bean wrote in his book *The Story of Anzac* (1921): 'The "**chooms**" were the first British troops whom the Australian soldier met, and his notions of the British private were to the end coloured by these recollections.' (p. 126)

doughboy

An American soldier. There are various theories as to the origin of this term. It first appears in a military context in reference to a U.S. Army soldier in the Mexican-American War in the 1840s. In the eighteenth century, British soldiers and sailors used the term *doughboy* for a fried flour dumpling, and in the United States a baker's apprentice was known as a *doughboy*. One theory was that because soldiers used pipe-clay on their uniforms in the nineteenth century, which turned doughy when wet, the name became attached to them. Whatever its origins, **doughboy** is particularly associated with the U.S. soldiers who fought in the Great War, and was a term the soldiers of the American Expeditionary Forces often used to describe themselves. Other names given to the American soldier include SAMMY and YANK.

Doughboy was picked up by the Australian press and was used through 1918 and 1919, albeit mostly by overseas correspondents. Its popularity with Australian soldiers is unclear. A short piece published in the Australian press in 1918 included the comment: 'The trouble is at present what to name them [the American soldiers]. "Sammy" it has been said decidedly, they dislike. "Yanks," which is the nickname suggested by their song, has a derogatory sound. ... Recent reports from the front refer to the American troops as the "**Doughboys**".' (Launceston *Examiner*, 25 October, p. 7)

Enzed

This term for a person from New Zealand was first used in the Great War by both Australian and New Zealand soldiers. **Enzed** (also occasionally written as **N.Z.**) might also be used attributively to describe someone or something from New Zealand. MAORILANDER is another popular name given to a New Zealander, and during the war was applied to a New Zealand soldier.

A 1917 newspaper article noted: 'The friendship between Australians and New Zealanders is now most noticeable. The forces call each other respectively "Aussies" and "**Enzeds**".' (*Bendigonian*, 20 December 1917, p. 21) Michael James Egan, an Australian soldier, observed in his diary in 1918: 'A lot of Tommy gunners in the next camp also a camp of **NZs** and a few Yanks, all Vicars gunners.' (Diary entry, 15 January, *WWI Diary of Michael James Egan*, p. 45)

frightfulness

The behaviour of the German Army was sometimes referred to as **frightfulness**. This was a term mostly used in newspapers and propaganda, rather than by soldiers. It was often connected to alleged German atrocities, especially against civilians, as well as the use of particularly vicious weapons or tactics on the battlefield.

A British article in an Australian newspaper reported that 'the Anzacs describe a new device of German "**frightfulness**" which they have called "the tortoise". A creepy looking thing on four legs was left lying on the parapets or in the trenches and other handy places when the Germans ran away. It was really a high explosive bomb, which burst on the slightest touch.' (Adelaide *Register*, 23 August 1916, p. 7)

Fritz

This name for a German, especially a German soldier, or for Germans collectively, was popular with both soldiers and the home front during the Great War. It was a diminutive of the common German name *Friedrich* (Frederick) and likely first appeared in the print media in 1915. During the war, this was probably the most popular name used to refer to the German enemy by the Australian soldiers, although BOCHE, HUN, and JERRY were all used. The country of Germany was sometimes known as *Fritzland*. A popular variant (and diminutive) was **Fritzie**.

Such nicknames for the enemy were common, but some were used more pejoratively than others. HUN, for example, was used frequently in propaganda and linked to negative images of Germans, while **Fritz** was often used in a fairly neutral way.

Sapper A.E. Hastwell, in a letter to home printed in the Adelaide newspaper the *Register* on August 15, 1916, wrote: 'We have a very exciting time all the while, blowing up **Fritz**, and he doing the same to us. It is all right so long as one is not caught. There is much of chance in the game of war though, and we left Australia to fight, not look on.' (p. 6) Arthur Howell, serving on the Western Front, wrote in his diary in 1917: 'Things were fairly quiet during the night except for **Fritz** shelling Flers with eight inch high explosives.' (Diary entry, 5 March, *Signaller at the Front*, p. 39) Private Jim Gaffney wrote to his father in 1918: 'Things do not look too bright on the Western Front, do they? But don't get downhearted, and think it means a victory for **Fritzy**. We have retreated, but are far from being beaten.' (*Urana Independent and Clear Hills Standard*, 26 April, p. 2)

Froggie

Froggie as a slang term for a French person dates back to the nineteenth century, and derives from *Frog*, 'a French person or person of French descent' dating to the seventeenth century. As a more general term of abuse it dates to the fifteenth century, and is a transferred sense of *frog*, 'an amphibian creature'. Both are derogatory terms that were used during the war for French people.

Stretcher-bearer William Slater wrote in his diary in 1917: 'In the afternoon Frank Shaw, Sgt Holgate and I go in to Armentieres to see if the graves are finished. We refuse to take delivery of the job for the **Froggie** has not done it according to agreement.' (Diary entry, 19 April, *War Diaries of William Slater*, p. 26) The troopship periodical *The Sardine* commented: 'Diggers during their early days in France were often amused by the ways of the **Froggies**.' (No. 6, August 1919, p. 4)

gyppo

A term for an Egyptian or Arab person; also Arabic (the 'Egyptian language'). It derives from *Egyptian* (*gyp* + *o*). It is first recorded in a British Army context in the late nineteenth century (often as *gyppie* or *gippie*) to refer to Egyptians, and often used in a derogatory or racist way. During the war, it was picked up by Australian soldiers. It was also used adjectivally to indicate something that was Egyptian. In the printed record, it is also often found with the spelling **gypo**.

A quotation from a book written by an Australian officer recorded the following observation, suggesting the stereotypes that were often applied to Egyptians: 'The louder the "**Gyppo**" sings the harder he works, and when the chant dies out you can guarantee

that "Johnny" is loafing.' (Adelaide *Advertiser*, 8 May 1919, p. 8)
Lieutenant A.E. Sheppeard, heading from Egypt to Gallipoli, wrote
in his diary: 'We had a great send off, the band played us out to the
tune of Tipperary. All the **gypo** kids can sing Tipperary but they only
do it in the hope of getting a piastre not for love.' (Typescript of
diary, p. 24, Papers, AWM 2DRL 10956)

Hoch

A term for a German, especially a German soldier, or the German
people, especially the German military. This came from the German
exclamation *hoch lebe*, 'long live', which was also used in a popular
1899 poem satirising the Kaiser, 'Hoch, Der Kaiser'. While used
by Australian and other English-speaking soldiers, this was less
common than names such as FRITZ or HUN.

Australian soldier Donald McHutchinson wrote home: '**Hoch's**
shells are falling thick and fast, and above all is the whish-ish-ish of
thousands of machine gun-bullets, a veritable ride of the Valkyries
through the dawning air.' (*Richmond River Herald and Northern
Districts Advertiser*, 25 December 1917, p. 2)

Hun

A term for a German person, or the Germans collectively. It was used
during the Great War, particularly within the context of propaganda,
and often referred to the German people collectively ('the **Hun**'),
while a term such as FRITZ was a term more often used specifically
to refer to German soldiers.

Hun derives from the name given to nomadic people from
Central Asia who attacked Europe and helped bring about the
collapse of the Roman Empire. The use of **Hun** to refer to Germans
was apparently brought about by Kaiser Wilhelm II, who in sending
German soldiers to China in 1900 to help suppress the Boxer
Rebellion, said that they should make a name for themselves just
as the Huns under Attila had. Rudyard Kipling then used the term
in 1902, helping to popularise the connection between Huns and
Germans. By the time of the Great War, it was a term associated with

German (especially Prussian) militarism. During the war, British, Australian, and other newspapers played directly on this connection to the Central Asian Huns, drawing a likeness between the Huns when they invaded the Roman Empire and the German military's behaviour during their invasion of Belgium and France. One of the charges levelled against the Germans was their destruction of historic buildings, especially the Library of the Catholic University of Louvain in 1914, and their killing of innocent civilians.

A poem written by a Perth resident ('A Patriot') in 1915 and printed in the Perth *Daily News* declared:

> In the name of the women and children,
> In the name of the nurses and nuns;
> The victims of unbridled licence,
> We are stirring at last, 'gainst the **Huns**! (12 November, p. 8)

Private Jim Taylor, a former journalist serving with the AIF in France, wrote back to his paper as the end of the war came closer: 'Don't be down-hearted at the position of affairs. Things are not really what they seem. ... The Hun has shot his bolt.' (*Brisbane Courier*, 14 June 1918, p. 8)

Hun hunt

To **Hun hunt** was to fight against the Germans; one who did so was sometimes known as a *Hun hunter*. The term was also used on the home front in Australia to refer to the targeting of German civilians for internment.

A cartoon in the Sydney *Sunday Times* illustrated a German being chased by a bayonet back to Berlin. The caption read: 'This is the game to play just now, and every Australian worthy of the name should practise it. **Hun hunting** is a legitimate pastime. The Hun asked for it in the first place.' (21 March 1915, p. 4)

Hunland

A name given to Germany and any area occupied by the German Army. This was a popular term during the war, particularly in the British and Australian press.

Corporal Eric Bell, a soldier from Katoomba, NSW, was described in the *Blue Mountain Echo* as having recently come 'back from **Hunland**': '[Bell] landed in France with the 5th Division in May, 1916, and after three months fighting was captured by the enemy, and for 2½ years was shuttlecocked through the prison camps of **Hunland**.' (8 August 1919, p. 5)

Jacko

This was a name used during the war for a Turkish soldier or the Turkish enemy collectively. It was one of several nicknames Australian and New Zealand soldiers gave to their Turkish enemy; others included JOHNNY TURK and ABDUL. It is of uncertain origin, although possibly a variant on *Johnny* in JOHNNY TURK.

Numerous letters and diaries from soldiers who fought at Gallipoli attest to the use of **Jacko**. Sergeant Lawrence, describing the fighting at Gallipoli, wrote in his diary: 'Every now and again there is a flash and a sharp clear bang followed almost immediately by a shower of sparks from **Jacko**'s parapet and a dull "whouf" which comes booming across the water.' (Diary entry, 19 September 1915, *Gallipoli Diary of Sergeant Lawrence of the Australian Engineers*, p. 91) In a letter reprinted in several newspapers in November 1915, Sergeant P. Gallagher who had served at Gallipoli wrote: 'There are occasions when other boats come round and **Jacko** does not miss his opportunity of shelling them, but as soon as they get within 100 yards of the Red Cross ship **Jacko** will instantly stop firing till they get clear again.' (*Kalgoorlie Miner*, 6 November 1915, p. 3)

Jerry

This term for a German, especially a German soldier, or for Germans collectively, appears for the first time during the Great War. It was not as popular in the Great War as it would be in the Second World War; HUN, BOCHE and FRITZ were more likely to be used, certainly by Australians. **Jerry** is probably an alteration of *German* but may have been influenced by the British slang word *jerry* meaning 'chamber pot' which the German infantry helmets (*Stahlhelme*) were said to resemble.

In a *Brisbane Courier* article in February 1919, a Brisbane soldier's letter from France recounted how moving through areas brought back memories of the fighting:

> All over the battle area the old familiar names appear on roads, trenches, dug-outs, dumps, and billets. But the limit was reached in Peronne. The battalion marched through it at night, during the late advance. **Jerry** was shelling in his usual careless fashion; it reeked with gas and the 'hum' of badly dead donks, and the shell holes, bricks, telegraph wire, and 'duds', which littered the streets caused much weird profanity from the half blind, gas masked 'diggers' moving towards Berlin. (15 February 1919, p. 6)

Jock

This is a common colloquial name for a Scotsman, used in England as early as the eighteenth century. It was first used to refer to a Scottish or Northern English sailor, but during the Great War it was commonly used to refer to any Scottish soldier, and subsequently any Scotsman.

Sergeant Cyril Lawrence noted in a letter home to his sister during a period of leave in Scotland: 'We called him [a taxi driver] **Jock**, as all Scotsmen should have that name. He was awfully surprised to find that we knew his name, and told us that it was Jock McDougall. Laugh—when I think of that morning I still laugh.' (Letter, 21 June 1916, *Sergeant Lawrence Goes to France*, p. 34)

Johnny Turk

Like ABDUL and JACKO, this was a name used during the Great War for a Turkish soldier, or the Turkish enemy collectively. The name *Johnny* was used in many combinations, generally as a term of familiarity, and in the sense of 'fellow' or 'chap'. The British and Australians used this to refer to other enemies: for example, in the Boer War, Boer soldiers were sometimes called *Johnny Boer* by British and Australian soldiers fighting in South Africa, and Banjo

Paterson wrote a poem 'Johnny Boer' published in 1900 indicating its popularity on the Australian home front during that war.

Johnny Turk was a term popular in the British and Australian press during the Great War. An article in the Tasmanian newspaper, the Launceston *Examiner*, recounted the arrival home of two soldiers, one of whom, Private Hubert J. Windred, had been wounded and sent home: 'He gave a description of the landing at Gallipoli, and regretted very much he was not fortunate enough to see the campaign through, as "**Johnny Turk**" had potted him.' (19 August 1916, p. 8) Australian soldiers in Gallipoli also used the term. Jim Osborn noted in his diary while at Gallipoli: 'Just got back at dugout when "**Johnny Turk**" started to shell the gully with shrapnel.' (Diary entry, 3 October 1915, *War Diaries of Sergeant Jim Osborn*, p. 27)

kultur

The Germans used the concept of **kultur** (in German, literally 'culture') to refer to the supposed supremacy of German civilisation; the British and other Allies used the term to refer to the perceived barbaric actions of the German Army, especially in relation to the Army's alleged perpetration of atrocities. It was widely used in propaganda and political discourse throughout the war years.

A Catholic chaplain from Australia, Thomas J. King, addressed soldiers at a service in 1918. He commented that 'Gallipoli, notwithstanding its military failure, marked the birth of Australian nationhood. He denounced German "**kultur**" as materialistic, unchristian, and sensualistic.' (*Tungamah and Lake Rowan Express and St. James Gazette*, 2 May, p. 3)

Maorilander

This was a term for a New Zealander. *Maoriland* for New Zealand is first recorded in Australian English in 1859 (and in New Zealand English in 1856), and **Maorilander** for a New Zealander in 1885. The name was often used by Australian soldiers to refer to New Zealand soldiers; they also used Enzed.

In a cable to the Australian press in June 1915, C.E.W. Bean wrote: 'The **Maorilanders**, after gallantly holding for eight hours a trench captured on the night of June 4, were driven out by tremendous fusillades of bombs last night.' (Rockhampton *Morning Bulletin*, 21 June 1915, p. 7)

poilu

A French soldier. It was a French Army slang term for an infantryman that pre-dated the war, and is a specific use of *poilu*, 'brave man', originally deriving from the sense of *poilu* in French, 'brave, virile'. The name was adopted by English-speaking soldiers, and was commonly used through the war, including by Australian soldiers.

Private Jim Taylor, a reporter who served with the Army Medical Corps in France during the war, wrote back to Australia: 'there is more than a bond of sympathy existing between the Australians and the **Poilus**. There is a subtle spirit of mutual admiration, and almost affection, on both sides.' (Brisbane *Queenslander*, 7 October 1916, p. 41)

Pommy

An Australian English term for a person from England. In Australian English, it usually referred to an immigrant from the British Isles to Australia, and dates to just before the war. While there are a number of popular etymologies for the term, most notably the notion that it is an acronym for *POME* (*Prisoner of Mother England*) referring to a convict, it derives from *pomegranate* (often with the variant spelling *pommygrant*), rhyming slang for 'immigrant'. **Pommy** is also recorded in New Zealand English.

Australian soldiers were not averse to calling the British soldiers **Pommies** (although it was never as widely used as Tommy), and the term was also used on the home front. Western Australian soldier and footballer, 'Chitter' Brown wrote from England in 1915: 'We are having a game of Australian football on Wednesday, and are going to show the "**pommies**" how we play our game.' (Perth *Sunday*

Times, 10 October, p. 16) A speech aimed at encouraging enlistment included the comment: 'Can you go about with an easy mind and think at the same time that the **"pommies"** are laying down their lives for you?' (*Dandenong Advertiser and Cranbourne, Berwick and Oakleigh Advertiser*, 25 January 1917, p. 2)

Sammy

This was a nickname given to an American soldier during the Great War, and appears to have been used by both British and Australians from the time of the American entry into the war in 1917, although it fell out of use not long after the end of the war. It was not as popular or widespread as the term YANK which had been around from as early as the end of the eighteenth century. **Sammy** derived from the American figure of *Uncle Sam*, which personified the United States. Fraser and Gibbons in *Soldier and Sailor Words and Phrases* write that the term was disliked by American soldiers.

An Australian newspaper noted a London *Times* correspondent in 1917 writing a story about 'the American **"Sammies"** (the new nickname of the troops from the United States)'. (*Port Pirie Recorder and North Western Mail*, 9 July 1917, p. 4) The name was applied regularly in the British and Australian press. The London correspondent for the Lismore newspaper, the *Northern Star*, wrote: 'I like the American **"Sammies"** with their slouched hats and their slang. Educated Americans do not apologise for the general use of slang terms. They tell you frankly that the British language is a dead one, and requires to make people sit up and take notice.' (15 May 1918, p. 4)

sausage-eater

A term for a German person, especially a German soldier. It derives from the stereotypical notion that Germans were fond of eating German sausage or *wurst*. It was a derogatory term used during the Great War.

Corporal C.H. Fisher wrote to his brother in Kerang, Victoria, with tales of the war. He noted: 'We have just had word through by wireless that we got three of Fritz's aeroplanes and a Zeppelin today. We have also learned that the British have got Bapaume, and a half dozen smaller places, in fact they have got the **sausage eater** on the run down there.' (*Kerang New Times*, 25 May 1917, p. 3)

squarehead

During the Great War, this was a name for a German soldier. The term, originally as meaning any German or Scandinavian person, appears to have had some currency before the war, although its origin is unclear (*Green's Dictionary of Slang* speculates that it may come from 'the severe "Prussian" haircut'). The wartime usage may have been influenced by the German infantry helmet (*Stahlhelm*) design: a squarish steel helmet (see also JERRY).

An Australian soldier, Private W. Sams, writing to a girl in the New South Wales town of Forbes declared: 'In our turn in the trenches, we have to stand up night and day with a rifle in our hands, so you can see there are better games than fighting Germans. But I do not intend to let any **squarehead** get me if I can avoid it.' (*Forbes Advocate*, 18 July 1916, p. 3) Another Australian at the Western Front, Archie Barwick, noted in his diary in June 1916: 'I think the **squareheads** are having a few more sleepless nights than they used to before the Australians came to France.' (*In Great Spirits: The WWI Diary of Archie Barwick*, p. 103)

Tommy

A name given to a British soldier. This term, short for *Tommy Atkins*, was used to refer to ordinary soldiers of the British Army from the early nineteenth century. Rudyard Kipling's use of **Tommy** and *Tommy Atkins* for a British soldier in his popular *Barrack Room Ballads* (first published in 1892) and various short stories helped to make the name common. Brophy and Partridge in *Songs and Slang of the British Soldier: 1914–1918* suggest the term was not popular with British soldiers: 'Never used by English troops except derisively or when imitating the style of a newspaper or a charitable old lady.' However, there is evidence that some British soldiers did use it of themselves, for example in their trench periodicals. For Australians serving in the Great War, the British soldier was most commonly called **Tommy**, and the term was ubiquitous in the Australian press.

An Australian sergeant wrote in his diary: 'Just finished breakfast when the Boche caused us to evacuate by dropping an 8 inch right alongside our dugout in a heap of smoke bombs. He put over about 40 rounds, and wounded a **Tommy** badly.' (Diary entry, 13 November 1917, *An Anzac's War Diary: The Story of Sergeant Richardson*, p. 66)

Early in the war, before terms such as ANZAC and AUSSIE had taken hold, there was some use of **Tommy** to refer to Australian soldiers as well, often as an *Australian Tommy*, a *colonial Tommy*, or as in C.E.W. Bean's *The Anzac Book*, even TOMMY KANGAROO. A report from Signaller A.A. Barber with the 10th Battalion of the AIF located in Egypt in April 1915 included the line: 'The Australian **Tommies**' eye glistens, and his tongue hangs out when he gets a letter from home.' (*Murray Pioneer and Australian River Record*, 1 April, p. 6)

Turkey

A term for a Turkish soldier. It was not as popular as some other terms such as ABDUL and not particularly well-attested, although evidence can be found for it being used by both Australians and New Zealanders during the Great War.

A poem, 'Australia's First Brigade', published in the Australian press in July 1915 included the verse:

> We've proved on Gallipoli how some of us can die.
> When, facing odds of ten to one, we made the **Turkeys** fly:
> And if their fleet will show itself upon the ocean blue
> We'll also prove to all the world we've got a navy too. (*Yea Chronicle*,
> 1 July 1915, p. 3)

Woodbine

This was a term used by Australian and New Zealand soldiers during the war to refer to an English soldier. It comes from the proprietary name *Woodbine*, a cheap brand of cigarette that many

British soldiers smoked. It is recorded in both W.H. Downing's *Digger Dialects* and Brophy and Partridge's *Songs and Slang of the British Soldier: 1914–1918*.

Aussie: The Australian Soldiers' Magazine commented in 1918 that 'Aussies don't like the tripe roared out of them by a barrack-room **Woodbine**.' (December, p. 16)

The usual nightly strafe: Trench and battlefield

Many soldiers dealt with death on a regular basis through the Great War and this shaped their culture in a variety of ways. One of the central ways it shaped the distinctive culture of soldiers was in shaping language and vocabulary. This chapter considers a range of terms relating to life and death in the trenches. Some relate more to the everyday life of the trenches (and should be considered alongside the terms about military life discussed in Chapter Two); others are more directly related to the realities of fighting and dying in the trenches. They can also be considered alongside the terms for weapons discussed in Chapter Eight.

Some of the words included in this chapter are concerned directly with death and being killed. They formed an important part of the soldier's vocabulary, as death was an ever-present reality for those who were sent into the front lines. A 1917 commentary on Anzac slang observed: 'At all times we shrink from the actual word death, and ever since man first began to clothe his language in poetry he has sought to take the sting, as it were, out of his word. ... [T]he soldier has evolved his own expressions.' The article went on to list a number of these: *so far so stopped one*, TOOK THE COUNT, *passed in his checks*, and GONE WEST. (*Cairns Post*, 26 April, p. 7) A number of other terms relating to death can be found in this chapter, including CHUCK A SEVEN, HANGING ON THE WIRE, and DEAD MEAT TICKET. They all perhaps demonstrate how soldiers might have been too superstitious to mention death directly, but did refer to it frequently through a variety of euphemistic terms.

Other words that are discussed in this chapter relate to various aspects of trench warfare. Some of these have become familiar to us, either because of their common use (now often figurative) in Standard English—for example, BARRAGE and CAMOUFLAGE—or because they are terms that we associate in the popular imagination with the Great War, such as DUCKBOARD, DUGOUT, and NO MAN'S LAND. Slang terms developed for fear, with soldiers described as sometimes 'having the BREEZE UP' or 'the WIND UP'. And soldiers engaged in other activities in trench and on battlefield, including stealing and looting from civilians or the Germans, described as RATTING or, more euphemistically, SOUVENIRING.

Many of the terms in this chapter are not exclusively Australian, and, as the experience of the trenches was one shared by a number of national armies, so was their vocabulary. Australian soldiers fought alongside British and New Zealand soldiers, and many terms were commonly shared between their vocabularies. But a few Australian terms developed or were popularised in relation to trench warfare: for example, the use of AUSSIE, 'a wound so severe as to get you sent back home to Australia', STOUSH, 'a fight', KING-HIT, 'a severe blow', and POSSIE, 'a position', are just a few of them. The latter three have all continued to be used in Australian English.

W.H. Downing's *Digger Dialects* records many terms not found elsewhere (except some of them were reproduced in A.G. Pretty's *Glossary of AIF Slang*—see the conclusion for a discussion of this relationship between the two), but both the terms and the definitions provided by Downing, who saw action on the Western Front, are evocative

of the realities of trench warfare, even as they seek to imbue death and
killing with dark humour:

> *Anzac soup*—'shell-hole water polluted by a corpse'.
>
> *Belgium*—'a fatal wound'.
>
> *belly-ache*—'a mortal wound'.
>
> *blow-to-fook*—'shatter to fragments'.
>
> *boy-with-his-boots-off*—'a shell which bursts before the sound of
> its passage through the air is heard'.
>
> *christen the squirt*—'to bayonet a man [for the first time]'.
>
> *cold storage (to go into)*—'to be killed in the 1916 winter'.
>
> *corpse factory*—'the Western Front'. [This term was also used
> extensively in the contemporary press during the war in
> reference to an alleged industrial installation used by the
> Germans to boil down corpses, and often cited as an example
> of German atrocities.]
>
> *fresh faces in Hell*—'a slaughter of Germans'.
>
> *mole-hole*—'a dug-out'.
>
> *smudged*—'killed by being blown to pieces by a shell'.
>
> *west o'hell*—'death; dead'.

Life in the trenches thus produced a language of its own, and the
evidence of these words as they are traced in many descriptions given
by soldiers in their letters and diaries provides insights into trench life.
While the full realities of trench warfare are perhaps impossible to grasp,
the language traced here captures some of the horrors and difficulties of
life for soldiers who saw active service during the Great War.

Aussie

A wound so severe as to send a soldier back to Australia (which
was often referred to as Aussie, see entry in Chapter One). This was
similar to the use of Blighty to mean a wound that got a soldier sent
to England for care and recuperation.

R.C. 'Cleve' Potter, an Australian serving in France, noted in his
diary: 'I turned my head silently towards Dick More, to see him grasp
at his face, and knew that he had received a 'Blighty', an **'Aussie'**
or a 'France', for the whole of his cheek had been blown away by

an explosive bullet.' (*Not Theirs the Shame Who Fight*, p. 191) The Tamworth newspaper, the *Daily Observer*, noted in 1918 that the husband of Mrs C. Griffin had 'received an "**Aussie**" wound, his leg being shattered'. (24 September, p. 6)

barrage

This term is first used during the Great War, probably around 1916. Derived from the French word for the action of barring something, and in Standard English as *barrage*, 'an artificial bar used in a river or watercourse', it dated to the nineteenth century. The military sense which developed from this is defined in the *OED* as 'a barrier of continuous artillery or machine-gun fire concentrated in a given area, used to prevent the advance or retreat of enemy troops, to protect troops advancing against the enemy, to repulse attacks by aircraft, and for destructive purposes'. Although a Standard English term now, and also often used in a figurative sense, at the time it was a new word that reflected the new type of artillery-based warfare that developed during the war. Different types of **barrages** were used to varying effect during the war, including *creeping barrages*, *lifting barrages*, and *box barrages*. **Barrage** is recorded in slang dictionaries of the Great War, indicating the contemporary perception that this was a slang term produced by the war.

Barrage was picked up in Australian newspapers from 1916 and became common in reports on the war in Europe, thus quickly becoming part of the lexicon. An example of its use is given in the poignant notice below:

> Mr. E.J. Bradley, of Ormond Road, Moonee Ponds, has been notified that his son, Corporal A.W. Bradley, has been posted 'missing' in France since August 4. He was engaged in work which involved passing through an intense **barrage** of heavy shells, and it is supposed that he was buried in the cavity caused by an explosion. His commanding officer speaks in glowing terms of the cool and brave deeds performed by the young soldier. (Melbourne *Argus*, 14 December 1916, p. 8)

Bert Bishop, an Australian soldier in Belgium, wrote in a letter home in 1917: 'About five o'clock, just as Wednesday's dawn was breaking, with a terrific thundering & crashing that shook heaven & earth our **barrage** started, whistles screeched, & we were away.' (Letter, 2 October, *Dear All: Letters from World War I—Bert Bishop*, p. 45)

beetle

A type of barge or lighter used for carrying troops at the Gallipoli landings and evacuation. It is unclear where the name comes from, although it likely derived from the appearance of the watercrafts; it does not appear to have been used after Gallipoli. Eric Partridge's *A Dictionary of Slang and Unconventional English* attributes the naming of this craft to Sir John Monash, although it is unclear where the evidence for this comes from.

An account of the Gallipoli evacuation noted: 'the queer picket boats known as "**beetles**" had been passing unobserved from the beach to the half dozen transports lying some two or three miles out.' (Perth *West Australian*, 16 February 1916, p. 5)

big push

A term that first came to prominence in 1915, and which initially referred to a planned military offensive as part of the Battle of Loos. It came to refer to any significant military offensive (real or planned) during the Great War; such an offensive might sometimes also be referred to as the *great push*. Soldiers in the trenches were always waiting for 'the **big push**'. Brophy and Partridge in *Songs and Slang of the British Soldier: 1914–1918* note with irony that the word *push* 'indicates the desired ideal rather than the actuality'. A British film released in 1917 was entitled *The Big Push*, and aimed to illustrate British military progress during the war; it was also shown in Australian cinemas.

Many Australian soldiers wrote home to talk about offensive movements during the war, and often talked about a **big push**. For example, after the Battle of the Somme in 1916, Australian Colonel-Chaplain F.W. Wray wrote back home to Bendigo: 'Our troops (the

Australians) suffered severely in the **big push** on the Somme. Each division went in twice, and our Australian boys have added to the great reputation they made at Anzac.' (*Bendigonian*, 23 November 1916, p. 31) Sapper S.R. Bennett wrote back to Australia in 1917: 'I am on draft with two Queensland telegraphists, and we were to have gone down to the Front last week, but were pulled out for some unknown reason. We will probably go forward next week and be there for the "**big push**".' (*Brisbane Courier*, 18 May, p. 8) In 1917, stretcher-bearer William Slater recorded in his diary: 'It is with a big lump in my throat and a pain in my heart that I bid farewell to those dear chums of mine who within a couple of days will be in the **Big Push**. Good luck to them all—a fervent hope for their safe coming out of it.' (Diary entry, 31 May, *War Diaries of William Slater*, p. 33) The term was not only used of actions on the Western Front, as the following comment in the soldier periodical the *Kia Ora Coo-ee* attests: 'During the "**big push**" from Beersheba the Camel Corps played an important part and upheld the reputation it made in Sinai Days.' (15 July, p. 13)

Big Stoush

The Great War was sometimes referred to by Australian soldiers as 'the **Big Stoush**'. The Australian English term STOUSH was commonly used during the war to refer to fighting, and the war in its entirety earned the nickname the **Big Stoush**.

South Australian soldier Private T.J. Lynch wrote to his aunt in 1917: 'We are going over to "The **Big Stoush**" next Saturday and I hear it's rather dangerous there. But heaven help poor Fritz when the 48th Battalion gets behind him, because we are all anxious to do a bit.' (Broken Hill *Barrier Miner*, 21 January, p. 3) Also in 1917, the troopship periodical *The Limber Log* noted of an NCO on board: 'That on conclusion of the **big stoush**, Ship's Sergeant-Major Odgers intends taking over the Four Courts Hotel. His vast experience in Australia, and latterly in the East, should enable him to cater for all-comers.' (p. 41)

Blighty

This was a wound serious enough to send a soldier to England for care and recuperation. The word comes from the use of BLIGHTY meaning England. (For the origins of the term, see the entry in Chapter Ten.) Such a wound was sometimes also known as a *Blighty one.*

Sergeant Richardson wrote in his diary: 'In about 15 minutes everybody returns and a few minutes later 4 men appear carrying a stretcher with some poor, unfortunate fellow who may get a **blighty** or perhaps a little wooden cross in France.' (Diary entry, 1 November 1916, *An Anzac's War Diary: The Story of Sergeant Richardson*, pp. 34–5) Archie Barwick wrote in his diary in May 1916: 'No matter how tired & sleepy you may be, when bullets or shrapnel are coming close you will do a get alright, no matter how much you would like a "**Blighty**". The meaning of "**Blighty**" is a nice little pet wound which will give you a trip to England. It is a great word among the Tommies.' (*In Great Spirits: The WWI Diary of Archie Barwick*, pp. 85–6)

bloodbath

A term found in Standard English from the nineteenth century, and meaning 'a battle or fight at which much blood is spilt; a wholesale slaughter, a massacre'. It seemed particularly apt when applied to the Western Front.

W.H. Downing records **bloodbath** in his *Digger Dialects* with the definition 'The Somme, 1916'. Indeed, during the Great War, most of the uses of the term found in the press can be found in early 1917, reporting on the fighting at the Somme, where there were especially high numbers of casualties. Downing also comments that this was 'originally a German expression'. While the *OED* evidence demonstrates that this sense was around since at least the nineteenth century, the British war correspondent Philip Gibbs did write that 'the German troops had invented a terrible name to describe this great ordeal; it was "The **Blood-Bath** of the Somme".'

(*Sydney Morning Herald*, 24 January 1917, p. 7) Much of the use of the term in the Australian press during the war seems to be by this particular British war correspondent.

box on

An Australian English term used in two senses during the war by Australian soldiers: the first was as a verb, meaning 'to fight', and especially 'to keep on fighting', the second was as a noun meaning 'a battle, a fight'. Both are first recorded in 1916, and both continued to be used in Australian English after the war.

An article in the Lismore newspaper, the *Northern Star*, in October 1916, noted that the 'Anzac view' was to '**box on**'. The article proclaimed: '"**Box on**"—that summarises just what the Australian would remark if asked his opinion in connection with the big war just now. ... There never existed a race of warriors so eager for the fray.' (6 October, p. 8) Percy Smythe, an Australian soldier, wrote in a letter home in May 1916: 'Have not seen Viv [his brother] since we went into the trenches. His brigade has had a bit of a "**box-on**" with Fritz.' (*Letters from Percy Smythe* [online]) In 1918, another soldier observed in a letter: 'Witnessed a big "**box on**" about six thousand feet above us, six of our planes attacked about five of theirs, and I was sorry to see Fritz come out victorious.' (*Letters from the Front*, 27 May, p. 179)

breeze up

The phrase 'to have or put the **breeze up**' was a variation of the more common 'to have or put the WIND UP', meaning 'to be afraid' or 'to make afraid'. See also VERTICAL BREEZE.

Lieutenant Crosbie Garstin, author of *The Mudlarks Again* (1919), records the following dialogue from 'somewhere in France':

'And how many hares have you killed?' Algy inquired.
'We haven't exactly killed any as yet,' said I; 'but we've put the **breeze up** on 'em—their morale is very low.' (Perth *Sunday Times*, 13 July, p. 15)

camouflage

This word, derived from the French *camouflet*, 'to blind', was first used in a military sense—to disguise any object used in war by means of paint, smoke-screens, or similar, in such a way as to conceal it from the enemy—during the Great War. It quickly came to be used in a figurative sense and came into Standard English.

In Australian newspapers reporting on the war, it was noted during 1917 that **camouflage** was a new word. The *Cairns Post* wrote in June that year: 'A new slang word, which is an equivalent for our longer phrase of "throwing the dust in one's eyes", comes from France, coined in the war. More literally, the new word which is **Camouflage**, means raising a smoke to fool the enemy, and the men who engage in this fascinating pursuit are the artists who fight the enemy with their brushes.' (30 June, p. 7)

chuck a seven

This term was a euphemism meaning 'to die'. W.H. Downing's *Digger Dialects* records a variant but very similar term, *throw a seven*. He also records *throw six and a half*, 'to almost die'. A possible etymology is suggested in the first quotation below.

A 1919 newspaper article on what they labelled 'Digger yabber', the slang of the Australian soldiers, wrote that the Australian soldier 'rarely ever says that a cobber has been killed, it's always " 'E's gone west", or " 'E's **chucked a seven**". The latter expression originates from the game of "hazard" in which, if you throw a seven, you are out of the game.' (Perth *Sunday Times*, 9 March, p. 7) An excerpt from the hospital magazine *The Harefield Park Boomerang* recorded that one patient had declared in his will: 'Should I **chuck a seven**, I leave all my dough to my cobber —' (*Brisbane Courier*, 18 April 1917, p. 10)

dead meat ticket

A slang term for a soldier's identity disc. First recorded in New Zealand English, **dead meat ticket** was used by Australian and

New Zealand soldiers during the Great War. The variants *cold meat ticket* and *corpse ticket* are found in British glossaries of the war. The grim fatalism of the soldier in the trenches is well illustrated in the use of this term.

One Australian soldier writing home in September 1916 explained the photo of himself that he was sending home: 'You will also notice the identification disc on my wrist. They used to be worn around the neck but there were so many men used to have the upper part of their bodies blown to pieces that all means of identification were lost, so now they are worn on the wrist. "**Dead meat tickets**" they call them.' (Letter, 8 September, *Four Australians at War*, p. 103) Private Roy Heron Stewart wrote home to say: 'I hope your parcel comes soon. No one else will be able to get it, because we have to show our identification discs (some of the chaps call them "**dead meat tickets**") or our pay book. This stops the crooks from getting our parcels.' (*Essendon Gazette and Keilor, Bulla and Broadmeadows Reporter*, 8 February 1917, p. 4)

duckboard[1]

This was a type of slatted timber path used in the trenches, usually in order to move men and materiel through wet or muddy ground. **Duckboards** were familiar to all soldiers who served in the trenches, and **duckboard** became a standard word of the war. Brophy and Partridge in *Songs and Slang of the British Soldier: 1914–1918* observe: '**Duckboards** were most useful, but they were heavy to carry, and they tended to slip under your feet in the dark, so that the loose end rose and hit you violently on the head.'

An Australian artillery officer's letter home told of his trench experiences: 'I shall never forget the night we had coming out— pitch dark, pouring rain, lightning flashes and a heavy gale blowing. We had to come out along the **duckboards** and had to use torches, even at the risk of old Fritz seeing us. Several times I was nearly blown off the duckboard into a shell hole full of icy water.' (Broken Hill *Barrier Miner*, 13 March 1918, p. 4)

duckboard²

A humorous term for the Military Medal. The Military Medal was introduced as an award for other ranks in the British Army (and Imperial forces) in 1916 for 'acts of gallantry and devotion to duty under fire'; it was later backdated for actions dating to 1914. Soldiers sometimes called the Military Medal a **duckboard**, presumably from the stripes of its ribbon resembling the slats of a DUCKBOARD¹.

A poem in the 1919 troopship periodical *The Karmala Keepsake*, 'That 1914 Rosette', included the verses:

> Oh! I'm just an Aussie soldier,
> Though I'm camouflaged a treat,
> With my ribbons and my badges,
> From my head down to my feet.
> I've a '**duckboard**' in its glory
> With a D.C.M. to boot,
> And there's 'rising suns' and 'Aussies'
> Tucked about my khaki suit. (p. 6)

An anecdote published in 1918 recounted: 'Our goat was grazing in the field when it started, and the shells fell around her. With a howl of anguish Darky forsook his dugout and rushed to scene of rescue. They both came in unharmed. He certainly deserved a "**duckboard**" (Military Medal, you know), but whoever heard of the decoration for saving a goat?' (Orange *Leader*, 28 August, p. 1)

dugout

A term in use before the war, this term for a shelter in the trenches became a familiar one through the war years. **Dugouts** were the primary place where soldiers lived while serving in the front lines of the trenches. They varied considerably in terms of their size and comfort levels.

Lance-Corporal Schuchard, a signaller with the Headquarters staff of the Australian 5th Light Horse, wrote home from Gallipoli: 'Eric Lascelles and I are in the one little **dugout**, and are as comfortable as can be. We boil our own billy, cook our own tucker, and are quite happy. We look straight out to sea—the bluest, most beautiful sea imaginable. The bullets and shrapnel blow around occasionally, but we are pretty safe in our little home.' (Melbourne *Argus*, 28 July 1915, p. 7) Sergeant H.H. Hutchinson wrote home from France with a story about his **dugout**: 'When I come back I'll bring you a pet rat. It has its home under my dugout. My **dugout** is 6ft. x 4ft., and 3ft. high, and three of us sleep together, so we haven't much room; but the closer we get, the warmer it is.' (Adelaide *Register*, 17 June 1916, p. 10)

fire trench

A type of trench, usually deep and narrow, from which firing at the enemy takes place. The term pre-dated the war, but was commonly used in describing aspects of trench warfare during the war.

A short item in the Melbourne *Argus* noted the anniversary of fighting at Quinn's Post at Gallipoli:

> On May 30, 1915, preparations were made in Quinn's Post to attack and destroy two enemy saps, the heads of which had reached within five yards of our **fire trench**. Two storming parties of 35 men went forward at 1 o'clock in the afternoon, cleared the sap heads, and penetrated into the trenches beyond, but they were gradually driven back by Turkish counter-attacks, in spite of our heavy supporting fire, our casualties being chiefly caused by bombs, of which the enemy seemed to have an unlimited supply. (30 May 1916, p. 6)

flare king

This was a term used to refer to a soldier whose occupation was to fire flares from the front line.

An Australian soldier serving on the Western Front wrote in a letter home in 1917: 'When the Australians first entered Bapaume they disturbed an old fellow who rejoiced under the name of "**Flare King**". ... I must explain to you what a **Flare King's** occupation is. At night each army, when facing each other in the trenches, have men who send up flares to enable them to try and see what the opposition is up to.' (*Southern Argus*, 12 July, p. 3)

full issue

A term for death used during the war: 'to get the **full issue**' meant 'to be killed'.

A letter written from the Western Front back to Australia recorded the term, as well as conveying the exhaustion and fatalism of some soldiers:

> For the Saturday we were out it rained like fury, and as we had to camp out in the open air, we got very little sleep, and I can tell you, that after two days and two nights' solid fighting, you want at least a couple of days' rest. With that sort of thing going on, do you wonder at us being tired of it all, and at times wish to get a '**full issue**—and finish'. Lots of the boys I know have welcomed death as the only means to get away from it all. (*Violet Town Sentinel*, 4 June 1918, p. 3)

A troopship periodical recorded a story of a soldier's death in 1919: 'When I went up I saw poor "Old" Bill huddled up near his gun. A whiz-bang had lobbed in the "possy", and he had received the **full issue**.' (*The Karmala Keepsake*, p. 8)

funk-hole

This term for a shelter, dugout, or any place to which one could retreat to safety was a popular term in use during the Great War. It typically referred to more shallow excavations, rather than deep, well-constructed dugouts. The *OED* first records its use in 1900, developing from the slang term *funk*, 'a state of panic or shrinking terror'. Thus a **funk-hole** was a place to escape from the sources of the terror. In their *Songs and Slang of the British Soldier: 1914–1918*, Brophy and Partridge note that '[n]o disparagement of the occupants is implied in this term'. **Funk-holes** were essential places of safety in the context of trench warfare. The term also came to be applied to any safe job or position away from the firing line.

The Adelaide newspaper, *The Mail*, included in a 1916 edition the following humorous item:

> A Property Notice from the Front.
> To Let, in Northern France.

This attractive and well-built dugout, containing one reception room, bedroom, and up-to-date **funk hole**. 4 ft. x 3 ft. All modern inconveniences, including gas and water. This desirable residence stands one foot above water level, commanding an excellent view of the enemy's trenches. Excellent shooting, snipe and duck. Particulars of late lieutenant, base hospital. (29 July, p. 11)

giggle house

An Australian English term for a psychiatric hospital. It derived from the stereotyped belief that people with a mental illness were prone to hysteria, and its use by soldiers is probably with reference to soldiers being hospitalised for conditions related to shell-shock. It first appears in the written evidence in 1919 in W.H. Downing's *Digger Dialects*, and is also recorded in a 1919 newspaper article on 'Digger Yabber'. The latter noted that an 'asylum is known as the rat-house or the **giggle house**'. (Perth *Sunday Times*, 9 March, p. 7) It is not otherwise particularly well-attested during the period of the war, although it becomes more common in Australian English after the war.

gone phut

This term was used of something having broken down or malfunctioned. The word *phut*, 'a brief plosive sound', is first recorded in the 1870s, and in the 1880s the phrase 'to **go phut**' developed in reference to a breakdown or a sudden failure. It was a popular expression with Great War soldiers.

A short piece in *The Dinkum Furf*, a troopship periodical, declared: 'A willing few have been working hard in the matter of Concerts. How about some of the dark horses having a go? It's up to some of you to do a bit for the amusement of the troops, you know. Why, our Sergeant Wilson's comedy in one act has **gone "fut"** for want of an energetic assistant.' (No. 3, June 1919, p. 2)

gone west

An expression meaning 'to have died'. It dates back several centuries, with the *OED* recording its first use in the fifteenth century. The term derives from the fact of the sun setting in the West. During the Great War, the expression was extensively used by soldiers as a euphemism for death.

Percy Smythe wrote in his diary in 1916 as he and his men were about to head for France and the Western Front:

> I suppose the Germans will subject us to a heavy bombardment as soon as we arrive in the firing-line trenches, to try to weaken our morale. We may also expect a gas attack. Anyway I suppose after a few months' time many of us will have '**gone west**', but we are all thankful to get away from here. If a person gets wounded or sick over there he will be all right for a trip to England. (Diary entry, 21 March, *World War I Diary of Percy Smythe* [online])

A reference to the death of an Australian soldier, Private Clement Henry Gamble, in the *Shepparton Advertiser* noted that 'Clem has fallen, or as the men at the front say, he has "**gone West**".' (8 November 1917, p. 3)

gun fodder

A term similar to *cannon-fodder*, defined in the *OED* as 'men regarded merely as material to be consumed in war'. **Gun fodder** dated to 1900, and was used during the Great War, perhaps because of its aptness to the nature of industrial trench warfare.

Corporal James B. Warren wrote to his relatives in Bendigo from France to say that the Germans were 'fighting in a don't care fashion. They advance in massed form, and are nothing else but **gun fodder**'. (*Singleton Argus*, 1 July 1916, p. 5)

hanging on the barbed wire

This phrase meant 'to be killed'. It derived from the fact that an attack on the Western Front would usually result in a number of men being killed and left entangled in the barbed wire that protected the trenches. Brophy and Partridge in their *Songs and Slang of the British Soldier: 1914–1918* write: 'Men were frequently caught in these [barbed wire entanglements] at night, and during day-time attacks, when they became easy targets for machine-guns. The dead bodies could not fall to the ground, but hung sagging in limp and often grotesque attitudes among the wilderness of wire. Hence it became a common euphemism for death, hard and bitter... .' There was also a popular war-time song called 'The Old Barbed Wire'.

An Australian newspaper report on how Australian soldiers repulsed a German attack in 1918 described the following: 'When the position was restored 25 enemy corpses were found **hanging on the barbed wire**. Our casualties were very slight.' (*Portland Guardian*, 8 March, p. 3)

hop-over

In the Great War, during a military action soldiers were expected to go over the sandbags that lined the trenches. An attack was therefore often referred to as a **hop-over**. There were a variety of similar terms used during the war such as HOP THE BAGS, OVER THE BAGS, and OVER THE TOP.

Australian Percy Smythe noted in his diary: 'News came through this morning that the "**hop-over**" proved entirely successful, all objectives, including the town of Passchendaele, being taken at an early hour.' (Diary entry, 6 November 1917, *World War I Diary of Percy Smythe* [online])

hop the bags

A term for the action of going over the sandbags that lined trenches as part of a military action. Similar terms include HOP-OVER, OVER THE BAGS, and OVER THE TOP.

Jim McConnell, writing in his diary in February 1918, described an incident: 'The next night four officers, four NCO's and a hundred men "**hopped the bags**". ... The object was to bring back as many prisoners as possible.' (Diary entry, 10 February, *Letters from the Front*, p. 109)

hot shop

A term for a place of danger, usually in reference to the front line of the trenches and fighting on the Western Front.

George Gideon of the 5th Division in the AIF wrote home to his mother from the front in France: 'I had a narrow shave once, and thought my light was going out; but I'm still going strong. It's what we call a very "**hot shop**"; but all the same it's enough to freeze you.' (*Essendon Gazette and Keilor, Bulla and Broadmeadows Reporter*, 18 January 1917, p. 6) Corporal C. Sharpe, also writing home to his mother in 1917, while on leave in England, expressed his concerns: 'I can tell you I don't want to go back to France in a hurry; it is a pretty **hot shop** there. They are giving us Australians plenty of fighting.' (*Braidwood Dispatch and Mining Journal*, 19 January, p. 2)

hurry-up

Often used in the phrase 'to give (someone or something) a **hurry-up**', this phrase was used in a wartime context to suggest that pressure was being put on the enemy.

Private Rod Hornsby from Bunbury, Victoria, who fought at Gallipoli wrote home to say: 'I can tell you the Turks got some "**hurry-up**" when we took the ridge.' (Perth *Daily News*, 5 June 1915, p. 11) Bert Orchard in his diary wrote: 'The left & centre attacked by a good number in afternoon, our guns gave them "**hurry up**" as they came over the hill and it was to see them now and again go up in the air.' (Diary entry, 1 May 1915, *Diary of an Anzac: The Front Line Diaries and Stories of Albert Arthur 'Bert' Orchard*, p. 51)

jumping-off trench

A shallow trench, intended to advance the front line a few yards forward prior to an attack.

An Australian, Corporal Philip Davey, won a Victoria Cross in 1918. His actions were described in the press:

> Cpl Davey, advancing alone against point blank fire, attacked the gun with grenades, and put out of action half the crew. He

returned to the original **jumping-off trench**, got more bombs, and again attacked the gun, whose crew had been reinforced. Cpl Davey killed the whole of the crew of eight men, captured the gun, and employed it in repelling a counter-attack, in which he was severely wounded. (Adelaide *Register*, 20 August, p. 6)

king-hit

This is an Australian English term, dating to the late nineteenth century, and referring to a 'sudden or damaging blow; a knock-out punch'. It was often used by Australian soldiers in a wartime context for its obvious relevance, and continued to be used in Australian English after the war.

Lieutenant Drummond writing home to his brother in Coffs Harbour from a hospital said: 'Was hit by a shell on the 20th in Dardanelles trenches; got a pretty good bump—punctured in half a dozen places, but not vital. The **king hit** was above the left ankle. The shell case broke the leg—a compound fracture. I was flattened out, but not knocked out.' (*Richmond River Herald and Northern Districts Advertiser*, 23 November 1915, p. 3)

mad minute

This term applied to a round of rapid firing or a period of frenzied bayonet practice. The tactic was pioneered by the British Army at the beginning of the Great War and became familiar to Australian soldiers.

An account by an Australian soldier at Gallipoli in 1915 included the comment: 'We had to hold the position with 200 rounds, and now and again we gave the enemy "the Englishmen's **mad minute**"—15 rounds rapid firing.' (Adelaide *Daily Herald*, 4 August, p. 6)

mopper-up

A soldier who was assigned to clear and occupy a military area, work known in the military as MOPPING UP.

War correspondent Keith Murdoch wrote in 1918: 'The men
go over the top fully organised for an offensive basis. Bombers,
signallers, **moppers-up** and stretcher bearers all are organised.'
(*Geelong Advertiser*, 9 March, p. 3)

mopping up

A term for the action or an act of dealing with pockets of resistance
that remain after a military advance. Those who undertook such
actions were known as MOPPERS-UP. Brophy and Partridge in *Songs
and Slang of the British Soldier: 1914–1918* write that this was a
'necessary operation if the assaulting troops were not to be fired on
from the rear'; they also comment that this 'domestic metaphor for a
murderous business is typically English'.

An item in an Australian newspaper reported on the following
engagement of Australian soldiers in France: 'Reaching Rainecourt,
the Australians swooped through, and established a new line well
eastward, leaving to other New South Wales troops the task of
mopping up the village. A solitary German machine gunner remained
hidden in Rainecourt for 24 hours, and shot spasmodically until
a thorough search disclosed his whereabouts.' (Adelaide *Register*,
19 August 1918, p. 5)

no man's land

The ground between two opposing (usually entrenched) armies.
The term dates back to the fourteenth century, and many early uses
refer to 'a place on a boundary or between boundaries'. It became a
familiar term during the Great War due to the nature of the trench
warfare that quickly established itself on the Western Front. It was
well-known both to the home front, who read about the war in the
press and in letters from their soldiers at the front, and was used by
soldiers. It is one of the terms most closely associated with the Great
War, particularly the Western Front, in the popular imagination.
During the war, **no man's land** on the Western Front might be
anywhere from 10 to 450 metres wide.

Private Newel Maskel wrote home in 1917 to tell his family about the death of his cousin. He told of his experiences at the front: 'I have had the pleasure of capturing a German prisoner. I was lying out in **no-man's-land** in a shell hole with a machine gun when he walked into me. When he was within a couple of yards I called to him, jumped up and caught him by the arm and placed my revolver against his head.' (*Shepparton News*, 6 December, p. 1)

over the bags

A variant of HOP THE BAGS, and an expression related to HOP-OVER .

Arthur G. Howell, an Australian signaller at the Western Front, recorded in his diary in 1917: 'The first division infantry went **over the "bags"** this morning, but down here we have not heard how the attack is progressing.' (Diary entry, 1 October 1917, *Signaller at the Front*, p. 56)

over the top

Like the terms HOP-OVER and HOP THE BAGS, this referred to an attack in the context of trench warfare in the Great War. To go '**over the top**' became one of the most well-known phrases of the war. Brophy and Partridge in *Songs and Slang of the British Soldier: 1914–1918* write in their entry for **over the top**: 'It was entering another world (and often literally, for the unlucky ones), an abrupt and absolute change to another sort of warfare.' Doyle and Walker in *Trench Talk* comment: 'Though death was often random and continual while in the trenches, there could be nothing to compare with the act of rising bodily out of the protecting earth and advancing into the face of enemy guns.' (p. 183) A saying popular with British soldiers during the war was '**over the top** and best of luck!'

Many Australian soldiers made reference to going **over the top** in their letters and diaries. Jim Osborn, also an Australian serving at the Western Front, noted in his diary: 'The German front line was just a mass of flame from our shell fire, and then it lifted, and at 9 pm we "hopped out" and "**over the top**".' (Diary entry, 18 August 1916, *War Diaries of Sergeant Jim Osborn*, p. 111)

parados

A mound of earth forming the back wall of a trench. It comes from the French, 'protection from the back'. A nineteenth-century military term referring to an elevation of earth used to protect a fortified position, it gained considerable currency during the Great War due to the nature of trench warfare.

A letter from Signaller J. Boase, who was serving on the Western Front, included the following description of battle:

> Meanwhile we are rushing for our line, losing men at every step. Time and again our view is utterly obscured by bursting shells throwing up columns of earth amongst us. Another hundred yards and we will be under shelter of the front line trench (if trench it can be called). Now for a final dash and over the **parados** we tumble, panting, breathless, and in many cases blood-spattered, and here we intend to remain for our term in the trenches. (Lismore *Northern Star*, 13 November 1916, p. 7)

Parapet Joe

A nickname given to a German machine-gunner, whose gunfire would prevent a soldier from looking over the parapet of a trench. This term is recorded in W.H. Downing's *Digger Dialects*, and was being used by Australian soldiers at least as early as 1916.

A 1917 'News from the Front' column in the Tasmanian newspaper, the *Zeehan and Dundas Herald*, noted: 'Have had the bullets whistling over my head in the trench like a swarm of bees around a man. One German in particular we call "**Parapet Joe**" can almost play a tune with his machine gun. Goes from one end to the other of our section, and just chips up the edge of the parapet right alone.' (22 March, p. 4)

pillbox

A small concrete fortification used as a gun emplacement or observation point. The term is a transferred use of *pillbox*, 'a small box, usually of a cylindrical shape, used to hold pills'. The first **pillboxes** were constructed by the German military in 1917, and were commonly referred to in descriptions of trench warfare along the Western Front. The term thereafter became Standard English.

An Australian press correspondent, writing from London in 1917, told of several cases of Australian soldiers' heroism: 'In another instance, the Western Australians found themselves held up in Glencorse Wood before a strong concrete **pill-box**, from the top of which a machine gun was playing on the attacking troops. The advancing troops were compelled to lie in shellholes. Then a corporal crept out and got near enough to throw a bomb, which killed the gunner and knocked out the gun. This feat allowed the advance to continue.' (Adelaide *Register*, 3 October, p. 7)

pipped

To be hit or wounded by a bullet was to be **pipped**.

An Australian soldier wrote home in 1916 to say: 'I thought I was going to be one of the lucky ones, but I was "**pipped**" the other day during a bit of a raid we made on Fritz.' (*Myrtleford Mail and Whorouly Witness*, 31 August, p. 3)

possie

First recorded in Australian English before the war as an abbreviation of *position*, the term **possie**, also commonly recorded with the variant spelling **possy**, was popular during the Great War with specific reference to 'an individual soldier's place of shelter or firing position'. Its use during the war likely popularised its more general use in Australian English after the war. Other variant spellings included *posy*, *pozzie*, and *pozzy*.

Private Will Snow wrote home in 1916 with the following description of his recent activities at the front:

> I went to get some water to have a wash yesterday. The well was a little distance from our '**possie**', down a bit of a communication trench, and it seems to be a favourite spot of Fritz's for dropping shells. However, as things were a bit quiet I sallied forth with my mess tin and was just returning when I heard a noise like a train in the air, so I promptly fell flat on my face. The shell exploded some yards to my left. (Lismore *Northern Star*, 2 August, p. 8)

In 1917, stretcher-bearer William Slater recorded in his diary: 'We are taken up to Kandahar Main Dressing Station [near Neuve Eglise] in cars and after a short rest go up into the line which is up on Messines ridge—country held by Fritz up to two months ago. Unbearable Trench is our "**possy**" and we found the name very apt.' (Diary entry, 11 July 1917, *War Diaries of William Slater*, p. 40)

rat

During the war, to steal something, especially from a corpse or the enemy, was sometimes known as **ratting**. The term existed in Australian English in the sense of 'to steal, to rob a person' from 1898, but in the wartime context this was used in particular reference to the taking of items from corpses or from the enemy (especially prisoners of war), as the following quotation suggests:

> What cheered our troops most was the Hun prisoners coming, or rather being driven, from everywhere. ... Souvenirs were the order of the day and I'll wager that amongst those thousands of Huns there was not one who was not '**ratted**' as the boys term it. They took crowns and gold braid off colonels' shoulder straps, as well as watches, revolvers and anything in the line of souvenirs. Some of them even got the famous iron crosses, and I saw one or two of them with the big-spiked helmets, with the eagle in front. (*Rochester Express*, 9 November 1918, p. 3)

Soldiers frequently sought to collect SOUVENIRS during the war.

rest camp

An ironic term for a cemetery. A *rest camp* was officially a camp where troops were sent when coming out of the lines.

Private F.E. Kennedy wrote home: 'To think that people should go through what the people of France have been through. ... A German after the war is over ought not get a space to move in; everywhere he goes he ought to be shunned: I was also having a look over a little British cemetery (which is known better to the boys here as a "**rest camp**"), and it looks well.' (*Bendigonian*, 1 November 1917, p. 4)

salve

The action of taking or misappropriating and making use of something that has no apparent owner might be referred to as **salving**. **Salve** is an abbreviation of *salvage*. This was often used in the context of salvaging various items for re-use, for example, from shelled houses or from the battlefield. See also SOUVENIR.

Arthur G. Howell, a signaller serving on the Western Front, noted in his diary in 1916: 'Made our dugout more comfortable by putting in a table which we **salved** from a ruined house on the way to Ypres.' (Diary entry, 7 September, *Signaller at the Front*, p. 23) In 1918, after the war had ended, there was a concerted effort to salvage and make use of items from the battlefield as this newspaper piece suggests:

> Huge quantities of goods of all kinds, representing vast sums of money are being **salved** daily from battlefields, roads, highways, railways, dumps, billets, ruined towns and villages. Special corps of salvage men have been formed, whose duties consist solely in collecting, sorting and distributing debris which even until recently was considered valueless and left unheeded. (*Stawell News and Pleasant Creek Chronicle*, 7 December, p. 1)

snodger

This Australian English slang term first appears as a noun in 1909 meaning 'an excellent thing', and possibly comes from a British dialect word, *snod*, 'sleek, neat, in good order'. It was used adjectivally during the war to refer to something, usually a shell, as being large or significant.

An Australian soldier writing home from France reported his friend as saying 'What a **snodger** of a shell' (*Burra Record*, 6 February 1918, p. 6), and an officer writing home commented: 'The men are quite jocular, and such remarks as "By —, that's a **snodger**. It nearly took me 'at," are heard when a whiz-bang or minnie pineapple or rum-jar comes a bit too close to be pleasant.' (*Richmond Guardian*, 3 March 1917, p. 2)

souvenir

Used as both a verb and a noun, this was an ironic wartime use of a Standard English term. Soldiers frequently **souvenired** a range of items while on service during the Great War, including taking battlefield **souvenirs**, taking items from German prisoners of war, and taking items from German trenches when they were captured. They might also '**souvenir**' items from local civilians. It is sometimes used in a similar way to SALVE, but might also frequently involve stealing or RATTING. Many of these items were sent home or were brought home with soldiers; some were turned over to the men who were establishing the Australian War Museum (later Australian War Memorial).

One Australian soldier noted in his diary: 'We had about a dozen prisoners coming towards us at the time, so we **souvenired** them to see that they had no bombs or revolvers about them. We **souvenired** a watch each, and I got a good pair of field glasses.' (Diary entry, 8 August 1918, *Letters from the Front*, p. 216) Another Australian soldier, Thomas Clair Whiteside, noted in a letter home in 1917: 'Fritz's dug-outs were full of **souvenirs**, and picks and shovels were lying about everywhere. Any amount of equipment and stuff to salvage.' (Letter, 3 March, *A Valley In France*, p. 83)

Souvenirs from the battlefield were also sent home to Australia for family members, or for soldiers to collect when they returned home, as this notice in an Australian newspaper suggests:

Mr. J. Short, of Bishopgate-street, has recently received a unique war **souvenir** from his son, Gunner Chas Short, on active service in France. The **souvenir** is one of the famous German Iron Crosses, of which so much has been heard during the war, and was acquired by Gunner Short during the Australians' fine success at the Hindenburg line in August last. (*Singleton Argus*, 5 November 1918, p. 2)

souvenir king

A person who took SOUVENIRS from the battlefield or the enemy was sometimes known as a *souvenirer*; one who was particularly prone to, or good at, souveniring was sometimes referred to as a **souvenir king**.

Aussie: The Australian Soldiers' Magazine noted in a humorous story: 'As a **Souvenir King**, a chap in my Batt. reigns supreme. He seems to have the idea that this war is being run for the sole purpose of providing him with Fritz automatic revolvers, field glasses and watches.' (September, p. 6) A 1919 newspaper item noted: 'The local branch of the Returned Soldiers and Sailors' League is to be asked to arrange a great display of war trophies, souvenirs, etc. As the Mid-Richmond had some noted "**souvenir kings**" at the front the result is likely to prove an exhibition of unusual interest.' (Lismore *Northern Star*, 1 November, p. 6)

S.R.D.

This abbreviation was stamped on rum jars from which rum rations were distributed to soldiers; it stood for 'Supply, Reserve, Depot'. While serving in the trenches, soldiers were usually given a rum ration at dawn and at dusk. **S.R.D.** was jokingly said by soldiers to variously stand for 'Soon Runs Dry', 'Seldom Reaches Destination', or 'Service Rum Dilute.' A collection of Australian soldier slang in the Perth *Sunday Times* included the 'Seldom Reaches Destination' interpretation. (9 March 1919, p. 7)

stonker

This term, used as a verb, means 'to kill, to defeat'. It derives from *stonk*, the stake in a game, especially in a game of marbles. **Stonker** continued to be used in Australian English after the war.

A 1918 newspaper article described the following: 'The cavalry detached one or two small parties to deal with a few loose bunches of Fritzes away from the village, and the rest of them went straight for the village at the gallop in extended order and promptly **stonkered** the Hun.' (Perth *Western Mail*, 30 August, p. 35)

stoush

This Australian and New Zealand English term as a noun meaning 'a fight' dates from the 1890s, and as a verb meaning 'to fight' dates from 1909. It was frequently used in the Great War by Australian soldiers to refer to the fighting of a battle. It possibly comes from the British dialect *stashie*, or *stushie*, meaning 'an uproar; disturbance'. The Great War was sometimes referred to as the BIG STOUSH.

Private C. Doyle, writing home from France in September 1916, said: 'The Anzacs are making a great name for themselves. They take stopping when they get a go on. I think this bit of **stoush** will be over by Christmas—let us hope so. I have had just about enough— two years a soldier.' (*Seymour Express and Goulburn Valley Avenel*, 1 September, p. 3)

stunt

This was a popular Great War term for 'an attack' or 'an advance' in a military context. The term possibly has its origins in American slang, where *stunt* was an American college slang term for 'a striking display or feat'. (See also the flying slang term STUNTING in Chapter Nine.)

Oliver Hogue, in his book *Trooper Bluegum at the Dardanelles* (1916), commented: 'I don't like the word "**stunt**"; it sounds like an American vaudeville turn. But somehow it attained a general vogue on Gallipoli, and it meant any of the little incidents, episodes, and brushes with the enemy which served to relieve the monotony of trench warfare.' (p. 186) In the 'Aussie Dictionary' provided in the first edition of *Aussie: The Australian Soldiers' Magazine* in January 1918, **stunt** was defined as: 'A successful enterprise or undertaking usually involving surprise. A large scale stunt lacks the latter and is termed a "push", and the element of success is not essential.' (p. 11)

suicide club

A term for a machine-gun company, a trench-mortar battery, or a bombing company; their work was considered to be more risky than the work of infantry soldiers because they were more likely to be targeted (and killed) by enemy fire. The term was in general use during the Great War. Fraser and Gibbons in *Soldier and Sailor Words and Phrases* write that it was 'applied usually, more or less in jest, to various "specialist" formations whose duties were, or seemed to be, of an exceptionally risky or dangerous nature, such as bombers, Machine-Gunners, Stretcher-Bearers'.

One 1916 Australian newspaper article noted: '**Suicide Club** is the facetiously pleasant name by which bombing parties go in the Army.' (*Warrnambool Standard*, 12 August, p. 10) In 1917, an Australian soldier, Private Harry Tribolet, writing home to Forbes, NSW, told his family that 'I have joined the machine gun section. The boys here call it the **Suicide Club**, but I am getting on all right with it.' (*Forbes Advocate*, 12 January, p. 4)

take the count

To **take the count** means to be knocked out or killed. This term dates back to 1902 and has its origins in boxing; during the Great War, it was used in reference to being wounded or killed in action.

A notice in the *Wangaratta Chronicle* in 1917 recorded the following information about Private Jim Cowan who had written home to his family to tell them of his experiences: 'He had just landed back after ten days' leave to England and Scotland, where he had a great time; but the killing part was going back to France. He landed back just in time to miss the big stunt, but on the way up

to the line got a shower of shrapnel and he nearly **took the count**.'
(12 December, p. 1)

tin hat

Also often with the variant **tin lid**, these terms were used for a steel
helmet, worn in the trenches, and which offered protection from
shrapnel. The steel helmet was introduced into the British Army late
in 1915 and quickly became much valued by soldiers, for obvious
reasons. Recorded British variants include *battle bowler* and *steel jug*.

Private F.A. Crawford, writing from France, described the
value of the steel helmet for soldiers: 'Many lives have been saved
by the introduction of the steel helmet, or the "**tin lid**" as the boys
call it, which will stop an almost spent bullet and shell splinters
which would otherwise inflict serious, if not fatal, wounds. Steel
helmets are worn by all troops in or near the trenches.' (Broken Hill
Barrier Miner, 22 July 1917, p. 3) A returned soldier in an interview
with the Victorian newspaper *Advertiser* said of the trenches: 'Rats
[in the trenches] were the main trouble ... So bad were they that no
food was safe in the dug out, so a bright spirit thought of hanging
it up in a **tin-hat** hung with wire from the cross beams of the roof.'
(12 January 1918, p. 2)

Tommy cooker

A term for a type of portable stove used in the front lines by soldiers.
This item was first used during the Great War and was used for
cooking or warming up food or tea. The name derives from TOMMY
(from *Tommy Atkins*), the popular name for a British soldier, and
cooker, a British English word for a stove.

Private W.H. Sutton, an Australian soldier in France, wrote
home to his sister, praising the **Tommy cooker**: 'I have just been
handed a cup of tea made on an Australian comforts fund **Tommy
cooker**. ... In our battalion the **Tommy cookers** are not the individual
property of any one man. They are treated as trench stores, and the
front line men hand them over to their relief.' (Launceston *Examiner*,
7 February 1918, p. 8) People at home often raised money to provide

Tommy cookers to Australian soldiers serving in Europe. In 1918 the following notice was printed in several Victorian newspapers, explaining just what the **Tommy cooker** was:

> At the Moonee Ponds Town Hall last Tuesday afternoon, an interesting demonstration of 'trench fuel' sent to soldiers for cooking purposes was given by Mrs Sloan. Six sheets of ordinary newspaper were rolled together tightly and pasted when in a solid roll. After being cut into pieces, measuring one inch long, they were saturated in melted paraffin wax and allowed to dry. When this preparation is completed the novel fuel will burn in a 'Tommy cooker' for 20 minutes, and will give heat equal almost to a Primus stove. The 'Tommy cooker' is merely a wire frame, in the centre of which the fuel rests, supports on each side holding the cooking utensils in place. (*Flemington Spectator*, 13 June, p. 3)

Tommy cookers were often so slow in heating as to be ineffective, and therefore often complained about by soldiers.

trench fever

A type of illness transmitted by lice and contracted by soldiers in the trenches.

An Australian newspaper noted of **trench fever**: 'This fever, as its name implies, is a war disease, and it is interesting to note that it is apparently a disease of the present war.' (*Horsham Times*, 15 February 1918, p. 3) A notice in the *Port Macquarie News and Hastings River Advocate* declared: 'Another of our soldiers with whom our sympathies are just now particularly enlisted is Corporal Ken. Dennis, a son of Mrs Dennis, of the local public school staff, who has been invalided to England from France, suffering a severe attack of **trench fever**, a notification to that effect having been received by his mother.' (15 December 1917, p. 4)

trench foot

A type of foot disease contracted by soldiers in the trenches due to prolonged exposure to extreme cold and wet, and as a result of poor sanitary conditions.

A 1915 article in the Perth newspaper, the *West Australian*, commented: 'Trench warfare has produced a special set of diseases ... . The medical papers are trying continually to find a proper name for it, the variations including "**Trench Foot**", "Chilled Foot", and "Water Bite".' (6 May, p. 8) Dr H.M. Moran, writing from the Middle East in 1916, noted: 'The wounded ... heal well—quite a contrast after the cases from France and Gallipoli, and we see no gangrene to speak of here, and very little "**trench foot**".' (Sydney *Referee*, 31 May, p. 12) Archie Barwick, serving on the Western Front in 1916, noted in his diary being lectured by a doctor on **trench foot** and how to prevent it: '**Trench feet** is a very serious thing: your feet swell up to an enormous size & you can't walk. This is caused by several things, such as boots too tight, poor circulation of the blood caused by overfatigue, no hot meals, wet feet & on top of all this the freezing cold.' (Diary entry, 4 December, *In Great Spirits: The WWI Diary of Archie Barwick*, p. 211)

vertical breeze

A term used during the war to mean 'a state of fear'. Brophy and Partridge in *Songs and Slang of the British Soldier: 1914–18* record that this was often used in phrases such as 'to suffer from a **vertical breeze**' or 'to have the **breeze vertical**'. It is thus similar 'to have the WIND UP', and probably related to it. See also BREEZE UP; WINDY. While recorded as airmen's slang in contemporary reports on flying slang, it was also used more widely, as suggested by the 1918 quotation below.

An Australian military padre's account of the Western Front included the observation: 'Every turn in the road was expected to reveal enemy patrols—the haystacks were viewed with suspicion, and the ground in the vicinity of depressions was avoided or approached with caution. The fact was lack of information had created a "**vertical**" **breeze**, which affected the majority of us.' (*Kyneton Guardian*, 29 October 1918, p. 4)

wind up

Usually in the phrase 'to have the **wind up**', this means 'to be afraid; feeling fear', and was first used during the Great War. Brophy and Partridge in *Songs and Slang of the British Soldier: 1914–1918* comment that 'to have the **wind up**' 'implied no disgrace, and could be mentioned casually in conversation'. Much of the Australian evidence suggests the term was used more commonly of the enemy, but might also be used of oneself. W.H. Downing's *Digger Dialects* records the variation *draft up*. See also VERTICAL BREEZE, BREEZE UP, and WINDY.

Australian officer Bert Smythe commented in his diary: 'As we passed down the sunken road 3 ft deep single file just out of sight of the enemy, he opened a fierce rifle fire the bullets of which swept right across the road & we had to take shelter for a while by sitting down. Fritz either had "the **wind up**" very badly, or else was expecting an attack.' (Diary entry, 9 April 1917, *Letters from Bert Smythe* [online]) One soldier from Kalgoorlie wrote: 'After our experience of the morning we had the **wind up** a bit about bombs, so we got into our dugout and waited for one to fall on the roof.' (*Western Argus*, 20 August 1918, p. 31)

windy

Related to 'have the WIND UP', this term is used to describe someone who is afraid, and was first used during the Great War. Brophy and Partridge in *Songs and Slang of the British Soldier: 1914–1918* note that unlike 'have the WIND UP', this term 'could be used of others in a derogatory sense'. However, the Australian evidence (as illustrated below) suggests that this was not always the case.

A soldier writing to the relatives of another soldier who had been killed in France wrote of him: 'We were on the Battery Staff together at Nieuport and Ypres, ... he was a man everyone felt could be depended on to do thoroughly and efficiently the job that was set him. And no matter if he felt "**windy**", he never showed it;

that's the hallmark of the brave man, isn't it?' (*Geelong Advertiser*, 29 July 1918, p. 6)

zero hour

The time at which an action, a battle or an attack commences. The term is first recorded during the Great War, thereafter becoming common.

A Queensland officer wrote back to Australia relating his first experiences of battle: '[T]he night preceding the attack, we had to get our men in the blackest of nights, in the rain, through mud often knee deep, to our place of assembly. Afterwards came the move on to the jumping off tape, and there await the **zero hour**, when the thunder of your own guns tells you that it is time to be up and doing.' (*Western Star and Roma Advertiser*, 7 September 1918, p. 6)

Passing Shrapnel Corner: Place names

It was common during the Great War for a range of places to be given nicknames by soldiers. Some of these names applied to a place that only had meaning in the context of the war, such as a particular location in a fighting area; others were corruptions or Anglicisations of existing place names. This chapter examines a number of these names. It is not comprehensive in its coverage of place names, but it aims to illustrate the different ways in which names came to be given by soldiers to locations.

For soldiers, naming places could create a sense of attachment to a place and serve to make it more familiar and normal and less alien to them. Place names in foreign languages could make soldiers feel far from home, but renaming places could help make them more familiar. They could also express feelings, such as sentiment, fear, or irony, for a place (and the actions being undertaken there). The naming of places could also serve to assert the dominance of the presence of the soldiers over a particular place or locality, a kind of 'conquest' of the area. In some places, such as on the Gallipoli peninsula, a series of Australian names overlaid a foreign terrain that was unfamiliar to the British and the Anzacs but nevertheless had a deep history.

In this chapter, a number of place names given and used by Australian soldiers are discussed. All the armies had their own particular place names, reflecting the places where they fought and with which they were most familiar. British soldiers referred to, for example, *Arm-in-tears* (for Armentières); *Balloo* (for Ballieul, a French town near Ypres); *Hazybrook* (for Hazebrouck); *Hop out* (for Hopoutre); *Lousy Wood* (Leuze Wood, where British soldiers fought during the Battle of the Somme in 1916); *Ocean Villas* (for Auchonvillers, a town near Arras); *Pop* (for Poperinghe, a town near Ypres where there were many camps for soldiers); *Roody Boys* (for Rue du Bois near Neuve Chapelle); *Ruin* (for Rouen), *Sally Booze* (for the village of Sailly la Bourse); and *White Sheet* (for the town of Wytschaete in Belgium).

Some of the names given by soldiers received some semi-official military status by being used on military maps. This varied: it was more likely such a name would be used for an area that had no other name or distinguishing marker.

Many of these names perhaps serve to reflect the fact that these places came to bear more relation to the world of the soldiers than to the pre-war reality of a place. Landscapes were changed dramatically as fighting, shelling, and the movement of soldiers and materiel transformed areas into the barren landscapes of the trenches.

Overall, place names given by soldiers tended to be of three different types. Firstly, some place names were given to a place on or near a battlefield where there was no other way of identifying it, except perhaps by a military marker or map co-ordinates. Names such as SUICIDE CORNER or SHRAPNEL GULLY are examples of this; these names also are indicative of the way soldiers connected these places with the reality of war and death.

Secondly, some place names were corruptions or Anglicisations of French, Belgian, or other names for existing places, villages, or towns. Existing names could be difficult to pronounce for many English-speaking soldiers with limited knowledge of foreign languages, and often little effort was made to pronounce such names correctly; in addition, they were often mangled for humorous effect, or in order to shorten the name. Examples of this include Moo-cow Farm (for Mouquet Farm) and Plugstreet (for Ploegseert).

Finally, soldiers could give names to particular locations within towns or existing foreign locations, often giving them entirely different names from their existing ones. In the Australian soldiers' case, for example, there are recorded instances where local streets in the town of Peronne were given names such as Roo de Kanga. These names were perhaps a form of staking out a territory for a particular national army.

Nicknames were also bestowed on individual trenches. An article published in Australian newspapers on 'Tommy slang' noted:

> Curious names have been invented for trenches. In many places, where the windings and turnings are most intricate, and a stranger is liable to lose his way, signposts are placed at the points of junction, and each passage and section of a trench is given a name, probably taken from the battalion which dug it or the officer who was in charge of the work. Very often the names selected are more pretentious. A plank pathway through a muddy wood will in all probability go by the title of 'Piccadilly' or 'The Strand'. A little log cabin or a dug-out under a breastwork of sandbags will be honored by the name of the Ritz or the Carlton. (Perth *Daily News*, 24 July 1915, p. 11)

Another piece from the Western Front in 1915 noted some names given to specific trenches by the British forces, including *Paradise Alley*, *Old Kent Road*, and *Hyde Park Corner*. (*Muswellbrook Chronicle*, 24 April, p. 4) Many of these trench names have not survived in the written evidence because they tended to be ephemeral, but again the phenomenon demonstrates the urge for soldiers to make familiar the unfamiliar, and orient themselves within the territory in which they found themselves.

Gallipoli and the Middle East

Australians first saw combat at the Dardanelles as part of the Gallipoli campaign in 1915. A variety of names were given to places of combat at Gallipoli. One Australian soldier wrote home to say: 'I am short of paper, and the Turks are doing a little gun practice outside. We have got all the places named. There is *"Death Trap Corner"*, *"Suicide Valley"*,

"Hurry-up Point", "Shrapnel Corner", etc.' (Healesville and Yarra Glen Guardian, 17 July 1915, p. 3)

Many of the names included by this soldier were unofficial nicknames for
locations adopted to help orient soldiers to the terrain in which they were
operating. Other names assumed a more official status and can be found
on maps of the period. A reporter, writing about the fighting in Gallipoli
in June 1915, noted: 'Every camp, hill, and gully, has now a distinctive
Australian name, such as Dead Man's Ridge, Bloody Angle, MacLaurin Hill,
Queensland Point, Hell Spit, Pluggers' Plateau, and Brighton Beach.' (The
Farmer and the Settler, 25 June 1915, p. 1)

A number of the place names used at Gallipoli were named after
individuals, usually officers. These include Courtney's Post, JOHNSTON'S
JOLLY, Monash Gully, Plugge's Plateau, and QUINN'S POST. Others, such as THE
PIMPLE and LONE PINE were given their names in relation to their physical
features. A number got their names from the nature of the fighting that
took place on or around the location: these include SHRAPNEL GULLY, REST
GULLY, Dead Man's Ridge, and Sniper's Ridge.

Some Australian soldiers served in the Middle East through the
rest of the war. Not many nicknames for this area survive in the records,
although one does: MESS-UP-POT-AMIA. This name reflects the humour that
was sometimes present in the activity of naming locations by soldiers,
also evidenced in a number of the names given to towns and locations
on the Western Front.

Discussed below are a selection of some of the more well-
known names given to places and locations encountered by Australian
soldiers serving in the Middle East and Gallipoli. This selection is not
comprehensive, but it does aim to demonstrate the various ways in
which place names functioned within soldiers' vocabulary.

∞∞∞

Anzac

The most famous place name connected to the fighting at the
Dardanelles was Anzac Cove, often abbreviated to and known as
Anzac.

One Australian soldier, Percy Smythe, wrote in his diary:
'Another rumour says we are to land at the place called **Anzac**, from
the initials of Australian and New Zealand Army Corps.' (Diary
entry, 26 August 1915, *World War I Diary of Percy Smythe* [online])

Archie Barwick, returning to Anzac Cove after a period of rest at Lemnos, wrote: 'When we left Lemnos we did not know properly whether we were going to **Anzac** or Salonika, but once we started we were not left long in doubt. We arrived off **Anzac** after dark—she was still in the same old place.' (*In Great Spirits: The WWI Diary of Archie Barwick*, p. 60)

C.E.W. Bean helped to immortalise the actions of the Australian and New Zealand soldiers who fought at Gallipoli. At the time of the evacuation, Bean wrote in his diary:

> So I have left old **Anzac**. In a way I was really fond of the place. I have certainly had some quite enjoyable times there in my old dugout–yarning to friends; or going round the lines. I can't pretend that I ever liked shells or attacks–but one came to put up with them as much as one does with the toothache ... . (Bean, 18 December 1915, Fewster (ed.) p. 254)

Anzac firmly entered the Australian imagination and continues to resonate as a location invested with special significance for Australians. Many Australians still travel to the Gallipoli area as a pilgrimage to the places where Australians fought.

Johnston's Jolly

This location, north of LONE PINE, was named after Lieutenant-Colonel George Jameson *Johnston* (1868–1949) who commanded the 2nd Field Artillery Brigade. It was the scene of fighting at the time of the Australian landing on Gallipoli. Historian of Gallipoli Michael McKernan explains: 'In calling for his gunners near Lone Pine to "jolly up" the Turks, Johnston prompted the troops to give this patch of land its name.' (*Gallipoli: A Short History*, p. 214)

A despatch by General Ian Hamilton was reproduced in the *Kalgoorlie Miner* in early 1916, describing the actions at Gallipoli: 'The entrenchment was evidently very strong; it was entangled with wire, and provided with overhead cover, and it was connected by numerous communication trenches with another point d'appui known as **Johnston's Jolly** on the north, as well as two other works on the east and south.' (21 March, p. 1)

Lone Pine

Lone Pine got its name from a popular song, 'The Trail of the Lonesome Pine'. The story related by Michael McKernan in his *Gallipoli: A Short History* (p. 215) is that when the soldiers landed on the peninsula, they looked up to see a single stunted pine tree rising above the scrub. This reminded them of the song, and hence the name. **Lone Pine** was the location of fighting in early August 1915; some of the fighting at this location was the fiercest of the Gallipoli campaign, with high numbers of casualties. **Lone Pine** is now the location of the Anzac Day ceremonies held at Gallipoli.

An account of the fighting around **Lone Pine** sent home to Australia by Sergeant-Major George Morris was printed in the Sydney *Sunday Times* in October 1915. He wrote: 'We have been having some very heavy fighting here in an attack on a place which we called "**Lone Pine**"—named that way on account of one pine tree on the ridge. We were successful, and are still holding the captured trenches, of which we took three times before we were stopped.' (17 October, p. 4)

Mess-up-pot-amia

Mesopotamia, a name for the Middle Eastern areas where soldiers fought during the Great War, was given a variety of names during the war. The British used the names *Mespot* and *Mess pot*. One Australian soldier however dubbed the area **Mess-up-pot-amia**:

> Five of us have just completed a seven days trip up the Tigris and we are now as far up country as the Turks will let us go. Maybe we will push on a little further shortly of our own accord. The rest of the boys are still back at the base, where we landed three months ago. They have not yet officially reached this country, and until they are officially here nothing can be done. Possibly the authorities will wake up some time before Doomsday, though I doubt it. We should have had Joe Girdham with us to ring the bell and announce to all and sundry the arrival of the 1st Australia wireless corps in **Mess-up-pot-amia**. (*Forbes Advocate*, 1 December 1916, p. 6)

The Peninsh

The Gallipoli Peninsula was sometimes known as **the Peninsh**, an abbreviation of *peninsula.*

One Australian soldier, commenting on a fellow soldier, observed the following:

> Keltie got his 'Blighty' and for the moment his interest in war vanished. They patched him up, and he made a third trip to Gallipoli. There must be few surviving soldiers of the A.I.F. can boast the distinction of three trips to the '**Peninsh**'. He met the battalion at Lemnos, where they were spelling, and went with them again to Anzac, where he was to the evacuation in December. (*Cairns Post*, 29 May 1919, p. 8)

The Pimple

A position near LONE PINE fought over by Anzac and Ottoman forces.

The *Bathurst Times* reported in October 1915 on some of the fighting happening at Gallipoli, saying: 'News has arrived of a great bombardment of a position to the right of Anzac, known as **the Pimple** on Oct. 6. Battleships, a destroyer, and our Anzac howitzers landed hundreds of shells for 45 minutes. ... The whole of **the Pimple** was covered with shells.' (27 October, p. 1)

Quinn's Post

This location, the scene of considerable fighting, was named after Major Hugh *Quinn* (1888–1915), who was killed on 29 May. It was the most advanced post of the line of Anzac forces. Quinn was North Queensland's heavyweight boxing champion, and was in command of C Company of the 15th Battalion.

A newspaper report in the *Bunbury Herald* on 24 June 1915 told of the actions on Gallipoli: 'The attack began at midnight, and the bombardment was unprecedented in vigour, and shells of all calibres were thrown. It was literally impossible to put one's head out of a dugout until the hail of shrapnel had abated ... in the morning an attack in great force was made by the Turks along the whole line, the main objective being **Quinn's Post**.' (p. 3)

Rest Gully

A gully that ran off SHRAPNEL GULLY.

Writing in 1916 of his Gallipoli experiences, Sergeant John H. Falconer, noted of his first arrival at Gallipoli: 'We formed up on the beach of Anzac Cove and after a very tiring march along the shore turned up into a gully called "**Rest Gully**" and there we dropped our kit, and were told we could rest until midday.' (J.H. Falconer, *On Active Service*) Writing of the Anzac withdrawal a few months later, Lance-Corporal T.A. Saxon wrote: 'We got our first relief from the firing-line and were sent to **Rest Gully** for a week, but if ever a place was misnamed it was "**Rest Gully**" (that is from our point of view) as from the time we got there till the time we left the Pen, we put in 18 out of 24 hours in fatigue work.' (*Euroa Advertiser*, 10 March 1916, p. 2)

Shrapnel Gully

This area received its name soon after the landing of the Anzac forces on the Gallipoli peninsula. Turkish guns regularly sent shrapnel down into the area. It was sometimes also known as *Shrapnel Valley*.

In his diary, Archie Barwick noted: 'It was just about this time [29 April] that General Bridges was killed in **Shrapnel Gully**, & everyone was sorry. The other Generals wanted him to withdraw all of us on the Sunday night ... but General Bridges said the Australians would never give in & if they had to die he would die with them, & so he did.' (*In Great Spirits: The WWI Diary of Archie Barwick*, p. 37)

Tom Skeyhill in his poem 'On Gallipoli' included the following verse:

> **Shrapnel Gully** is on their right,
> Courtney's Post is to their head,
> The wide Mediterranean at their feet,
> And the blue sky overhead. (*Preston Leader*, 9 October 1915, p. 5)

The Western Front

Australian soldiers in France and Belgium had a range of names for places they encountered while serving on the Western Front. Some are well-attested and often mentioned by soldiers, such as SAUSAGE VALLEY, MOO-COW FARM, and SUICIDE CORNER. These well-attested terms related to towns or areas over which soldiers were fighting, or they were, like SUICIDE CORNER, a name that might be applied to any area that was particularly dangerous.

Others, such as *Wallaby Alley* and *Possum Lane*, are not well-attested in the printed record, although when Australians entered Peronne, they clearly named the streets there in their own Australian fashion. As mentioned at the entry for ROO DE KANGA, the street sign put up by the Australian soldiers survives, having been collected by those who established the Australian War Museum (later Australian War Memorial). The following short piece, taken from the *British-Australasian* and reprinted in the *Western Champion* in 1919, captures the way Australian soldiers sought to rename these streets in ways that reminded them of home: 'The Rue de Kanga, mentioned some weeks ago, is not the only good Australian street that has grown up in a single night, so to speak, in the wake of the Australian Imperial Forces in France. *Dingbat Avenue*, *Wombat-road*, Wallaby-alley, and Possum-lane are a few of the signposts that the "digger" has left behind him.' (15 February, p. 10)

Casualty Corner

An area on the road that ran through SAUSAGE VALLEY, a valley that led to the battlefields at Pozières. Casualty Corner was subject to considerable shelling by the Germans, hence the name.

Arthur Howell, writing in his diary in 1916, wrote: 'When we got as far as **Casualty Corner** the enemy began to shell the cross roads and in the space of a few minutes the place resembled a shambles. ... The place is well called **Casualty Corner**.' (Diary entry, 22 July 1916, *Signaller at the Front*, p. 17) A month later, on leaving Pozières and the Somme, Howell wrote in his diary: 'Such places as "Sausage Valley" "The Rock" "**Casualty Corner**" and the "Pozieres Cemetery" are engraved indelibly on the minds of everyone who was there.' (Diary entry, 27 August 1916, p. 22)

Hellfire Corner

According to Fraser and Gibbons in their *Soldier and Sailor Words and Phrases*, **Hellfire Corner** was a place in The Salient, where a railway line crossed the Menin Road near Ypres. The Menin Road supplied the trenches, and thus was constantly under bombardment by German forces. Initially a nickname, it became official when it began to appear on military maps. However, there were probably a number of **Hellfire Corners** named by soldiers on the Western Front.

Arthur Howell wrote in his diary in 1917: 'The enemy was shelling round the dressing station round "**Hellfire Corner**" and I had to leave the road and go through the mud overland.' (Diary entry, 7 October 1917, *Signaller at the Front*, p. 57) Another soldier, writing in 1918, recounted: 'The resultant getting to the dressing station without being blown to eternity by the machine guns or the shells playing all round you was one of the worst ordeals. How I got off that front alive beats me, especially around such places as **Hellfire Corner** and Shrapnel Gully.' (Perth *Sunday Times*, 7 July 1918, p. 3)

Huns' Walk

This referred to a German trench line, which Australian forces aimed to capture during the Battle of Messines in 1917.

C.E.W. Bean in both his war correspondence and his later official histories of the war wrote about **Huns' Walk**: 'The 47th [Battalion] had to maintain the difficult struggle at the point where the 3rd and 4th Australian Divisions joined. It attacked opposite **Huns' Walk**, and reached the support trench of the second German line.' (Adelaide *Register*, 28 May 1918, p. 5)

Moo-cow Farm

This was Mouquet Farm, an area near Pozières, which saw an action take place as part of the larger Battle of the Somme, in August

1916. Three Australian divisions were involved: the 1st, 2nd, and 4th Divisions. Australian soldiers dubbed the area '**Moo-cow**' **Farm**.

> The Australians stuck it; guessing what the bombardment foreboded, they held on in the trenches, and dug themselves in in the shell craters and the old German trenches, with bombs ready and machine guns handy. The attack was between the windmill and Mouquet Farm. The Australians nickname the latter "**Moo-cow Farm**". (*Brisbane Courier* 15 August 1916, p. 4)

Plugstreet

Ploegsteert, a village in Belgium near Armentières. Ploegsteert Wood was part of the Western Front and saw a great deal of fighting through the early part of the war; it later became an area where soldiers might rest before going back to the front lines. It was perhaps a name better known to British soldiers (because of their involvement in the fighting there), but was reported on widely in the Australian press.

An Australian chaplain from the Nepean area in New South Wales who served with the Canadian forces wrote back to Australia: 'We spent three months in "**Plugstreet**", and had many exciting experiences and lost many good men.' (*Nepean Times*, 4 March 1916, p. 8)

Pozzie

An abbreviation of the name of the French town of Pozières, the location of fierce fighting involving Australians.

The hospital periodical, *The Harefield Park Boomerang*, included a poem with the following verse:

> When nights were cold and beer was bad
> I'd lecture and bully our old man 'Dad';
> I never saw **Pozzie** or inside hell,
> But I wore gold stripes on my left lapel—
> That's what I did in the war, dinkum;
> That's what I did in the war. (1 August 1917, p. 13)

Roo de Kanga

A street sign placed after Australian soldiers captured the town of Péronne in 1918 dubbed the street the **Roo de Kanga**, with 'Roo' being a play on the French word for street, *rue*. The street sign was collected, and later put on display at the Australian War Memorial.

A British article in the Australian press noted: 'And of a sudden one comes on the largest notice board of all. The effect is like that of a clean and merry wind blowing through a swamp. The board bears the title "**Roo de Kanga**", and it marks the Australian conquest of the ruins on September 1.' (Perth *Daily News*, 17 December 1918, p. 4) Another article reported: 'Coming through again in daylight three weeks later, the place had been tidied up, the streets repaired and swept, and the following names were seen on official signboards: "**Rue de Kanga**" (main street), "Emu Alley", "Diggers-road", "Dingbat lane", and "Platypus street".' (*Brisbane Courier*, 15 February 1919, p. 6)

Sausage Valley

This was a name given to a valley south of the village of La Boiselle near Pozières. It was probably named because the Germans flew an observation balloon (a SAUSAGE) near the valley, but see also the Melbourne *Argus* quotation below, which suggests a different origin.

In his diary, Arthur Howell wrote: 'After leaving Albert we proceeded to the position at a trot. We are on the slope of **Sausage Valley** which is nothing more than a mass of tangled barbed wire, shell holes and graves.' (Diary entry, 19 July 1916, *Signaller at the Front*, p. 17) A few months later, the Australian press reported:

> **Sausage Valley**, it should be explained, is a depression behind the position from which the original attack on Pozieres was made. It was at that time the principal artillery position behind the Anzac lines, but as the attack was pushed beyond Pozieres the guns were advanced from the valley to the crest of the ridge east of it. The Australians say it is called **Sausage Valley** because it is next to Mashed Valley; and Mashed Valley gets its name from its proximity to **Sausage Valley**. Both are bits of Anzac nomenclature,

as is Dinkum Gully, so called because it is quite straight. All these names now appear on the military maps of the district. (Melbourne *Argus*, 12 October 1916, p. 9)

Shrapnel Corner

A location in the Ypres salient that was subject to regular bombardment and shelling by the Germans.

Arthur Howell wrote in his diary in October 1916: 'Some of the gunners went into Ypres today all coming home laden with stuff from the canteen. They were hurried along by a few air bursts as they were passing "**Shrapnel Corner**".' (Diary entry, 30 September 1916, *Signaller at the Front*, p. 25)

Suicide Corner

A number of locations on the Western Front were named **Suicide Corner**, the most famous being a location in the Ypres salient. Like SHRAPNEL CORNER, the name makes reference to the danger of passing through the location due to the heavy shelling of the area.

A soldier on the Western Front wrote in November 1916: 'We live in little dug-out shelters behind the pits, and some of the soldiers sleep in parts of the ruined town behind us. They have some great names for some of the spots. "Shrapnel-road", "**Suicide Corner**", "Ratrun Villa", "Daylight Crescent" (where daylight is about the only thing to see, the houses having been blown to bits).' (Launceston *Examiner*, 25 November 1916, p. 9) In 1917, stretcher-bearer William Slater noted in his diary: 'More brick-bag filling at "**Suicide Corner**" which as the name indicates is a pretty unhealthy part of the globe.' (Diary entry, 24 May 1917, *War Diaries of William Slater*, p. 32)

Wipers

Ypres, a town in Flanders in Belgium. **Wipers** was a popularly used corruption of the name, and was made famous by the publication of the British trench paper *The Wipers Times*.

The Australian press made many references to **Wipers**, usually in reproducing pieces from British newspapers, and thus the name became well known to an Australian audience. Australian soldiers also knew it. Captain H. Alan Currie (possibly Henry Alan Currie, an Australian who enlisted in the British Army in 1915) wrote in 1916: 'I went up to "**Wipers**" the other day. It is a big city, absolutely deserted ... .' (*Camperdown Chronicle*, 25 April, p. 4) In *The Harefield Park Boomerang*, a hospital periodical, an anonymous verse included the following lines: 'Far, far from "**Wipers**" I long to be, | Where German snipers can't snipe at me.' (Vol. 2, No. 7, July 1918, p. 134)

The daily hate: Weapons and the technology of war

The Great War saw a proliferation of weapons and technologies that profoundly changed the nature of warfare. Of all the areas that generated new words and slang, this was perhaps the one that was most prolific. A large proportion of the terms included in this chapter refer to weapons, including guns, bombs, grenades, and other technologies for killing. They reflect the industrialised nature of the war, as well as the importance of these weapons in shaping the experience of war. The ubiquity of terms for shells, guns, and artillery suggests the centrality of these weapons in trench warfare and, by extension, in the lives of soldiers. Soldiers frequently commented on the range of weapons, including artillery guns and shells, in their accounts of the war.

Heavy artillery was critical to the Great War, and a key to British victory lay in their capacity to increase the weight of their artillery which Germany could not keep up with; in addition, the accuracy and effectiveness of artillery improved over the course of the war. The British forces fired over five million tons of ammunition during the war. Artillery played an important tactical role in the war, as it was used to try to destroy trenches and enemy guns; for soldiers, they were a pervasive feature of their lives in the trenches.

The artillery developed in the Great War was destructive and powerful. Not only did it have a real physical impact on soldiers—the mutilation or complete obliteration that might come with being hit by a shell—shelling had devastating psychological effects on soldiers. Soldiers in trenches under heavy bombardment suffered the most. They were helpless to do anything, and they were subject to the constant noise and fear generated by an artillery barrage. War became depersonalised, with soldiers feeling that their own actions had little effect. Shells might contain a range of materials: for example, high explosives, shrapnel, or chemicals (gas).

The lexicon of Great War weaponry was therefore rich, with many nicknames being applied to guns, shells, and other technologies of the war. Soldiers sometimes commented on the number of names given to guns and other weapons. For example, Archie Barwick, who served on Gallipoli and the Western Front, noted the numerous nicknames given to Turkish guns at Gallipoli in July 1915:

> We christened a few of the Turkish guns, some of the names ran like this: Beachy Bill of course takes pride of place, the most destructive gun on the peninsula; Percy Jones, a fairly silent fellow; Harry Lauder, a shell which used to sing when it came along; Asiatic Annie from the Chanak forts, a big shell which never done any harm, because it always landed very thoughtfully where there happened to be no one; Wheelbarrow Jack, a big shell which used to be shot from a mortar—it was round like a football, & used to make a creaking noise on its way to the trenches. (*In Great Spirits: The WWI Diary of Archie Barwick*, p. 45)

This is just one such observation on the many names and words for weapons given during the war.

The use of nicknames perhaps helped in making these weapons less intimidating to soldiers. A shell known as a WOOLLY BEAR, for example, was perhaps made more 'familiar' by such a name. BEACHY BILL might be the gun that ended a soldier's life, but the nickname helped a soldier to regard it with humour, even a perverse kind of affection, rather than dwelling on the fear it might generate. While later wars would produce much technical jargon for weapons and other technologies, the Great War is notable in the ways in which the unfamiliar and depersonalised weaponry of war was made more familiar.

Most of the terms in this chapter are slang, and only a couple, such as TANK and BLIMP are (or became) Standard English terms. While it is possible to identify terms as referring to particular types of guns, grenades, or shells, it should be noted that individual soldiers might use the same term for different types of weapons, or use different terms for the same weapon. For example, a BLACK MARIA could be a gun or a type of exploding shell. Therefore it is not always possible to precisely define some of the terms recorded in this chapter. This vocabulary reflects the ways in which these weapons defined the experiences of trench warfare for soldiers; but it also suggests that soldiers were not always completely familiar with the weapons and shells that they encountered—unsurprising in the environment of the trenches.

A variety of terms about war and warfare came from, and were shared with, the British army. Some, however, seem not to have made their way into the Australian soldier's vocabulary, at least in the printed evidence. Some terms used by the British army do not turn up in the Australian evidence, except in newspaper articles taken from the British press or in British slang dictionaries. These include *creeping Jimmy*, 'a type of high velocity shell which gave no warning of its approach'; *grass-cutter*, 'a type of aerial bomb'; *hairbrush*, 'a grenade with a slab of gun cotton on the handle'; and *policeman's truncheon*, 'a type of grenade'.

W.H. Downing also includes a few terms that don't appear elsewhere in the written evidence. These include: *comforts funds*, 'shells'; *flying incinerator*, 'an incendiary shell'; *mouth-organ*, 'a Stokes shell', which Downing comments as being 'so called from the peculiar note caused by the air passing through the holes around the base of the shell as it rises'; *pea-shooter*, 'a German anti-tank gun'; and *typewriter*, 'a machine-gun'.

coco

Annie from Asia

Annie from Asia, sometimes **Asiatic Annie**, was a name given to
a large gun that fired on Australian troops at Gallipoli. This is one
of several nicknames given to guns at the Dardanelles; the more
frequently mentioned of the guns is BEACHY BILL.

John L. Treloar in his diary kept at Gallipoli noted that 'the gun
which fires the big shells [has been christened] **"Annie from Asia"** '.
(*An Anzac Diary*, p. 141) In a 1918 newspaper article, reference
was made to a speech by an army chaplain wherein he explained
'the various names which were humorously given the guns of the
Turks—"Beachy Bill", **"Asiatic Annie"**, "Tired Tim"—and described
at length the experiences of men in the trenches and behind the
lines'. (Adelaide *Register*, 3 May, p. 25)

Bangalore torpedo

This was a tube-like device, using explosive charges, used to clear
a pathway through a barbed-wire entanglement. It was invented in
1912 by an officer with the British Indian Army, and used during
the Great War.

An account of Australians fighting on the Somme in 1918 noted
some of their exploits, including their use of a **Bangalore torpedo**:
'Three engineers were sent out prior to a raid to clear the way for
their fellow men. They placed a **Bangalore torpedo** under the wire,
but being sighted were bombed by the enemy.' (*Bendigonian*, 4 July
1918, p. 10)

Beachy Bill

Beachy Bill, sometimes abbreviated to **Beachy**, was a name given
to a Turkish gun that fired on Australian soldiers at Gallipoli. The
name probably derives from the fact that many soldiers were fired
on while situated on the beaches. Nicknames for guns and other
weapons are a common feature of soldiers' slang as mentioned in
the introduction to this chapter, but **Beachy Bill** was perhaps the

best known of all the guns to Australian soldiers and most often mentioned in their accounts of the Gallipoli experience.

C.E.W. Bean noted in his diary on 14 December 1915: 'Except for **Beachy** the night is very usual. The ordinary fitful rifle fire—a 30 shot a minute night.' (*Bean's Gallipoli: The Diaries of Australia's Official War Correspondent*, p. 246) *The Anzac Book*, a book put together by Bean, and which included contributions from many of the soldiers who served at Gallipoli, included a poem that mentioned the infamous gun:

> There's a certain darned nuisance called '**Beachy**,'
> Whose shells are exceedingly screechy;
> But we're keeping the score,
> And we're after your gore—
> So look out, '**Beachy Bill**', when we meet ye. (1916, p. 96)

Private Roy Richards writing to his mother back home in Australia told her of the gun: 'The Turks have a ½ in. gun, and we call it "**Beachy Bill**". It has been in action six months, and sweeps our beach day after day, and we cannot locate it. This gun has cost the Allies a couple of million in shells without counting the casualties of our men.' (*Bendigonian*, 16 December 1915, p. 24)

Big Bertha

This was a nickname given to a German long range gun, and was especially used of the German guns that bombarded Paris. It is speculated in the *OED* that the name derived from *Bertha* Krupp von Bohlen und Halbach, one of the German Krupp family who owned the steel works that produced many of the German armaments used in the war; however, *Bertha* was a common German name and many guns were given generic names during the war. Although more commonly used by British soldiers than Australians, the term appears in both the Australian press and in soldiers' accounts.

The Australian press noted in 1919: 'Senator Pearce, Minister of Defence, is sending to Australia seven hundredweight of brass from the "**Big Bertha**" captured at Proyart. It is intended for conversion into commemoration tablets.' (Lismore *Northern Star*, 12 August,

p. 5) The troopship periodical, *The Sardine*, included the following humorous story:

> One of the Yanks who had just arrived in France, and was attached to our unit, had rather a lot to say about the new gas they had brought from America, when one of the Diggers said, 'Well, how good is this gas?' The Yank said it is that good if it gets in your Pay Book it will kill your next of kin or stop your allotment. 'Well,' said the Digger, 'that is nothing. Have you heard of "**Big Bertha**", that fires 75 miles in Paris?' 'Sure!' says the Yank. 'Well, that is nothing,' says the Digger, 'we have a gun that fires 128 miles, and the recoil brings up the ammunition and takes back the wounded.' (No. 6, August 1919, p. 7)

big stuff

Large shells or a heavy artillery shelling was sometimes known to soldiers as **big stuff**.

Private Bert Saxon wrote home to Australia from the Western Front: 'Fritz gave me a scare the other day. I was working away on the road when he started to send some **big stuff** over, and the pieces were flying all around us, one piece lobbing in between three of us. I don't know how it was that one of us did not get it.' (*Euroa Advertiser*, 27 July 1917, p. 4) A 1918 article on 'trench talk' noted that: 'Any misfortunes that the "**big stuff**" may bring are spoken of lightly in the trenches.' (Adelaide *Register*, 12 March 1918, p. 6)

Black Maria

A name given to two types of German armaments on the Western Front: the first was a particular type of heavy German shell that on exploding emitted volumes of dense black smoke (and were similar to JACK JOHNSONS or COAL-BOXES), and the second a large-calibre German howitzer gun. *Black Maria* is a slang term dating to the nineteenth century used to mean both a police van and a type of card game; it is unclear what influences these senses had on the military sense.

An article in the Australian press dating from 1915 explained the exploding shell for their readers:

> TNT, which enters largely into the manufacture of high explosive shells and hand-grenades, is perfectly harmless under ordinary conditions. Only when it is detonated has it the tremendous effect which carries devastation far and wide. When detonated, however, the explosion is of great violence, and gives the characteristic black smoke which is the origin of the endearing titles by which the shells are known in France and Flanders—**Black Marias**, Jack Johnsons, or coal-scuttles. (*Dandenong Advertiser and Cranbourne, Berwick and Oakleigh Advocate*, 18 November 1915, p. 6)

Another article, excerpting from a soldier's letter (the soldier was an Australian serving in a British regiment), mentions the gun: 'The Germans have got a huge gun in position somewhere near here which we call "**Black Maria**", and she leaves her card on us at "frequent and uncertain intervals".' (*Kalgoorlie Miner*, 7 January 1915, p. 2.)

blimp

A slang term for a non-rigid airship. The origin of the word is uncertain. In the Great War, such airships were used primarily for scouting purposes along the British coastline by the British Royal Naval Air Service in order to deal with the German U-boat threat. **Blimp** came into popular usage during the war, and continued to be used after the end of the war.

An account published in the *Geelong Advertiser* described the way **blimps** worked for an Australian audience: 'Day is breaking with a drizzling rain and a sea-mist as I climb into my seat in the "**blimp**". (A "**blimp**" is a streaming silvery-looking cigar-shaped balloon with an aeroplane minus the wings fixed underneath, and our job is scouting over the home seas for submarines.)' (3 August 1918, p. 9)

coal-box

This was a particular type of low-velocity German shell that emitted black smoke. The name derives from the black smoke produced when the shell exploded. Although the *OED* defines the **coal-box** as a type of shell, a 1916 British trench slang glossary defined it differently: 'According to some a big shell, but generally understood to be a sort of high-explosive shrapnel which seems to burst in the air with a cloud of thick black smoke which whirrs around like a catherine wheel.' (*The War Budget*, 23 March 1916, quoted in Doyle and Walker, *Trench Talk*, p. 164) Brophy and Partridge in *Songs and Slang of the British Soldier: 1914–1918* note that it was used for both a kind of shell and the shell-burst itself.

Percy Smythe, an Australian soldier serving on the Western Front, wrote the following in his diary: 'Soon afterwards Fritz began to make things uncomfortable by sending over 9.2 inch high explosives, or "**coal-boxes**", and high explosive shrapnel, which make an effective combination, for if one gets down low in the trench to avoid the shrapnel, he is liable to be buried by the other brutes of things.' (Diary entry, 24 July 1916, *World War I Diary of Percy Smythe* [online]) Private 'Chum' Stott wrote to his father in Tasmania about how he and his fellow soldiers were 'up to our thighs in slush, and were just being relieved when Fritz put a "**Coal Box**" (big shell) right in the middle of seven of us. It blew one poor devil clean up in the air, and out of the trench, killing him outright.' (*North Western Advocate and the Emu Bay Times*, 10 February 1917, p. 8)

crab

This term was used for an artillery shell, and was likely an abbreviation of *crab-shell* referring to an artillery shell (and a punning allusion). However, Fraser and Gibbons in their *Soldier and Sailor Words and Phrases* suggest that **crab** was a shortened form of *crab-grenade*, 'a type of German grenade' that resembled a crab. Brophy and Partridge in *Songs and Slang of the British Soldier: 1914–1918* record the term DRAW CRABS, 'to attract fire from the enemy artillery by exposing oneself on ground under observation'. The phrase draw the crabs, 'to attract enemy fire', was also used during the Great War.

Captain W.A. Thompson wrote that **crabs** was 'the euphonious title given by the "digger" to a shell'. (*Albury Banner and Wodonga Express*, 28 February 1919, p. 28) A letter from gunner 'Sol' Green, reprinted in the *Dubbo Liberal and Macquarie Advocate* in 1918 saw him write: 'They [workers of the Australian Comforts Fund] saw more than their share of shells, on account of so many people visiting the dug-out to get a hot drink, and, as we term it, "**drawing the crabs**" meaning, of course, shells.' (28 May, p. 2)

crump

This was a term used during the war to refer to the sound of a shell or shell-burst. It likely derived from a nineteenth-century sense of *crump* meaning 'a heavy hit or fall', but perhaps also in allusion to the sound they made. **Crump** was also used as a verb meaning a shelling.

In 1916 C.E.W. Bean described a bombardment in France: 'We can hear the **crump**, crump, crump of heavy explosives almost incessantly. I fancy our heavy trench mortars must have joined in.' (Rockhampton *Capricornian*, 26 August, p. 24)

crump-hole

A name given to a shell-hole or crater made by a shell, and deriving from the use of CRUMP to refer to an artillery shell.

A Sydney doctor wrote a powerful description of the aftermath of the Somme printed in the *Sydney Morning Herald*: 'The trenches were only a succession of **crump-holes**. The German dead lay piled up in heaps, two, three and four deep, having met their death from bullet, bomb, bayonet, and shell fire.' (6 September 1916, p. 7)

dud

During the Great War, this term was used of an artillery shell that failed to explode. It might also be applied to a soldier who was sick, unable to fight, or otherwise inefficient in their duties. Of unknown origin, it can be found in slang to refer to 'a counterfeit thing' from the late nineteenth century, as well as used contemptuously of a person (*OED*). After the war, the more general use referring to something or someone inefficient or useless became common.

One soldier wrote the following in his diary while serving on the Western Front: 'Morning Germans putting shells near this place but not near enough to be dangerous. Mostly **duds**.' (*Diary of Henry Scharrer Bloch*, 23 April 1916, p. 38)

egg bomb

This was a term for a particular type of small bomb or grenade, approximately the size of an egg. Brophy and Partridge in *Songs and Slang of the British Soldier: 1914–1918* explain how it worked: 'A smart tap on the boot severed a wire and started the ignition before the bomb was thrown.'

An Australian soldier, Private D. Hellings, writing to a friend in Swan Hill from Belgium in June 1918, described a capture of a German strong point: 'We were dressed in steel armour, which covered the body front and back, and with blackened faces and hands, some armed with rifle and bayonet and others with clubs and revolvers, and all had pockets filled with **egg bombs**, we were ready to serenade Fritz.' (*Swan Hill Guardian*, 24 June, p. 2)

flying pig

This was a nickname given by soldiers on the Western Front for a particular type of shell from a German *Minenwerfer*, a type of trench mortar (see also MINNIE). The name likely derived from the appearance of the large shell. Fraser and Gibbons in *Soldier and Sailor Words and Phrases* provide a description: '[I]ts corpulent elongated form (2 feet long) and tail with steadying vanes ... suggested the appearance of a pig in the air.' A 1917 report on trench warfare in France also added to this description: 'The "**flying pig**" is nothing more nor less than an aerial mine in the literal sense, and the huge hole it makes is actually a mine crater. ... [It] is designed so that the explosion does not occur until the projectile has been allowed to penetrate deeply into the earth, in order that the full force may be concentrated against a subterranean structure such as a German dug-out.' (Perth *Daily News*, 24 December 1917, p. 7)

football

A name for a particular type of trench mortar shell. It derived from their size and shape.

Percy Smythe, an Australian soldier, noted in his diary: '[A] heap of dirt came tumbling down into our position. I thought we had stopped a "75", but it turned out to be a "**football**", an extra large bomb fired from a trench mortar. Nobody was hurt by it.' (Diary entry, 5 September 1915, *World War I Diary of Percy Smythe* [online])

gazump

A large artillery shell. The word possibly derived from the sound of the landing of such a shell. W.H. Downing in *Digger Dialects* records the variant *gezumpher*.

Australian soldier Vere Dubout, writing from a French hospital in October 1917, told his story: 'That night he put over an intense barrage on us, and about 8 o'clock my mate and I were buried by a big **gazump**, which missed our hole by 4 feet, and blew all the side in on us; before we could get clear of the mud and slush another one roared down again almost on top of us, chucking about another ton of mud on us, which was luckily soft.' (*Melton Express*, 12 January 1918, p. 3)

Gentle Annie

A name given to the first armoured motor-car produced in Australia for fighting purposes in 1916. W.H. Downing in *Digger Dialects* suggests that the name was applied to a large Howitzer gun that fired on Bailleul in early 1918, but there is no further evidence for this recorded in Australian sources. 'Gentle Annie' is the title of a popular song of the period, and probably influenced the name.

The Australian armoured car was given some press coverage, as it was a new and unfamiliar type of military technology. It was observed as being:

... of different design from those motors at Cape Helles which were attached to the Royal Naval Air Service, and which were turret shaped armored bodies, mounted on Rolls-Royce chassis; it is different, too, from the French and Belgian of a similar type, which have little or no shield for the rapid firing gun. ... As the work proceeded various difficulties had to be overcome and modifications made on the original plans, but the result was Tuesday the nearly completed armored car, nicknamed by its crew, **Gentle Annie**. She weighs a ton and half. (*Nhill Free Press*, 11 February 1916, p. 3)

granny

This was a nickname given to a large Howitzer gun used at the Western Front, probably one of 12 or 15 inches in size. It was sometimes also referred to as *grandma* or in full as *grandmother*. An alternative name for this gun is LAZY ELIZA.

An Australian soldier from Ballarat wrote home from the front to report: 'I am quite used to guns now and when "**granny**" speaks— that is the big gun down in the gully—well, the earth trembles. I'll bet she makes Fritz hop.' (*Ballarat Courier*, 17 January 1917, p. 4)

hate

This was a term (used as a noun) for a bombardment or artillery shelling. It came from the German 'Hymn of Hate against England' (composed by Ernst Lissauer in 1914), referring to the shelling of British soldiers, which was popular in Germany and received with much righteous outrage in the British and Allied press. The Hymn of Hate was notably satirised in the popular British periodical *Punch* in 1915, which played on the notion that Germans were motivated entirely by a blind hatred of England. **Hate** then came to be used to mean a bombardment, specifically against Allied troops. A.G. Pretty's *Glossary of AIF Slang* also includes *hate stuff*, defined as 'ammunition fired by the enemy'. (See also the similar term HEAVY STUFF.)

Hate was used by Australian soldiers in reference to shelling both in Gallipoli and on the Western Front. One soldier, writing to his sister at home in Australia, said: 'The Light Horse fellows are around on the right, and I don't see them often. Old Johnnie (that is our name for the Turk), puts over the usual "**hate**" (shrapnel) every day but we are all dug in, and soon get out of the way.' (*Gippsland Farmers' Journal*, 14 December 1915, p. 4) Another soldier writing home from a hospital in London after fighting on the Somme commented on it: 'It is a gruesome place, and a mucky one. It is also a very lively place when the daily "**hate**" is on.' (Rockhampton *Capricornian*, 31 March 1917, p. 16)

heavies

This was a term for heavy artillery, or shells from heavy artillery. It was in use in the British Army from the late nineteenth century. It was widely used during the Great War, including by Australian soldiers. During the war, especially on the Western Front, heavy artillery was extensively used by each side to attack each other's positions. See also HEAVY STUFF below.

Australian soldier Bert Smythe, serving in France in 1917, wrote in his diary the following observation of the shelling: 'Fritz threw a lot of whizz-bangs at us just sweeping the surface also a few **heavies**. His balloons up all day. Several in front quite close & two on our right fairly close. This position must be a big salient for he seems to be in front & on both sides of us.' (Diary entry, 13 April, *Letters from Bert Smythe* [online]) William Campbell Young in 1918 in his diary noted: 'Fritz concentrated two of his "**Heavies**" on to the next farm to ours and got eight direct hits, making life not worth living in it.' (*World War I Diary of William Campbell Young*, p. 25)

heavy stuff

A variant of HEAVIES, **heavy stuff** referred to large shells, or a heavy shelling.

In 1917, Private James Sheldrick wrote home from France to his sister in Australia to say: 'There is some strain on the nerves during a heavy bombardment, when hundreds of shells are being thrown about. Our artillery is very searching and effective, and the

Hun is not entirely impotent. He uses some **heavy stuff**.' (*Burrowa
News*, 7 September, p. 3) A brief anecdote in *Aussie: The Australian
Soldiers' Magazine* noted: 'Fritz had been sending **heavy stuff** over
into an area that he had previously left alone, so Mulga Bill decided
to dig in and live in a dugout instead of a tent.' (4 April 1918, p. 3)

iron foundry

A term for a heavy artillery shell used on the Western Front.
W.H. Downing in *Digger Dialects* defines it as 'a very heavy shell';
Brophy and Partridge in *Songs and Slang of the British Soldier:
1914–1918* included the term *iron foundries* in their collection,
which they define as 'heavy shelling'.

One soldier wrote home to his brother about his own experience
with an **iron foundry**:'On one particular occasion, while six men, Including himself, were going to the front trenches, an "**iron foundry**" burst
alongside them.' (*Townsville Daily Bulletin*, 26 January 1917, p. 5)

iron rations

A term for artillery shells. During the war, IRON RATIONS was also a
name for a type of emergency rations given to soldiers. (See entry in
Chapter Two).

Percy Smythe, an Australian officer, wrote home to his family
from the Western Front:

> There was a number of big 9.2 inch howitzers just in rear of where we
> were working, and each time they flung their massive '**iron rations**'
> over to the German lines we could see the projectile whirling away
> and growing smaller and smaller till it passed the culminating
> point and vanished from sight. These shells are so heavy that two
> men are required to lift one of them, so what enormous power
> must be concentrated in that small charge—power sufficient to
> throw one of those heavy missiles a distance of half a dozen miles
> and more. (Diary entry, 9 November 1916, *World War I Diary of
> Percy Smythe* [online])

Arthur G. Howell wrote in his diary in 1916: 'The enemy artillery woke up a bit last night and later on our guns sent them some "**iron rations**".' (*Signaller at the Front*, 6 October 1916, p. 26)

Jack Johnson

This nickname for a particular type of heavy German artillery shell was commonly used, especially on the Western Front. It derives from the famous African-American heavyweight boxer, *Jack Johnson* (1878–1946), who had the nickname 'the Big Smoke'; the shells named for him emitted heavy black smoke when they exploded. Johnson became heavyweight boxing world champion after beating Canadian boxer Tommy Burns in Sydney, Australia, in 1908 to win the title. Australian soldiers first used the term at Gallipoli.

Jack Johnsons were just one of many different types of shells experienced by soldiers during the war, but was one of the terms most commonly known and used. They were a key feature of life under fire as evidenced in this quotation from Sergeant Cyril Lawrence as he describes the fighting at the time of Ypres-Passchaendale: 'The crashing and jolting is indescribable—in two minutes it has become impossible to see more than 15 yards in any direction—flying clods and dust mixed with the enormous black soot clouds from Fritz's "**Jack Johnsons**" and the white suffocating fumes from our own shells.' (Letter, September 1917, *Sergeant Lawrence Goes to France*, p. 134)

jam-tin artillery

A term used at Gallipoli for some of the soldiers in the trenches who made use of JAM-TIN BOMBS against the enemy.

Private B.A. Clarke who served at Gallipoli wrote: 'The trenches here are only six or eight yards distant, and sometimes a pair of beady eyes was visible for a moment as they peered at the top mirror of my periscope. They don't stop long, because our **jam tin artillery** is pretty effective.' (Adelaide *Chronicle*, 23 October 1915, p. 45)

A variant term in the British press, and reported in the Australian press, is *Ticklers' artillery*. An Australian newspaper column explained:

> We had not heard of such a unit among the armies that are called Kitchener's, nor of any noted commander who rejoiced in the name of Tickler. And when we read that 'Tickler's artillery' are not artillery at all the mystification was the greater. The title, it seems, is another example of the wit of Tommy Atkins. Tickler is the name of a well-known line of jam makers. A good deal of jam made by this firm was served out in tins, and when the tins were emptied of their sweetness they were filled with explosives and converted into hand grenades. 'Tickler's artillery' is the name which a wag in the trenches has conferred upon the men who throw the hand grenades. (*Stawell News and Pleasant Creek Chronicle*, 6 November 1915, p. 3)

jam-tin bomb

A type of grenade made using a jam tin. They were generally crude bombs, used early in the war before sophisticated grenades were available, and often manufactured in the field. They could be quite dangerous to the person who made them, due to their makeshift nature.

In August 1915, writing in his diary at Gallipoli, Archie Barwick commented: 'At this time we were using nearly all **jam-tin bombs** made by ourselves; they are very effective if they lob in among men, but are dangerous to handle for sometimes they don't look to be alight, & all the time are burning.' (*In Great Spirits: The WWI Diary of Archie Barwick*, p. 54) A newspaper piece from 1916 noted: 'The **jam-tin bomb** is no longer the summum bonum of the bomb world—the one one makes oneself and fills with bits of scrap-iron and old nails; but numerous cylindrical fellows, and round ones, and egg-shaped ones have taken their place. And each of these has to have a detonator put in before it can be used.' (*Urana Independent and Clear Hills Standard*, 14 April, p. 4)

Jericho Jane

A name given to a Turkish gun that operated in 1918 in the Jordan Valley. It is a name similar to BEACHY BILL and BIG BERTHA.

In November 1918, the *Kia Ora Coo-ee*, reporting on the achievements of the Anzacs in Palestine, noted that in their operations 'they discovered a long range navy gun lying on its side, a piece known to us as "Nimrin Nellie" and "**Jericho Jane**", with which the Turk had made our camps near Jericho dusty and unpleasant'. (15 November, p. 7) Sapper C.F. Fitzpatrick from Windsor, NSW, wrote home from Palestine to say: 'Just as "Beachy Bill" became so well-known on Gallipoli, so will "**Jericho Jane**" be remembered by those of our troops who were concentrated in the Jordan Valley. ... The damage done by this weapon was infinitesimal, and it was so much ammunition wasted by the enemy.' (*Windsor and Richmond Gazette*, 25 April 1919, p. 8)

Jewel of Asia

A name given to a big gun that fired on soldiers at Gallipoli. There is a popular song of this title, composed in 1896 by Harry Greenbank and which featured in the Edwardian musical play *The Geisha*. The play was performed in Australia in 1915, suggesting its ongoing popularity and familiarity to Australian audiences. There was perhaps also a touch of irony in the use of the name, given the deadly nature of the weapon.

In a despatch from Gallipoli, war correspondent Ashmead Bartlett wrote: 'There is one gun known as the "**Jewel of Asia**", which continually drops shells but with a minimum of result. You hear the shriek of its arrival, and the explosion, followed by a cloud of sand, out of which emerge figures of men and animals who should have been killed or injured, but who very seldom are.' (*Western Star and Roma Advertiser*, 10 July 1915, p. 6)

Lazy Eliza

A name for a gun used on the Western Front. As suggested in the quotation below, it usually referred to a 15 inch gun, also called GRANNY. **Lazy Eliza** appears to be a term primarily used by British soldiers, but W.H. Downing in *Digger Dialects* includes *Lazy Lizz* as a name for a type of heavy long distance shell.

A London newspaper report in the *Maitland Weekly Mercury* noted: 'Beaumont-Hamel was built of its own stone taken from quarries which comprised a semi-circle of enormous caverns. The caverns are covered with stone, so effectively that they were proof against damage, even by "grandmother" or "**Lazy Eliza**", as the Tommies have named the bombarding 15-inch guns.' (25 November 1916, p. 12)

minnie

This was the name given to the German trench mortars known as *Minenwerfer*, and is an abbreviation. It is another example of the variety of terms given to shells and artillery during the Great War. The **minnie** was one of the most destructive and most feared weapons of the war.

Sapper R.W.P. Fairlam wrote home in 1917 describing the **minnie** to those back in Australia:

> It is rather a queer sensation in the trenches when Fritz sends over some of his shells. He has some they call '**minnies**' they are terrors. They do not travel very fast but they make a hissing noise and come along in a wobbly course generally three or four all sent one after the other. You can see them coming if you are quick, but it is hard to tell where they will land, the only thing to do is to wait, then flop down flat and chance to luck. (*Moorabbin News*, 31 March 1917, p. 2)

A poem by a soldier named Bill, printed in the troopship journal, *Homeward Bound* in 1918, included the lines: 'Our flight in the darkness when **Minnies** come nigh, / Is made bright by the light of the Very's on high.' (p. 36)

mother

A name for a large howitzer gun at the Western Front. This was a smaller gun than that dubbed the GRANNY (or *Grandmother*).

A newspaper article published in Australia in 1915 noted some of the names of guns used at the Western Front: 'A certain heavy howitzer, whose dull boom is easily extinguishable [sic] above the reports of any other piece, is affectionately termed "**Mother**".' (*North Western Advocate and the Emu Bay Times*, 12 March, p. 3) In 1917, a reviewer of a book about the war wrote: 'Out in France our boys know all about the "**Mother**" guns—the giant 9.1 howitzers which every day send over ton upon ton of high-explosive shells to carry death and devastation among the German trenches.' (*Colac Herald*, 3 September, p. 4)

oil can

A particular type of German trench-mortar shell. The name derived from its shape, which resembled an oil can. They were fired from German *Minenwerfer*, known to the Anglophone troops as MINNIES.

An article highlighting slang from the trenches in Australian newspapers in 1918 recorded: '**Oil Cans**.—The projectile favoured by "Minnie," shaped like an oil-can, about 2ft. by 1ft., and exceedingly full of "bust".' (*Malvern Standard*, 24 August 1918, p. 6)

pig-stabber

A term for a bayonet. Recorded in W.H. Downing's *Digger Dialects*, this was a variation of *pig sticker*, recorded in the *OED* as dating to the nineteenth century.

An Australian signaller wrote of his experiences at Gallipoli: 'I set out with my **pig-stabber** ready and the magazine full of "Turkish delight", and reached a communication trench going off from the main trench. There I found a Turk in a good hole throwing bombs.' (Adelaide *Daily Herald*, 6 January 1916, p. 2)

pineapple

This was a name used during the war for a variety of grenades and trench-mortars, including the British Mills bomb and the German *Granatenwerfer* (trench mortar), used during the war. The term derived from their appearance. Brophy and Partridge in *Songs and Slang of the British Soldier: 1914–1918* describe the **pineapple** as 'a German mortar bomb with a wind vane', hence suggesting that its appearance resembled a pineapple. A.G. Pretty's *Glossary of AIF Slang* defines it as a 'light German trench mortar shell, grooved into sections to ensure a fragmental burst'.

Lieutenant J.R. Charlton, an Australian officer, wrote home about his experiences on the Western Front:

> 'Fritz' sends over a trench mortar bomb, which we call 'the **pineapple'**, because it resembles a pineapple in shape. Some of our lads were worrying 'Fritz' with rifle grenades, when he sent us back a few '**pineapples'**. His ranging is bad, and one 'dud' landed in 'No Man's Land.' When it was getting dark I went out and got it. I took the detonator out, and now have the bomb as a souvenir. (Broken Hill *Barrier Miner*, 29 July 1917, p. 2)

pip-squeak

This was a name given to a particular type of high-explosive, high-velocity shell used at the front. The term probably derived from the high-pitched noise the shell produced.

An Australian soldier who enlisted in England wrote home to Australia describing some of the shells encountered on the Western Front: 'To begin with, there is our ubiquitous friend the "**Pip- squeak"**, so called because he is so small. He is about nine inches long and three inches in diameter, and is fired from the 77 mm gun. He is used on those frequent occasions when the Hun cannot see what he is firing at, but feels it incumbent upon him to shoot merely to annoy the British.' (*Gippsland Times*, 11 October 1917, p. 3)

plonker

This was a term for an artillery shell. It is an Australian English word, first recorded during the war. It comes from *plonk*, 'to hit or strike', a British dialect word. Brophy and Partridge in *Songs and Slang of the British Soldier: 1914–1918* record *to plonk*, 'to shell'. *Aussie: The Australian Soldiers' Magazine* included the following story in a 1918 edition:

> Two officers were occupying a shell-hole. Fritz was putting over some big stuff. Every time a **plonker** landed near them, one of the officers energetically fired his revolver into the air. 'What the blank are you doing that for?' asked the other. 'Retaliation, my boy, retaliation! We must retaliate at all costs!' And he vigorously fired two more shots into the air, as the dirt from a 5.9 showered over them. (18 January, p. 3)

plum pudding

A name given to a particular type of trench mortar bomb. W.H. Downing in *Digger Dialects* describes the **plum pudding** as 'a spherical iron shell filled with explosive and projected by means of a trench mortar towards the enemy trench'.

Private Hughie Turner wrote home: 'After throwing shells over all day, he managed to find a "**plum-pudding**" dump which was near our dugout, and caused a terrible explosion.' (*Cairns Post*, 3 October 1917, p. 4)

potato masher

A name given to a particular type of hand or stick grenade, so called because of its physical appearance. It was a device used during the war by the German army and was familiar to Australian soldiers.

Percy Smythe recorded in his diary: 'Saw something rolling towards me along the top of the bank on the right of the road, a few yards away, and suddenly realized that it was a German "**potato-masher**" bomb. I sprang back and turned to shout a warning to the men coming behind. The grenade exploded, and a small piece of the casing buried itself in my cheek. Took a Mills bomb from my pocket to send after the Huns, but could not get the confounded pin out.' (Diary entry, 1 September 1918, *World War I Diary of Percy Smythe* [online])

Quick Dick

A name given to a gun used at Gallipoli. See also BEACHY BILL and ANNIE FROM ASIA.

An Australian soldier writing from Gallipoli talked about various names for the guns used by the Turkish forces at the Dardanelles: 'All the Turkish guns have their pet names, such as Asiatic Annie, **Quick Dick** (who is a particularly nasty ... you sort of don't know he's here until he has gone past); then there is Aerial Archibald, the anti-aircraft gun, and Gentle Annie whom one can hear coming for a long time.' (*Coleraine Albion and Western Advertiser*, 15 November 1915, p. 3)

quickfirer

A term for a rapid-firing gun, especially a machine gun. It was in use from the late nineteenth century, but was still popular during the Great War.

In 1914, not long after the war began, an Australian newspaper noted the invention of the Caldwell Quickfirer Field Gun. A newspaper article commented that: 'This marvelous production of an Australian brain, the inventor being an Australian (Mr. T.F. Caldwell), excels anything of the kind in **quickfirers** ever produced.' (*The Newsletter: An Australian Paper for Australian People*, 3 October, p. 4)

rum jar

This was a name given to a particular type of German artillery shell, so-called because of its shape. Rum jars (jars for holding rum) were a common sight in the trenches, as a small rum ration was often dispensed.

Corporal Jack Turner, an Australian soldier, wrote the following poem, published in an Australian newspaper in 1918:

When Fritz is starting something
and his guns are on the bust
When the parapet goes up in chunks,
and settles down in dust,
When the roly-poly '**rum-jar**' comes
a-wobbling thro' the air,
'Til it lands upon a dugout—and the
dugout isn't there;
When the air is full of dust, and
smoke, and scraps of steel and noise
And you think you're booked for
golden crowns and other Heavenly joys,
When your nerves are all a-tremble
and your brain is all a-fret—
It isn't half so hopeless if you've
got a cigarette. (Carnarvon *Northern Times*, 22 June, p. 6.)

sausage

This was a term for an observation balloon, usually referring to a
German observation balloon rather than a British one, although both
had a similar shape. It is possible that the use was reinforced by a
stereotypical and derogatory reference to Germans as SAUSAGE-EATERS
used during the Great War. Both sides put up observation balloons as
a means of gathering information about enemy forces and positions,
and this information was particularly useful for ensuring effective
deployment of artillery.

A newspaper article from 1916 reported: 'But when you look
up at the "**sausage**" shining in the sunshine three or four miles away,
and know that there are eyes in it which can see you and report your
movements to the nearest battery, you begin to be uncomfortable.
They have so much advantage of you, those eyes in the sky.'
(Adelaide *Register*, 16 October, p. 6) Sergeant Cyril Lawrence, an
engineer with the AIF, wrote in his diary on 3 July 1916: '[Attacks
by British planes] will cause Fritz to scratch his head and think
and he will certainly not be so keen on putting his "**sausages**" up.'
(*Sergeant Lawrence goes to France*, p. 40)

strafe

Originally a slang term for 'a fierce assault' or the action of 'attacking
fiercely', **strafe** became Standard English in the twentieth century,
particularly in reference to an attack from a low-flying aircraft. Its
origin is in the popular German phrase *Gott strafe England* ('may
God punish England') used by the Germans in 1914, and made
use of in the British press, often for propaganda purposes. It rapidly
spread into common soldiers' usage in the trenches, as well as being
used in newspaper reports on the war.

In 1916, Sergeant Cyril Lawrence noted in his diary: 'Nothing
has happened since I went away except that one night, the night
I left in fact, they dropped the usual **straffe** round the billet and
succeeded in wounding one horse and one man in the behind.'
(Diary entry, 15 June, *Sergeant Lawrence goes to France*, p. 38)
A 1918 newspaper report noted: 'A Sydney captain said the
Bosche hereabouts [Morlancourt sector] got their wind up when
we advanced our line 700 yards, preceded by a barrage not heavier
than the usual nightly **strafe**. Pandemonium reigned in the Bosche
trenches.' (*Geelong Advertiser*, 17 May, p. 3)

tank

An armoured motor vehicle that moves on a tracked carriage and
is mounted with a gun. The British Army introduced the **tank** in
September 1916. They conjured up for many the *land ironclads*
imagined by H.G. Wells before the Great War, and a variety of
names were given to them, including *landships*, *motor monsters*, and
land dreadnoughts—all of which are names that can be found in
the Australian press through the war years. As the development and
manufacture of the vehicles was kept secret, the name **tank**—which
commonly means an artificial reservoir or cistern—was used. The
name stuck.

A 1916 article on the **tank** described the new invention to an
Australian readership:

'Tanks' is the slang word that the army staff has applied to these strange creations of machinery, but they look less like tanks than anything else in the world. It is hard to say what they look like. They have been compared both to armadillos and measuring worms, and to many other weird creeping or crawling objects of natural history. (*Yea Chronicle*, 14 December 1916, p. 6)

An Australian soldier's diary of serving in a **tank** was published in Australian newspapers in 1917. He wrote: 'The blessed old tub gave a sudden jerk. God in Heaven, thought I, it's good-bye to earth; but it wasn't. Only some Hun dead and wounded we skidded into. The rain of bullets resumed. It was like as if hundreds of rivets were being hammered into the hide of the **tank**. We rushed through.' (*Tungamah and Lake Rowan Express and St. James Gazette*, 4 January, p. 6) Archie Barwick, writing in his diary in October 1916, on first seeing a **tank**, noted: 'They are ponderous affairs & nothing but a direct hit from a shell would stop them for they are all steel, a proper land dreadnought.' (*In Great Spirits: The WWI Diary of Archie Barwick*, p. 196)

taube

This term was used by soldiers for a German plane. *Taube*, meaning 'dove' in German, was the design of an early monoplane. The name came to be applied to any German plane used by the Imperial German military forces for a variety of purposes including reconnaissance, bombing, and fighting.

Many Australian soldiers' letters and diaries make reference to **taubes**. Percy Smythe recorded the following observation in his diary in 1916:

By the time we got to our camping grounds the rain had gone and the sun shone intermittently through the clouds. One after another our balloons went up, until the sky was dotted with them. The aeroplanes also got busy, and soon a **Taube** came over, but two of ours took after him, and he had to get lively. There was an interesting chase for a while, but the **Taube** flew into a cloud and dodged our machines. (Diary entry, 2 November, *World War I Diary of Percy Smythe* [online])

toothpick

A term for a bayonet. A number of such names were given to bayonets, including PIG-STABBER. Other terms recorded in British evidence include *meat-skewer*, *cat-stabber*, and *tin-opener*. **Toothpick** is attested in the Australian evidence during the war.

Private Arthur Bishop from Fremantle, W.A., wrote home to his mother about his perception of alleged German atrocities: 'Fritz forced the civilians into a barrage and bayoneted a lot. ... Yes, I would give it to them on the point of a **toothpick** (bayonet).' (Perth *Daily News*, 11 January 1919)

whizz-bang

This name given to a particular type of small-calibre shell fired from a light field gun (nearly always applied to the German 77mm field artillery gun) was a popular one during the war. It was used by British soldiers on the Western Front, and was taken up and used by Australian soldiers. The name derives from the sound that was made by the shell: it *whizzes* through the air and is followed by the *bang* of the explosion. The term is also found in American English from around the time of the war, referring to a person or thing that is impressive or successful. During the war, the variant spelling **whiz-bang** was also used.

Captain Hugh Knyvett described the experience of being shelled by **whizz-bangs**: 'I sat with my "dixie" of stew and lid of tea in the open doorway of a dug-out, and the **whiz-bangs** passed within twenty yards of me and pelted me with pieces of dirt, but nothing hard enough to break the skin struck me.' (*'Over There' with the Australians*, p. 145) Private Harry Cadwallader commented on the sounds of the artillery and other weapons in a letter home in 1916: '[T]he minute you turn in of a night, no matter how the artillery is bombarding or how near the **Whiz Bangs** are coming and the continual rattle of musketry and machine guns, they sound like the crack of a heavy stock whip as they cut through the air.' (Letter, 3 May 1916, AWM PR01199)

The term **whizz-bang** lent itself to a range of things at the front: images exist of a place in France renamed '**Whizz-bang** corner' by the soldiers, and there was an Australian concert party 'The **Whiz Bangs**' that entertained soldiers during the war.

woolly bear

A name given to a particular type of German artillery shell that gave off thick white smoke when bursting. The term sometimes was used in reference to the smoke or shell-burst itself. Its origin is uncertain.

A newspaper report noted: 'The "**woolly bear**" is so named because of the pretty effect it makes when bursting in the air.' (Perth *Daily News*, 14 March 1917, p. 3) An Australian officer, Lieutenant H.H.P. Hamilton, in an account of his experiences of battle published in the *Brisbane Courier*, quoted a young soldier as saying: 'I must get back before they send those **woolly bears** (big shrapnel) over.' (24 October 1918, p. 7)

Zepp

An abbreviation of *Zeppelin*, a type of dirigible airship produced in Germany. Zeppelins were used by the Germans during the Great War as a means of dropping bombs on the enemy; this included using them in air raids over England which caused much destruction and led to some civilian casualties.

Arthur G. Howell wrote in his diary in 1916: 'More good news from other parts of the line and also news of the destruction of two **Zepps** in England.' (Diary entry, 7 September 1916, *Signaller at the Front*, p. 23) Private M. Ferguson wrote home to Australia in the same year to say that he was in England and that 'I would very much like to see these places in peace sometimes, as now the lights are all dulled at night on account of the **Zepps**. I have not seen a **Zepp** yet, but have seen the results of their bombs in places around Woolwich Arsenal.' (*Riverina Herald*, 27 December 1916, p. 2)

CHAPTER

9

*Language of the air
and sea:* Words of the
Australian Flying Corps
and Royal Australian
Navy

Flying Corps slang

The Australian Flying Corps (AFC) was formed in 1912. During the Great War, it played a valuable role in the war effort. Some 3720 men served in the AFC, both in the Middle East and, from 1917, on the Western Front. About 500 of these were fliers, the rest served with the ground crew. The AFC made important contributions to victories in both these theatres of war through 1917 and 1918.

Casualties were particularly high as a percentage of the men who flew. One hundred and seventy-nine Australian airmen were killed, wounded, or taken prisoner. Aircraft could not only be shot down by the enemy, but planes could easily suffer mechanical problems and crash. Accidents often took as many lives as combat. Flying during the war was thus a particularly risky endeavour, although the war in the air attracted a certain glamour. Flying as a new technology captured the public imagination, and generated a new language of its own.

During the war, air power became increasingly valuable to modern warfare. At first, planes were primarily used for the purpose of reconnaissance; later in the war, they were also used for bombing. The Royal Flying Corps and the Australian Flying Corps engaged in a variety of activities including intelligence gathering, which was especially important for directing artillery fire, ground attack, and aerial bombing.

Flying, and especially flying within a military context, developed a jargon all of its own. Many of these jargon terms related to the mechanics of planes, and are therefore best considered as technical terms. But there was also a set of slang terms that quickly evolved to deal with various aspects of flying and the war in the air. Some of the popular flying terms pre-dated the war, but many were unique to the context of a war in the air.

A 1917 article on the 'new vocabulary' of the airmen noted that 'no one can claim the invention of so many strikingly original terms as the air services. This language was, the article declared, 'entirely meaningless', but to the initiated, 'it is full of expressiveness and beauty'. (*Western Argus*, 11 December 1917, p. 36) Another article dubbed this vocabulary 'Airmanese', and described it as 'the newest, most expressive, and most comprehensive slang of the war'. (*Manaro Mercury, and Cooma and Bombala Advertiser*, 17 June 1918, p. 2)

A number of flying terms used in the war became popular, some forever associated in the popular imagination with the war, such as DOGFIGHT and ACE. There were also a number of words to describe the manoeuvres of flying, which we would today find common and still use, such as to BANK or to NOSE DIVE.

The language of flying was of interest to the general public through the war years, as evidenced by a number of articles on the topic, many of them of British origin, published in Australian newspapers. These articles sometimes provide the best evidence that certain terms were in circulation during the war; however, some of them are not attested in Australian evidence otherwise. They were known to an Australian audience, thanks to these articles, and were probably familiar to, and used by, men of the Australian Flying Corps. They include:

> *chukka*—'a patrol over enemy lines'.
>
> *crash merchant*—'a pilot who often crashes his aeroplane'.
>
> *hickboo*—'a battle; a term used when enemy aircraft are about'. One contemporary article noted: 'If Zeppelins or Taubes are on their way, a "hickboo" is on.' (*Farmer and Settler*, 21 March 1919, p. 8) Another article on 'sky slang' argued that the word was 'a distortion of an Indian word, meaning an eagle'. (*Kalgoorlie Miner*, 10 July 1917, p. 3) Brophy and Partridge in *Songs and Slang of the British Soldier: 1914–18* record the term as *hickaboo*.
>
> *humming bird*—'an enemy aeroplane'.
>
> *Hun*—'a pilot in training'. The author of a 1919 article on 'service slang' noted: ' "The nickname," a full-fledged flying man told me, "probably has its source in the Hunnish tricks which these fledglings exercise upon His Majesty's valuable aircraft, since at the opening stages of their career most of them crash fairly frequently." ' (Perth *Daily News*, 23 January 1919, p. 4)
>
> *jink*—'to suddenly turn and dive'. An Australian newspaper reported on British pilots in Italy: 'There was one British machine that was the marvel of all beholders, jinking about just over our heads, rolling over and over and gambolling in the air like a kitten on a rung.' (*Bendigonian*, 12 December 1918, p. 23)
>
> *penguin*—'a former pilot with a job on the ground that doesn't involve flying'.
>
> *pylon pilot*—defined in the contemporary evidence as 'a gentleman who prefers flying before a large and admiring crowd'. (*Globe and Sunday Times War Pictorial*, 17 June 1916, p. 1)
>
> *quirk*—'a novice flyer'. Also used for a certain type of aeroplane.
>
> *rumpty*—defined in one contemporary article as 'a particular machine in which most novices make their earliest venture in the air'. (*Western Argus*, 11 December 1917, p. 36)
>
> *spikebozzle*—'to bring down an enemy aircraft, especially a Zeppelin'. Wilfred Granville records this in his *A Dictionary of Sailor's Slang* (1962) with the definition 'render ineffective; sabotage'. He suggests that it derives from the combining of *spike*, 'a gun', and bam*boozle*, 'to cheat'.
>
> *tripe hound*—'a name given to the Sopwith tri-plane'.

As part of a collection of 'slang and peculiar words' gathered by the Australian War Museum (the compilation of which is discussed in more depth in the concluding chapter), a *Glossary of Terms used in Australian Flying Corps* was put together to accompany A.G. Pretty's *Glossary of AIF Slang*, the only such collection of Australian flying terms. This collection includes a range of technical terms, for example, *map squares*, defined as 'the squares of the map conforming to the grid lines of division of the map of France', and *Scarfe mounting*, defined as 'a patent moveable gun mounting for Lewis gun used by Observer capable of adjusting to allow [the] gun to be fired from any position except underneath the plane'. However, it also includes a good number of more interesting terms. This glossary is one of the most useful compilations of flying corps slang for the period, and certainly the most valuable collection we have of Australian material.

The *Glossary of Terms used in Australian Flying Corps* includes a number of terms that have not been located in other printed evidence; some of these are worth mentioning here, because of the way they provide insight into the experience of aerial warfare and being a pilot during the war. The original definitions from the glossary are provided:

arsy tarsy—'upset, unsettled, different to ordinary conditions, to fall "arsy tarsy", to tumble down'.

got him cold—'To be in such a position in aerial combat that the attacker cannot fail to bring down his adversary. The reverse of had me cold where a lucky escape is described by one who has escaped.'

Mr. Sandbags—'On arrival of new pilot at a Squadron flying two seater machine the Squadron C.O. usually insists that before taking an Observer with him, the Pilot shall show his ability to fly and land first and the sandbags are placed in Observers seat to substitute the Observers weight.'

P.B.O.—'Usually refers to Poor B— Observer, used in banter with pilots or others.' [This referred to the Observers who went up in planes with the pilots. It is a variant of P.B.I. (See entry in Chapter One.)]

split arse—'Describing some sudden quick movement in flying either in combat, practising or amusement.' [Partridge in his *A Dictionary of RAF Slang* defines it as an adjective denoting 'daring', 'addicted to stunting', and hence 'reckless'. It is also recorded in W.H. Downing's *Digger Dialects* as *split-ass*.]

ace

A term for a particularly talented and successful pilot who shot down a large number of enemy planes (five or more). Its origin is uncertain. *Ace* meaning 'an expert' was American slang dating to the nineteenth century, but Brophy and Partridge in *Songs and Slang of the British Soldier: 1914–1918*, and Fraser and Gibbons in *Soldier and Sailor Words and Phrases*, speculate that the war-time use of **ace** came from the *ace* in a deck of playing cards (which may be the ultimate origin of the American term anyway).

In 1919, the *Wyalong Advocate* noted the arrival in Melbourne of Captain A.H. Corby D.S.O., D.F.C, who was described as 'the Australian flying "**ace**", who has downed more enemy aeroplanes than any other officer in the Australian Flying Corps'. (24 June, p. 1)

archie

The term **archie** was used during the Great War as both a noun and verb in reference to anti-aircraft fire, and was used both by fliers and by soldiers. Its origin is uncertain; however, the most common story is that it derived from a popular British music-hall song, 'Archibald, certainly not', written by George Robey in 1911. The song told the story of a hen-pecked husband whose wife thwarted his plans for their honeymoon and declared 'Archibald, Certainly Not'. British aviators responded to the supposedly ineffective German anti-aircraft fire with the same declaration. A famous pilot of the war, Amyas E. Borton, who was later made Air Vice-Marshal, supposedly shouted out the song while dodging enemy fire, thus beginning the use of **archie** for enemy anti-aircraft fire. In the Second World War, **archie** was largely replaced by the American term *flak*.

The term reflects the changing technology of warfare that marked the Great War experience. It was the first war to make significant use of the aeroplane as a tool of war: firstly for reconnaissance purposes, and then for attacking other planes and dropping bombs. Anti-aircraft guns developed in response to this and thus became a feature of modern warfare.

Viv Smythe, an Australian soldier who served on the Western Front made this observation of the **archies**:

> The weather has been very cold and wet, but today is gloriously fine and so comes out our friend the Taube [German plane]. We know he is about because we hear the anti-aircraft guns ('**Archies**') and see the white puffs of their shells mottling the sky. Those who have strong sight can pick out the tiny speck that all the commotion is about, flying so high that, with the slight haze the heat has brought forth, any but large objects below must be indistinguishable. Perhaps they are merely out for 'moral effect' to hearten their troops who must be sorely disappointed to see so many of our machines flying so low while theirs hardly ever venture out. If so, the height they keep at is explicable, and is regulated by the range of our '**Archies**'. (Letter, 23 September 1916, *Letters from Viv Smythe* [online])

An account of aircraft trying to dodge **archie** was published in the *Cairns Post* in 1918: 'Pilot banked and ruddered, changing direction, still losing height. With eyes only for their villages, they kept on, "**Archie**" catching up to them again, passing ahead of them, bursting all around them.' (9 May, p. 2) It was also used as a verb to refer to the act of firing anti-aircraft guns: 'A German 'plane is being "**archied**" to the north, and there is a barrage of "**archies**" being put up behind it.' (H. Dinning, *By-ways on Service: Notes from an Australian Journal*, p. 240)

The *Glossary of Terms used in Australian Flying Corps* includes *black archie* and *white archie*, the colours in reference to different exploding shells of the anti-aircraft guns.

bank

To **bank** is to incline an aeroplane at an angle to the horizon, usually in order to turn. This is a standard flying term dating to before the war. According to the *OED*, it is first recorded in 1911.

'Trooper Bluegum' (Oliver Hogue) described his experiences going up with the Australian Flying Corps in Palestine: 'How the airmen must look down on the poor cameliers. We circled and

banked; flew before the breeze at anything over a hundred miles an hour.' (*Sydney Morning Herald*, 15 February 1918, p. 6)

bus

A term for an aeroplane. Dating back to 1910 (*OED*), it became common during the war, although it didn't remain so, being superseded by *kite* in the Second World War. The *Glossary of Terms used in Australian Flying Corps* also records '*the old bus*', defining it as: 'A term used by a pilot to affectionately describe his machine which may have gone through many combats with him and he becomes attached to his own particular old bus.' Another word for an aeroplane mentioned in glossaries of flying slang from the war is *crate*.

Air Mechanic Bruce Beard, serving with the Flying Corps in the Middle East, wrote in a letter home to his brother: 'He [a German pilot] tried too hard to get away after he was well beaten in the scrap, and instead of landing quietly when he had the chance and becoming a prisoner, he kept trying to get out of range of our **bus**, so our pilot got busy again with the gun and no doubt the Hun got shot as his machine suddenly dived to earth from about 5000 feet'. (*Shepparton Advertiser*, 25 February 1918, p. 3)

circus

During the Great War, this was a name given to an aerial squadron. The quotation below from F.M. Cutlack provides a full description of a Great War flying **circus**. One of the most famous of the war was Baron von Richthofen's group of flying aces. Brophy and Partridge in *Songs and Slang of the British Soldier: 1914–1918* speculate that the name derived either from the circling around of the aeroplanes, or from the bright colours in which aeroplanes were painted.

F.M. Cutlack reported from France on the activities of the Australian Flying Corps and provided a definition of a **circus** for his readers:

The Australian Flying Corps is well represented in a certain wing of the Royal Air Service, which has been doing heavy execution among the Germans in the past fortnight. In six days this wing shot down 61 enemy machines, which either crashed down or were put out of control, and probably destroyed. As is usual when our men have a specially successful period, an avenging '**circus**' arrived a few days ago. A **circus** is a selected number of crack airmen, flying the type of machine which each man prefers individually, and acts as a combination under a famous leader. (Adelaide *Daily Herald*, 25 March 1918, p. 5)

cream puff

A term for a shell burst produced by anti-aircraft fire.

E.C. Newell, from Melbourne, wrote home to his parents: 'If a lot of our friends who are staying at home knew what a great time we are having they would hurry up and enlist. I have been interrupted with my letter, having to fire a few "**cream puffs**" at Fritz to try and keep him quiet.' (*Preston Leader*, 3 February 1917, p. 2)

dogfight

A term for an aerial battle conducted at close quarters, and first used during the Great War. It continued to be popular and was used again in the Second World War.

A report on Australian activity in Palestine in 1918 related: 'The Australian pilot then went for one of the next two 'planes, and sent the selected machines crashing to the ground between Burin and Tulkeram. The other Australian having shot down the two-seater in the Hanutah area, joined his comrade in the "**dogfight**".' (Adelaide *Register*, 31 August, p. 8)

egg

A slang word for an aerial bomb. The first evidence recorded in the *OED* is from 1917. It sometimes also referred to a sea mine in British Royal Navy slang. Australian soldiers primarily appear to have used it in reference to an aerial bomb. This is one of several terms used during the war that reflect the advent of aerial bombing. The dropping of aerial bombs was sometimes referred to as 'laying **eggs**'.

A 1918 review of a book by a British Flying Corps airman in an Australian newspaper noted: 'Bombs, by the way, are "**eggs**" in the language of the air.' (*Shepparton Advertiser* 30 May, p. 1) An Australian soldier, writing to the *Sydney Stock and Station Journal* from the Middle East in 1917, said: 'To add to our discomfort, Taubes come flying over us and drop bombs—a proceeding known throughout the army as "laying **eggs**".' (16 March, p. 5)

flaming onions

This was a term for a particular type of incendiary shell used by the Germans. Such shells were used to direct German anti-aircraft artillery to aeroplanes. In appearance, they looked like a string of fireballs.

The *Bairnsdale Advertiser and Tambo and Oreo Chronicle* describing the life of 'a man at the front' wrote of the airman:

> But the airmen live in a cleaner atmosphere, in spite of shrapnel barrages and **flaming onions**, which, after all, are more fearsome than deadly. **Flaming onions** are green balls of lighted phosphorous—said, by some, to be strung together in batches of a dozen or so on wires, which are fired at our airmen like rockets in hopes of them falling across their machines and setting them on fire. (20 July 1918, p. 3)

flat spin

A **flat spin** is a spin in which an aircraft descends in tight circles while not departing greatly from a horizontal attitude. It is later also used in a figurative sense meaning to be in an agitated state of mind.

A Sydney aviator, Lieutenant J.H. Butler, who had been fighting in Palestine, recounted for the newspaper: 'You can fly by the stars, but you are apt to do a **flat spin**—the nose of the machine spins round out of control, does the lead-leaf act, and after falling about 500 feet, you finish with a spinning nose dive. Not too pleasant. It happened once to me.' (*Richmond Guardian*, 19 October 1918, p. 6)

flip

A trip, usually a short one, in an aeroplane was sometimes known as a **flip**.

Flip was explained for an Australian audience in an article about service slang: 'A pilot never announces his intention of making a flight in such commonplace parlance; he tells his companions that he is "off for a **flip** upstairs".' (Perth *Daily News*, 23 January 1919, p. 4)

full-out

A pilot who was very keen to fly was sometimes referred to as (a) **full-out**. During the war, an aeroplane that was going at full throttle was sometimes described as going *full out*, and the term likely derived from this.

In 1918, an article on flying observed that: 'The nerve strain of flying is enormous, but people who are "**full out**" and really fond of it are not constantly aware of it—fortunately.' (*Cairns Post*, 19 September, p. 3) A 1919 article on 'service slang' noted that **full-outs**, 'it need scarcely be said, usually succeed in getting themselves disliked, especially by junior officers, who are consequently expected to evince a similar enthusiasm in their country's defence and welfare'. (Perth *Daily News*, 23 January, p. 4)

ground strafe

A term for a low-flying attack made on gun positions, trenches, or transports, or the practice of doing this. One of the quotes below suggests that this kind of attack might also sometimes be called a **ground stunt**.

A report on British and Australian fighting in France in August 1918 recorded the following: 'Our airmen were "**ground strafing**" all day, and caught a transport column in a cutting.' (*Farmer and Settler*, 27 August 1918, p. 2) A member of the Australian Flying Corps wrote a description for the Brisbane newspaper the *Queenslander* of 'what is known as a "**ground strafe**" or "**ground stunt**" '. He described part of this action thus: 'A party of infantry and transport is proceeding slowly along a road. Down goes my nose, and I put a burst into them from my machine gun, and they scatter and take cover—one on a horse is thrown.' (5 April 1919, p. 17)

hedge-hopping

To fly very low, and therefore to be so low as to appear to be hopping over hedges. This term was first recorded during the Great War.

An account published in Australia explained the manoeuvres employed by the fliers of the Australian Flying Corps:

> 'Hedge-hopping' is the art of flying low and following the contours of the country only a few feet from the ground. This necessitates 'zooming' over hedges and other obstacles, then dropping back to the low altitudes. It is a dangerous pastime, as the slightest error in judgment will inevitably result in a bad crash. (Perth *Daily News*, 3 January 1919, p. 5)

nose dive

A term for a rapid descent of an aeroplane. Now Standard English, and also used figuratively, it was first used just before the war and popularised during the war.

Familiar to flyers, this term was used often in descriptions of aerial combat. A story of aviator Lieutenant H.H. Turk—an Australian serving in France—and his experience of aerial combat noted his coolness and self-control: 'While aloft, he descried a hostile 'plane, and, detaching himself from the squadron, he immediately gave chase. ... After a period of fighting he forced one of the enemy machines to descend, but had the misfortune to have his steering controls shot away, and his machine, deprived of its rudder, made a spinning **nose dive** towards the earth.' (*Cairns Post*, 4 December 1916, p. 2)

pancake

A term used to describe the emergency landing of an aeroplane. It pre-dated the war, but is mentioned in various accounts of flying slang during the war years.

An account of fighting in France in 1914 reported in the Australian press described a pilot of the British Royal Flying Corps having to land his plane behind enemy lines: he 'managed to "**pancake**" his machine down to earth'. (*Kalgoorlie Miner*, 28 September, p. 5)

side-slip

A term for a sideways motion of an aeroplane. Recorded from before the war (1911) as a noun, it was used in descriptions of flying and aerial combat during the war.

C.E.W. Bean, writing of the exploits of Australian airmen in the Royal Flying Corps, included the following description of aerial combat:

> In one of these raids opposite Ypres the airman approached a German balloon which was being drawn down under such a barrage of fire that it seemed impossible to get near it. By the time he was over it was within 300 feet of the ground. In the midst of the barrage he pretended that one of the shells had hit him, and came **side-slipping** down towards the earth. (Perth *Western Mail*, 4 January 1918, p. 35)

spin

A term for a steep descent of an aeroplane that, according to the *OED* definition, 'describes a helix at an angle of attack greater than the stalling angle.'

A 1916 collection of flying slang noted: 'A "**spin**" is perhaps the most unpleasant sensation possible in mid-air. It usually occurs, after over-banking, with the result that the aeroplane spins around like a top, and finally crashes to earth.' (*Globe and Sunday Times War Pictorial*, 17 June 1916, p. 1) Sometimes the manoeuvre was used as a trick, as suggested by this account by F.M. Cutlack: 'Three others [enemy planes] attacked one Australian machine, which descended with a **spin**, affecting to be out of control, escaped, and flew home.' (Broken Hill *Barrier Miner*, 31 March 1918, p. 4)

stunting

A term for the performing of flying tricks or aerobatics. It is first recorded in 1914.

Flight-Lieutenant George Walsh, wrote home to his parents in Toowoomba, Queensland, about his flight experiences: 'Straight flying, of course, gives little sensation, but "**stunting**" does. However, one gets used to it, and it becomes second nature.' (*Catholic Press*, 27 June 1918, p. 50)

Naval slang

The language of the Royal Australian Navy (RAN) is difficult to trace for this early period. While the British Royal Navy and the Merchant Navy had many of their own words and phrases, and these were likely shared, at least in part, by Australian sailors, these words are hard to trace in the printed evidence, especially in a purely Australian context. As Sidney Baker argues, in his book *The Australian Language*, 'Australian and English naval traditions are closely akin', and, as a result, 'the Australian sailor used a good deal of the slang originated by the English sailor'. (p. 183)

The Australian navy, which at this time was very small, functioned as part of the British Royal Navy during the Great War. The RAN was established in 1911, with the centrepiece being the battle cruiser HMAS *Australia* which was commissioned as the flagship of the RAN in October 1913. The HMAS *Sydney* famously sank the German ship SMS *Emden* in 1914. The RAN played an important role in providing support and convoy duties throughout the war, undertaking patrols as part of the blockade of Germany, and undertaking some anti-submarine warfare.

Naval slang occasioned some commentary in the British and Australian press during the war, although never as much as did Flying Corps slang. One article observed: 'Sailors, as everyone knows, are of a race apart, and, this being the case, they naturally speak a language of their own—a language which in some respects would sound strange and uncouth to the average "long-shore loafer", as Jack dubs anyone who has not been initiated into the mysteries of the sea as practised in the Royal Navy.' (*Albury Banner and Wodonga Express*, 3 January 1919, p. 20) Another article noted the language of the Navy as being 'to the shore-going ear ... both uncouth and bewildering'. (*Malvern Standard*, 11 October 1919, p. 5)

A 1915 article on the slang of JACK TAR (the popular name for a British sailor, dating back to the eighteenth century), commented that 'Jack Tar has a language all his own', and proceeded to describe a number of the vocabulary items that made up this language. One of the most prolific source of naval slang terms was food: 'Tinned beef is ironically known as "the accident", baked meat as "the burnt offering", and vegetables as a "schooner on the rocks", while "Fanny Adams" has been for ages the nickname of tinned mutton.' The author also noted the terms *flogging the cat* for what he described as a grumbler's 'growlings', and to *lie under the truck* referred to a spell of bad temper. (*Wyalong Advocate and Mining, Agricultural and Pastoral Gazette*, 31 July, p. 7)

Another article on 'lower deck slang' similarly recorded a range of slang terms for food:

> Meat in a dish without 'trimmings' is denominated a '*straight-rush*', and if a bluejacket does not fancy his dinner sufficiently well to eat it he '*gives it a march past*'. Plum-pudding is '*figgy duff*'; bloaters are called '*Spithead pheasants*', '*dead marines*', or '*two-eyed steaks*'; whilst a kipper is 'a *half-timer*', blancmange '*chicken fool*', tapioca pudding '*squeaker*', and cabbages, etc., '*bunny's meat*'. (*Gundagai Independent and Pastoral, Agricultural and Mining Advocate*, 17 October 1918, p. 7)

And yet another article noted the terms *ordinary seaman's delight* for sausage, *humming bird* for a bloater fish, and *wardroom end* for rump steak. (*Malvern Standard*, 11 October 1919, p. 5)

A variety of terms for the various positions in the Navy were also to be found, argued the author of the 1918 article reprinted in the *Gundagai Independent and Pastoral, Agricultural and Mining Advocate*:

> The captain of a warship is known as '*the owner*' to all under him, whilst the commander—who ranks next the captain—is '*the bloke*.' '*Number one*' or the '*first luff*' is the first lieutenant. '*Flag Jack*' means the flag-lieutenant to an admiral. '*Gunnery Jack*' is a ship's gunnery-lieutenant. '*Torps*,' her torpedo officer. '*Padre*,' '*the sky pilot*,' and '*Holy Joe*' are all three of them nicknames for the chaplain. Mid-shipmen are called '*snotties*,' and the paymaster, '*the pusser*'—pusser being the old title of officers belonging to the accountant branch. (17 October 1918, p. 7)

A few other terms used by the British Royal Navy during the Great War, although they have not been traced in the wartime Australian evidence except in articles about naval slang, include: *doohickey*, first recorded in naval slang, this word for 'any small object; a thingummy' became popular; *dibby*, 'a spoon'; *hostilities*, 'a sailor who has joined the Navy for the period of the war only'; *hunting flotilla*, 'a flotilla of destroyers engaged in submarine-hunting', found in Australian news reports from Britain; *poultice walloper*, 'a sick-berth attendant', there is some evidence that this was also used for those who worked in the British Royal Army Medical Corps; *rag-tearer*, 'a naval signalman', also referred to as a *bunting-jerker*; and *shave irons*, 'service chevrons'.

These wartime articles and summaries suggest that the naval slang of the Great War was rich, but it remains elusive to the modern lexicographer. While Australian sailors may well have known many of these terms, our ability to trace contemporary usage is somewhat limited.

Many of the terms discussed below are either particularly well-known general terms, such as JACK TAR, or are official terms of the war reported on in the Australian press, such as DAZZLE PAINT. They are therefore not as revealing of the culture of the average sailor as we might like, but they do suggest something of the impact on the Australian vocabulary of the emerging Australian navy and its participation in global affairs during the Great War.

bluejacket

A term for a sailor, used in the British Navy and taken up and used in the Australian Navy. It dates back to the eighteenth century.

The *Singleton Argus* noted in 1915: 'A young **bluejacket** on H.M.A.S. Australia, writing to his parents, says the ship in three months has travelled 40,000 miles, which is rather a remarkable record even for the British Navy.' (22 June, p. 1) An article from 1916 described the modern naval personnel: 'The modern **bluejacket** must be a well-educated man, particularly if he wants to obtain promotion.' (Adelaide *Register*, 1 July, p. 6)

dazzle paint

A term for the camouflage paint applied to ships during the war. A 1919 article explained:

> Dazzle-painting, the art of disguising ships at sea, was invented by Lieut.-Commander Norman Wilkinson, O.B.E., R.N.V.R. As is now well known, it dismissed the hope of making ships invisible, and aimed at a distortion of hulls, bridges, &c., in order to confuse the enemy submarine into erratic shooting, and to prolong his observations, giving thus a chance to the attacked to spot its danger and possibly of tackling the submarine with its guns. (Adelaide *Register*, 21 July, p. 2)

Another article from 1919 noted the ships that had been **dazzle painted** in Sydney Harbour for the war were being restored to their normal appearance, and noted that some would likely regret the removal of the paint: 'To see a great liner in her camouflage was to be reminded of a very dignified and imposing lady reluctantly masquerading at a fancy dress ball in a fantastic futurist costume.' (*Sydney Morning Herald*, 2 September, p. 6) These ships were sometimes known as *dazzle ships* or *dazzled ships*.

Fanny Adams

A term for the tinned or potted meat served on ships. It probably derives from *Fanny Adams*, a girl who was murdered in 1867 and her body butchered. There is also likely a connection with *F.A.*, 'fuck all'. It was a popular naval slang term.

A 1915 article on life aboard a troopship noted: '[T]he hot savoury dinner of the first day or two gives way for good to bully beef of great resisting properties, "**Fanny Adams**", and tinned unmentionables, garnished with sad-looking preserved spuds.' (*Berwick Shire News and Pakenham and Cranbourne Gazette*, 23 June, p. 4)

hush-hush ship

A ship so named because its details were secret during wartime.

An Australian 1919 newspaper report noted: 'The aeroplane ship is the natural outcome of the old seaplane carrier. It is popular to talk of such ships as **"Hush! Hush!" ships**.' (Perth *Daily News*, 5 February, p. 7)

Jack Tar

A term for a British sailor. It was well-known to Australians, and dates back to the eighteenth century. There was no equivalent term for an Australian sailor during the Great War, although **Jack Tar** was sometimes applied to them.

A newspaper report in August 1915 noted a Western Australian sergeant, who had been at Gallipoli, paying 'a high tribute to the **Jack Tar**, who landed the Australians at Gaba Tepe'. (Adelaide *Register*, 26 August, p. 10) A British naval captain commented in 1916 on Australian sailors: 'We cannot yet rap into their heads that everything on board a warship has to be done by schedule, and that if a particular duty is down to be done at a particular hour, it must be done then or else it will put the whole routine of the ship out of order. That is the difficulty we have to contend with with the Australian **Jack Tar**.' (Ipswich *Queensland Times*, 9 June, p. 6) A 1919 article on 'Grand Fleet slang' warned, however, never to call a navy man a '**Jack Tar**' as it was an insulting term. (*Malvern Standard*, 11 October, p. 5)

mucko

An able seaman was sometimes called a **mucko**, from the idea that they engaged in work that was *mucky*.

An article in the *Singleton Argus* noted that sailors preferred not to be called JACK TARS and would rather be a ' "matelot" (or "**mucko**" more often), and he doesn't mind the collective use of "Jack Tars" when applied to him and his mates, but he certainly does resent being hailed by utter strangers as "Jack" '. (13 October 1917, p. 2)

panic party

A term for a group of crew members assigned to pretend to leave a ship in a panic in order to fool the enemy. Q SHIPS were the ships used for this tactic.

The activities of the Q SHIPS were widely reported in the Australian press. A story about the winning of a Victoria Cross by a New Zealander who helped to sink a submarine had a fellow New Zealand crew member describing the event: 'About two minutes later the submarine opened fire, the time being then 8.40 p.m. She fired three shells over us, and then to their credit be it said, waited until our **panic party** had launched the boat and pulled clear of the ship, after which the submarine started to shell us in earnest.' (*Kalgoorlie Miner*, 25 June 1919, p. 6)

Q ship

A **Q ship** was a merchant ship with concealed weaponry used to lure submarines into surfacing to attack. They were sometimes also known as *mystery ships* or *trap ships*. Wilfred Granville in his *A Dictionary of Sailors' Slang* (1962) explains: 'Guns were concealed under dummy hatches and deck houses. When a U-boat signalled her to stop and abandon ship, a boat with a panic party left the **Q-ship** and rowed off to a safe distance. On board remained the gun's crews, closed up, waiting for the order to open fire on the submarine when—as usually happened she came nearer. When the U-boat presented the right target position she was sometimes sunk or very severely damaged by the Q-ships' fire.' Granville also argues that the 'Q' comes from the Latin *quaere*, enquire.

A 1919 news report on Commander C.G. Matson, who had links to Melbourne, noted that during the war he 'was employed by the Admiralty in connection with the mysterious **"Q" ships** which did so much towards vanquishing the German U boats'. (Broken Hill *Barrier Miner*, 8 February, p. 10)

shovel engineer

A humorous term for a stoker, the person responsible for feeding and tending a furnace on board ship.

A newspaper article from 1916 had this to say of naval stokers:

Of these 'others' none has a better claim to be lifted from the obscurity which enshrouds the 'unwritten and unsung' than the naval stokers, whose splendid work, done under the most trying conditions, has been a material factor in winning the victories afloat that have come to us during the war. Stokers are not 'bluejackets'—that term applies to sailors only—but there are more stokers than sailors aboard some of his Majesty's ships. Nor, by your leave, are stokers to be described as 'the black squad,' for that appellation belongs to the firemen of the mercantile marine. 'Clinker-knockers' and '**shovel engineers**,' if you like, but not 'black squad' unless you wish to give offence. (*Maitland Weekly Mercury*, 5 August, p. 16)

theatre ship

A ship especially equipped to provide theatrical entertainment to sailors.

The phenomenon was reported on in the Australian papers in 1917. One paper noted:

Apropos of amusement for the Fleet, a correspondent sends a satisfactory report of the efforts made in somewhat difficult circumstances. 'The larger ships are even, many of them, fitted up with their own cinematograph, and there is also a **theatre ship** with stage and every other contrivance complete, which goes the round of the other craft, and pulls up alongside, so that officers and men may go aboard to enjoy the performance.' (Orange *Leader*, 21 December, p. 1)

Aussieland, the diggers' home sweet home: Home and home front

CHAPTER

10

Soldiers had mixed feelings about home and the home front, expressed in some of the slang terms examined in this chapter. The home front, too, had a range of terms that helped to define their wartime experiences.

Home was for many soldiers a source of emotional support, signified in letters and parcels received. In soldier culture, home was often highly sentimentalised. Historians have examined how dreaming of home could often be essential to a soldier's psychological well-being and survival. Many soldiers in their letters, diaries, and soldier publications, expressed their desire to return to what they often called the 'Sunny land of the South', AUSSIELAND. They also hoped for a visit to BLIGHTY (England), another 'home' with which many soldiers identified. Most of all they wished for a return to CIVVIES.

But aspects of home could also incur the resentment of many soldiers. For example, SHIRKERS and SLACKERS were frequently criticised by soldiers (especially in a volunteer army), as well as by those on the home front. Along with the targets of complaint mentioned in the chapter on BRASS HATS, these figures were much reviled by many soldiers.

At home, civilians became familiar with many of the terms already examined in this book through the press, through letters from their loved ones who were serving, and through soldier publications sent home to family members. As they read about the war in these various sources, they became familiar with the language of death, weapons, and military life.

Some terms generated during the war reflected the particular home front experience. The debate over conscription, for example, tore Australian communities apart as strong feelings for and against the introduction of conscription were stirred up: ANTIS—those opposed to conscription—were targeted by those who thought conscription should be introduced. Two conscription referendums were held, but the introduction of conscription was defeated both times. The divisive and heated politics of war also saw terms such as RED-RAGGER being used, as well as words such as SHIRKER and SLACKER that were also used by soldiers. Those who morally objected to the war were often dismissed as CONCHIES or might be given a WHITE FEATHER. Many of these terms were thus highly charged with political meaning during the war years.

The war also made its mark in other ways. Efforts on the home front were important. ANZAC BUTTONS were purchased to raise funds for soldiers, and some women became involved in war work and were known as SISTER SUSIES. One of the lasting impacts of the war on Australian society and culture is reflected in the language surrounding commemoration. ANZAC DAY, from 1916, became a sacred day for many Australians as it became an occasion for collective mourning, and ANZAC DAY MARCHES and ANZAC SERVICES have been held since 1916.

anti

An abbreviation of **anti-conscriptionist**; in the context of the Great War, this was someone opposed to conscription. In Australia, conscription—compulsory military service—was bitterly contested during the war and was a divisive political issue. Britain introduced conscription in January 1916, and New Zealand in May 1916. Two conscription referendums were held in Australia, the first in October 1916 and the second in December 1917. In both referendums, the popular vote narrowly rejected the introduction of conscription. **Anti** and **anti-conscriptionist** were terms used to describe those who opposed conscription and who campaigned for the 'no' vote during the referendum campaigns.

Australian newspapers were filled with debates and discussion over conscription. The *Albury Banner and Wodonga Express* printed the following commentary criticising anti-conscription campaigners: 'The **anti-conscriptionists** appreciate their moral and numerical weakness, and they have set to work, with their evil propaganda, to win over to their side men and women against whose loyalty not a word can be said. They are, in short, inviting loyalists to desert and to become the confederates of the infamous I.W.W. [Industrial Workers of the World, known as the "Wobblies"].' (20 October 1916, p. 18) Another newspaper, the *Gilgandra Weekly*, quoted a Dubbo newspaper: 'The Dubbo "**Antis**" are bringing returned men to oppose the sending of reinforcements to relieve the war-weary men in the trenches and give them a furlough in Australia.' (7 December 1917, p. 6)

Soldiers voted in the conscription referendums, and some followed the debates closely. Stretcher-bearer William Slater, who was elected as a Victorian Labor State M.P. while serving overseas, was avidly interested in politics. He wrote in his diary after the second conscription referendum: 'Greatly elated to see that conscription looks like being defeated. I'm the only "**anti**" here out of six of us.' (Diary entry, 22 December 1917, *War Diaries of William Slater*, p. 67)

Anzac button

A button (or badge) bought in Australia to raise money for soldiers and returning veterans of the war. Such a button was often sold and worn on and around ANZAC DAY; the earliest references to **Anzac buttons** and Anzac Day show that the date (which came to

be 25 April, the anniversary of the Gallipoli landing) was not yet
settled, as suggested by the following quotation from a regional
Victorian newspaper:

> The various tents which administer so much to the comfort and
> care of our soldiers, whether in camp in the States, in Egypt, or
> at Gallipoli, being in need of assistance, the Lord Mayor's central
> button committee has fixed on to-day, Friday, 17th inst., as 'Anzac
> Day', and have issued a special 'remembrance button' to be sold
> throughout the Commonwealth at the usual price of one shilling,
> the proceeds to be divided between all the tents working for the
> welfare of those under arms ... . The Mayor was authorised to
> order 1000 **'Anzac' buttons**, which has been done. (*Gippsland
> Mercury*, 17 December 1915, p. 3)

Another sense of ANZAC BUTTON, referring to a nail used in place of a
trouser button, is also found in soldier slang. (See entry in Chapter
Two.)

Anzac Day

A day to commemorate Australian sacrifices at Gallipoli in 1915 was
observed from 1916, both on the home front and by soldiers. From
1927, all Australian states observed 25 April as a national public
holiday. During the war years, **Anzac Day** was both an opportunity
for remembering and grieving for loved ones who had been killed,
and a means of raising funds for soldiers still serving, or returned
and wounded veterans. New Zealand similarly observes **Anzac Day**.

In 1916, Australian soldier Roy Whitelaw wrote in a letter
home: 'Tomorrow (25th) will be **Anzac Day**, we will have a holiday
and sports and finish up at night with a concert. I will tell you all
about it in my next letter.' (Letter, 24 April, *Somewhere in France*,
p. 53) The troopship periodical *The Persique* commented on the
anniversary of Gallipoli two years later:

> Today we celebrate the third anniversary of the Landing on
> Gallipoli. To the Australian, it means more than the beginning
> of a campaign in a War of many campaigns. ... For on that day,
> we raised our claim for Nationhood. ... There is a tendency for us

to regard our adventures in a heroic light, but, when we realise
what the past three years have been to us, and what they have
been to the men who have fought throughout these years, it will
be less self-satisfaction that we celebrate **Anzac Day**. (No. 8,
25 April 1918, p. 1)

Anzac Day march

A march that takes place to commemorate ANZAC DAY. War veterans
participate in a march as part of the various ceremonies that take
place on the day.

London was the scene for early **Anzac Day marches,** as illustrated
in this quote: 'Brilliant sunshine prevailed to-day, and enormous
crowds assembled along the route of the **Anzac Day march** of the
Australian troops. Thousands thronged the precincts of Westminster
Abbey and cheered the troops.' (Launceston *Examiner*, 27 April
1916, p. 5)

Anzac leave

This was special leave given to Australian soldiers who had enlisted
in 1914, so that they could return home to Australia in 1918.

In 1918, a number of notices of the return of these soldiers
were published in the Australian press. The Adelaide *Advertiser*
noted the arrival of a number of soldiers: 'The arrivals consisted of a
dozen 1914 men on special "**Anzac**" **leave**, and about 75 invalided
soldiers, all of whom appeared to be well on the way towards recovery
from wounds or sickness. Relatives and friends were eagerly on the
lookout for them, and reunions of a most happy character were
witnessed.' (17 December, p. 7)

Anzac service

Also known as the **Anzac Day service**, this is a ceremony held on
ANZAC DAY to commemorate those lost at Gallipoli (and later to
honour all Australian war dead). The first service was held in 1916
on the first anniversary of the Gallipoli landing.

A piece in the Australian press just after Anzac Day in 1916 reported on the Cairo ceremonies: 'Thousands attended the **Anzac service**, including the Consuls and the Allies' representatives, and detachments of the Anzacs. The Bishop of Jerusalem presided. Messages were read from the Prime Minister of Australia, Hon. W.M. Hughes, and Senator Pearce.' (*North Western Advocate and the Emu Bay Times*, 27 April 1916, p. 1)

Aussieland

A variation of AUSSIE, 'Australia', this term first appeared at the end of the war.

An Australian soldier in France wrote home to say, 'Our chief topic of conversation these days is the early prospect of return to dear old **Aussie-land**. The mere thought of it sends thrills of joy through one, and, like children, we count the days to the time we leave these shores.' (*Shoalhaven News and South Coast Districts Advertiser*, 10 May 1919, p. 4) A troopship periodical contained a sentimental poem that included the following verse:

> Old Afric's shore is far behind,
> We're sailing o'er the foam;
> Upon our way to **Aussie land**,
> The Diggers' Home Sweet Home. (*The Boomerang*, New Year Number, 1920)

Blighty

The term **Blighty** came to have several different meanings during the Great War for Australian soldiers. It is an Anglo–Indian alteration of the Urdu word *bilāyatī*, meaning 'foreign, especially European', which in turn derived from the Arabic *wilayat*, 'province'. It was probably first used by the British Army when serving in India, but gained wide currency during the Great War meaning 'home' (England). Brophy and Partridge's gloss on **Blighty** in their *Songs and Slang of the British Soldier: 1914–1918* is evocative of the distance between the front lines and home: 'He [the soldier] had entered another, insane, existence, ugly, precarious, fatiguing, bearing hardly any resemblance to his normal life. ... **Blighty** to the soldier was a sort of faerie, a never-never land.'

For most Australian soldiers, **Blighty** was not home, but it did have special meaning for many who had family or were born in England. At the very least, a visit to **Blighty** offered a much appreciated respite from the front lines and military life. The term **Blighty leave** was also used by soldiers for a period of leave in England. Australian Roy Whitelaw wrote in a letter home to his family: 'It is very nice getting photos of you all, should I be lucky enough to get **Blighty leave** or go near any decent sized towns I will get my photo taken and send one along.' (Letter, 19 December 1916, *Somewhere in France*, p. 87) William Slater, a stretcher-bearer with the AIF, wrote in his diary: 'We get a surprise as a Blighty boat leaves and takes six from our ward but I am not among the fortunates. Talk about lead-swinging. It is one of the funniest things out to see all the fellows using their heads to get across to **Blighty** and I don't blame them either.' (Diary entry, 3 August 1917, *War Diaries of William Slater*, p. 44)

Another sense of BLIGHTY, as a wound severe enough to send a soldier to hospital in England, also came into currency during the war. (See entry in Chapter Six.)

civvies

This term for civilian clothing (also known as *mufti*, a term that dates back to the early nineteenth century) was part of British Army slang and dates back to the late nineteenth century. It was picked up and used widely during the war, including by Australian soldiers.

Advertisers in Australia made use of the term **civvies** in reference to clothing, as suggested in this advertisement dating from 1919:

> The good ships of transport bearing their precious freight of Australia's best sons, returned from duty done. Thousands of hearts leap forth in joy to greet them, and the delights of home-coming are mingled with thanksgiving for peace, as we see the eagerness of our boys to lay aside the stern habiliments of war and don their longed-for **civvies**. Hundreds of returned men when choosing peace time suits have proved the wisdom of the advice

to save time and money by going to Lance and Co.'s. (Lismore
Northern Star, 10 November, p. 4)

civvy

This term for a civilian, dating back to the nineteenth century, was
popular during the Great War. It is an abbreviation of *civilian*. The
related term CIVVIES is also used to refer to civilian clothing, and
more generally returning to civilian life ('returning to CIVVIES').

A soldier's poem from 1915, 'At the Dardanelles', which was
printed in an Australian newspaper, included the verse:

Sometimes we get some rooty,
The **civvies** call it bread,
It ain't as light as feathers,
And it ain't exactly bread. (*Queanbeyan Age*, 26 November, p. 5)

C.O.

Abbreviation of *conscientious objector*, a person who refused to serve
in the armed forces on the grounds of conscience. This abbreviation
was used in both England and Australia during the Great War. See
also CONCHY.

A 1916 newspaper piece from New South Wales revealed something of popular attitudes to conscientious objectors in Australia
during the war:

What is the conscientious objector? Well, he may be described as
a miserable waster who would sooner see his women ravished and
his children 'pinked' on the point of a bayonet rather than he should
take up arms in their defence. ... [One such man being interviewed
was asked] 'But suppose the Huns invade Australia? Won't you
fight to defend your womenfolk?' 'I shall not,' retorted the **C.O.**,
'if my women are murdered and outraged like the Belgians, it will
merely be the expression of God's will. I would not raise a finger
in their defence. I would rather die a martyr.' (*Cumberland Argus
and Fruitgrowers' Advocate*, 12 July 1916, p. 2)

cold foot

A term for a cowardly soldier, or a person who, although eligible for military service, fails to enlist. It comes from the American expression *to have cold feet*, around before the Great War. The term **cold foot** (also **cold footer** and the adjectival **cold-footed**) appears to be Australian, and was also used on the home front as an insult to men who had not enlisted or who supported anti-conscription. W.H. Downing's *Digger Dialects* records **cold footer** with the definition 'a *carpet knight*', a term for a stay-at-home soldier.

An Australian soldier wrote home from the front in 1918 to say: 'Our guns were sending over a few shells the other night, and the noise they were making made one wish he was a **cold-foot** back in dear old Ausy.' (*Cumberland Argus and Fruitgrowers' Advocate* 3 July, p. 3) The term **cold foot** was perhaps sometimes applied unfairly as this 1917 letter to the editor of the *Bendigo Advertiser* suggests: 'I have been much annoyed by the driver of a butcher's cart who calls me "**Cold-foot**", and asks me to enlist. I have offered and been rejected four times. This ought to protect me from further annoyance. If not I know what course to take.' (23 October, p. 4)

Cold footer is also well-attested in Australian sources. One writer quoted from a letter written by a Victorian officer in France: 'We are up to the knees in mud, real mud, remember; M-U-D that sticks to one closer than a **cold footer** in Australia to his comfortable job.' (*West Gippsland Gazette*, 14 August 1917, p. 5) A small item in the hospital periodical *The Harefield Park Boomerang* recorded a fictional argument between a soldier and a man at a race track: 'One of the mob of **cold-footers**, holding a race-card in his hand, addressed the soldier: "Who do you think will win the war, soldier"? he asked. "By the look of you mob," answered the returned man, "I should say Germany." ' (Vol. 2, No. 7, July 1918, p. 119)

The use of **cold-footed** to refer to someone cowardly (or at least not in the firing line) is attested in this quotation from the diary of Australian soldier Archie Barwick from May 1916: '3 of us got into a row over the saluting yesterday. I don't mind saluting a soldier, but hang these flash **cold-footed** crowd that hang well behind the firing line & have all the skite.' (*In Great Spirits: The WWI Diary of Archie Barwick*, p. 90)

conchy

Abbreviation of *conscientious objector*, a person who refuses to serve in the armed forces on the grounds of conscience. Like C.O., this was used in both Britain and Australia during the Great War. The variant spelling **conchie** also appears in the printed record.

As Australia did not introduce compulsory enlistment in the war (unlike Britain), there was less debate about those who identified as conscientious objectors. A 1919 commentary on war slang observed: 'To the uninitiated the slang word **conchy** might suggest some connection with a shell (of the sort found on the seashore, not on the battlefield), but in future dictionaries of slang he will find it explained as "conscientious objector".' (Brisbane *Queenslander*, 2 August, p. 41)

Another term for a conscientious objector, mentioned in Brophy and Partridge's *Songs and Slang of the British Soldier: 1914–1918* and A.G. Pretty's *Glossary of AIF Slang*, is *Cuthbert*. Pretty defines it as: 'A man with a cushy job in a government office, especially one who avoided military service on the score of occupation. Personal name supposedly suggestive of effeminacy.' Fraser and Gibbons in *Soldier and Sailor Words and Phrases* note that this term was coined by a cartoonist named Poy, who depicted Cuthberts as 'frightened looking rabbits'. While mentioned in these various war slang dictionaries, *Cuthbert* is not found in Australian evidence.

Coo-ee march

A recruiting march that began in the New South Wales town of Gilgandra and ended in Sydney, where men enlisted to serve in the AIF. Many such SNOWBALL MARCHES (as they were dubbed) were held through the war, including the KANGAROO MARCH. Such marches were one method employed to encourage enlistment, although they often had mixed results.

The *Gilgandra Weekly* noted in January 1916: 'Tooraweenah ... gathered all its beauty and its chivalry to wish God speed to the boys who were going out to fight for Australia, home and beauty. The **Coo-ee march** had emitted a spark that caused a huge conflagration of enthusiastic patriotism throughout the Commonwealth, and Tooraweenah, being very close to the emitting spark, caught alight like tow.' (14 January, p. 9)

Gallipoli Day

An early name for ANZAC DAY. It made direct reference to the men lost during the Gallipoli campaign.

The *Barrier Miner* newspaper described some of the celebrations for **Gallipoli Day** in the town of Broken Hill in 1916: 'A memorial procession will take place through the main streets of the city on Sunday next, and will be followed by a memorial service in the Proprietary Paddock, to commemorate the landing of the Australians on the Gallipoli Peninsula.' (17 April, p. 2) A month previously the same newspaper noted that one boy scout troop 'will march in the procession on **Gallipoli Day**'. (28 March, p. 3)

Kangaroo march

A recruiting march that began in the New South Wales town of Wagga Wagga and ended in Sydney, where men enlisted to serve in the AIF. The recruits were given the name *Kangaroos*. A number of such SNOWBALL MARCHES were held; see also COO-EE MARCH.

A notice in the *Goulburn Evening Penny Post* in December 1915 observed that the 'Kangaroo' recruits, who numbered over 200, were due to arrive in Goulburn. It informed readers that: 'Sergeants Cross and Coates, who recently returned from the front and have been giving some stirring addresses along the route of the **"Kangaroo" march**, will address a public meeting at Rogers' Corner on Saturday night.' (16 December, p. 4)

The Little Digger

A nickname given to Australian Prime Minister William 'Billy' Hughes during the Great War. Replacing Andrew Fisher, Hughes was Prime Minister from October 1915 until 1923. Hughes made particular use of the name in courting the returned soldiers' vote during the 1919 federal election campaign.

In a statement aimed at returned Australian soldiers published before the election in 1919, Hughes declared: 'You and your comrades have spoken of me as **"the little digger"** and "the friend of the soldier". Nothing that has come to me by way of good fortune, no honour bestowed upon me, has made me one half as glad and proud as to know that the men who have saved Australia think me worthy of their friendship.' (*Sydney Morning Herald*, 11 December, p. 8) A Sydney *Sunday Times* article from a few days later noted that the secretary of the Returned Soldiers' League thought that since Hughes had attended many soldiers' gatherings, 'there can be little doubt that **The Little Digger** has the soldiers at the back of him at this election'. (14 December, p. 2)

red-ragger

A term, usually derogatory, for a person who identified politically as a socialist or communist. This term is predominantly Australian, and first came into use a few years before the Great War. It refers to the red flags waved by those who supported revolutionary and left-wing political movements. During the war, the government was especially censorious of radical left-wing politics and there was a crackdown on organisations such as the Industrial Workers of the World (known as 'Wobblies').

Right-wing newspapers were especially condemnatory of radical politics as evidenced in the following commentary, typical of the time: ' "Anzacs of industrialism" is the name given to the **red-raggers** of Broken Hill in an appeal for funds to assist them to remain on strike, and also to hold up the making of munitions, to prolong the war, and cause unnecessary pain and death to our brave boys at the front.' (*Maryborough and Dunolly Advertiser*, 9 February 1916, p. 1)

shirker

This originally Australian and New Zealand English word refers to 'one who evades their responsibilities', and was used during the war specifically to refer to someone who failed to enlist. It was often used in the context of referring to someone who was in a particular job (for example, working in factories or in office jobs) and who used this as their reason for not enlisting to fight.

Attitudes towards **shirkers** were often damning, as the following letter to the editor from 1915 suggests:

> Under present conditions **shirkers** cannot be shifted, but at the close of the war another aspect will open. Our boys who have gone to the front (only some of them, maybe) will be returning, and then will be the time to deal with the **shirker**. Every business firm in Australia should see to it that no billet shall be held by a **shirker** that can be filled by a man who has served his country in its hour of need. (Melbourne *Argus*, 24 April 1915, p. 19)

Sister Susie

A term for a woman who was involved in war work, or who supported the war in some way. It appears to have particularly been used in reference to women who were involved in a broader patriotic effort beyond assisting immediate family members. It derived from a 1914 song by Herman Darewski and R.P. Weston, 'Sister Susie's Sewing Shirts for Soldiers', which referred to a Red Cross worker.

Australian newspapers published a short item in January 1915 noting the song's popularity and that it was a song for the women of Australia, as well as England. They speculated that it was becoming as popular as 'Tipperary', albeit 'more difficult to sing'. (*Camperdown Chronicle*, 21 January 1915, p. 6) Subsequently, the term gained some popularity in Australia to refer to women who supported the war effort, particularly through knitting socks for soldiers. In 1918, a newspaper item expressed concern that fewer women seemed to be engaged in this knitting due to the cost of wool: 'It is not that "**Sister Susie**" or the host of other woman friends or relatives of our soldiers have become tired of knitting socks, or are becoming neglectful of their soldier friends abroad. The trouble is that wool has reached a price beyond the scope of the average woman's purse.' (*Border Morning Mail and Riverina Times*, 24 May 1918, p. 3)

slacker

A term for someone who avoids work, **slacker** was used in Australia during the Great War in the same way as SHIRKER, to mean someone who evaded military service.

Sergeant Cyril Lawrence lamented in a letter home in November 1917 that: 'We can't go on for ever like this and the old Hun, drat him, is nothing like finished yet ... [the] world cannot afford to lose all these good and valuable lives whilst the **slackers** remain behind.' (Letter, 5 November, *Sergeant Lawrence goes to France*, p. 146) A Victorian politician, E.E. Heitman, enlisted in 1918. Giving a public address in Melbourne, he told his listeners that he 'had no sympathy for the war weary. ... He would rather lay down his life in the greatest cause the world had ever seen, and leave a noble heritage to his family, than be branded as a traitor and **slacker** in the hour of the nation's greatest need.' (Melbourne *Leader*, 11 May 1918, p. 25)

snowball march

A march held to encourage recruitment, particularly from rural areas. Specific **snowball marches** were held during the Great War, such as the COO-EE MARCH and KANGAROO MARCH.

A notice placed in the *Nhill Free Press* informed the public: 'The State Recruiting Committee is arranging to collect a number of volunteers in the Nhill and Kaniva districts, when plans will be made for a **snowball march** from Nhill to Melbourne to gather recruits.' (2 March 1917, p. 2)

white feather

Men who were not in uniform during the war were sometimes given a **white feather**, often by women. This signified their perceived cowardice. The use of a white feather to symbolise cowardice has a long history, dating back to at least the eighteenth century in Britain. The white feather was commonly used in Australia, as well as in Britain, during the Great War.

Feathers were sometimes given to men who were in fact soldiers wounded or on leave, or ex-soldiers. A piece in an Australian newspaper commented on this phenomenon:

> The idiotic practice of indiscriminately distributing **white feathers** appears to afford a peculiar pleasure to some people who have impudently taken on themselves the role of judging who should enlist for active service. If through an unfortunate lack of brains, this appears to them an effective means of aiding the recruiting movement, they might at least make enquiries as to whether their victims had not already offered to fight for King and country. (*Hamilton Spectator*, 2 August 1915, p. 4)

Conclusion
Recording and remembering the language of the soldiers of the Great War

ANNIE. — "Annie from Asia"; a Turkish gun emplaced on the Asiatic side of the Dardanelles which used to bombard the British lines at Cape Helles in 1915.

BEACHY. (or "Beachy Bill") The Turkish guns emplaced in the Olive Grove [Gallipoli] which caused considerable casualties at Anzac, mostly on the beaches.

N.B.G.   No bloody good.

ALLY SLOPERS CAVALRY.   the Army Service Corps

POMPEY.   The nickname given to Brig-Gen. Elliott of the 15th A'Bde [probably derived from "Pompey" Elliott, the well-known captain of the Carlton (Vic) Football Club].

SQUARE PUSHING.   see TRACKING SQUARE.

MALEESH   Arabic term much used by the Light Horse & troops in Egypt, in the same way as the troops in France adopted. SAN-FAIRY-AN.

NOBBY   Nickname usually given to men named Clarke. [of naval origin]

MADAMOISELLE FROM ARMENTIERES   The beginning of a ribald song much sung in France.

APRES LA GUERRE.   The reply usually given to embarrassing questions (especially from French mademoiselles); also the beginning of a soldier's song.

From near the beginning of the Great War, attempts were made to collect, record, translate, and interpret the new words and language that developed as a result of the war. As discussed in the introduction, many reports in the press reflected a fascination with the language generated by the war. In 1919, a reporter argued that: 'Somebody should compile a pocket dictionary of terms and expressions in common vogue amongst demobilised men, and so enable the average citizen to enjoy five minutes' conversation without conjecturing the meaning of five words in every six.' He added that at some point in the future, soldier slang might get into a dictionary: 'Meanwhile the civilian suffers through his lack of acquaintance with the military dialect.' (*Western Argus*, 9 December, p. 4) A returning soldier wondered what would become of 'the "rough stuff" that has served us so faithfully?' The author speculated that an 'enterprising "digger" may publish a selection of choice war words set to music for abuse in Australia'. (*The Dinkum Furf*, No. 3, June 1919, p. 1)

A number of dictionaries were indeed compiled in the aftermath of the war, and the language, especially the slang, of the war has continued to be a source of fascination for many. This book concludes with a brief history of these various dictionaries.

The first dictionaries of Great War slang

One of the first dictionaries of war slang to be published in the immediate aftermath of the war was W.H. Downing's *Digger Dialects*. Walter Hubert 'Jim' Downing (1893–1965) enlisted in the AIF in September 1915. Serving in the 57th Battalion, he saw action on the Western Front, and was awarded the Military Medal for his bravery at Polygon Wood. He returned to Australia in February 1919. He wrote a fictionalised memoir of his wartime experiences, *To the Last Ridge*; the publisher he first approached, Lothian, was uncertain as to whether they would publish it, and instead asked him to compile a dictionary of war slang which they thought would sell well. Downing agreed, and it was later said that he compiled the dictionary over a weekend. *Digger Dialects* appeared in 1919. *To the Last Ridge* followed in print in 1920. Downing went on to work as a solicitor, dying in 1965.

Downing's book was an extraordinary record of what he knew of soldiers' language in the Great War, compiled while his memory of the conflict was still fresh. J.M. Arthur and W.S. Ramson, who edited a new edition of it in 1990, called the dictionary in their introduction 'a major document of Australian social history', and commented that Downing was 'an extraordinarily acute observer of language in action'. Downing in his introduction to the volume saw the words he had gathered as reflective of the 'little communities' formed by the soldiers and their 'keen and vigorous mentality'.

Downing's dictionary contained many words, with often witty definitions. Some of the irony that marked later literary representations of the Great War can be seen in some of his definitions, but it is also an entertaining and socially perceptive dictionary. Most importantly, it helped to record many of the distinctively Australian terms in use during the war that might otherwise have been lost. Reviewers of the time were fascinated by the book. One reviewer commented that it reflected the 'Australian sense of humor, inventiveness, and mental picturesqueness' and demonstrated how soldiers had given a 'new vigor and terseness to the Australian language'. (*Dungog Chronicle*, 24 December 1919, p. 3)

Downing's book was a full dictionary. Other early collections of slang often appeared as appendices to memoirs of the war. One example of such a glossary was that included with Arthur Guy Empey's memoir *'Over the Top'*, published in 1918. Arthur Guy Empey, an American soldier in the US Cavalry, joined the British Expeditionary Force in 1915 after the sinking of the *Lusitania* and served as a machine gunner in France before being discharged after he was wounded at the Somme. He published a book about his experiences that was hugely popular, especially in the United States, and he was active in recruitment drives in the United States for the rest of the war. After the war ended, he wrote screenplays and a variety of pulp fiction.

The book included what he called 'Tommy's Dictionary of the Trenches', probably aimed at explaining the slang of the trenches to an American audience. Empey commented in a brief preface to the dictionary that he had 'gathered [the terms] as I lived with [Tommy Atkins] in the trenches and rest billets, and later in the hospitals in England where I met men from all parts of the line'. He added: 'Tommy is not a sentimental sort of animal so some of his definitions are not exactly complementary [sic], but he is not cynical and does not mean to offend anyone higher up.' (p. 281)

Empey's collection is relatively brief. He includes a lot of military 'technical' terms, including ranks. However, his definitions are often clever and distinctive, and conveying cynicism and humour in how he interpreted a term. Some of his glossary entries include:

> *aerial torpedo*—'A kind of trench mortar shell, guaranteed by the makers to break up Fritz's supper of sausages and beer'.

> batman—'A man who volunteers to clean a non-commissioned officer's buttons but who never volunteers for a trench raid. He ranks next to a worm.'
>
> char—'A black poisonous brew which Tommy calls tea.'
>
> D.C.M.—'Distinguished Conduct Medal. A piece of bronze which a soldier gets for being foolish.'
>
> R.I.P.—'It means "Rest in peace", but Tommy says like as not it means "Rest in pieces", especially if the man under the cross has been sent West by a bomb or shell explosion.'
>
> trench—'A ditch full of water, rats, and soldiers.'
>
> wire—'See barbed wire, but don't go "over the top" to look at it. It isn't safe.'

Empey also provides an interesting insight into how an American regarded life in the British Expeditionary Force, and how he regarded the language that was used.

Another early vocabulary compiled in the immediate aftermath of the war was the collection made by the staff of the Australian War Museum (now Australian War Memorial). The librarian of the Museum, Albert George "Pret" Pretty, compiled a *Glossary of Slang and Peculiar Terms in Use in the A.I.F.* The motivation for making this compilation is unknown; perhaps there was a desire to collect these slang terms as part of the collection of the records of the war, one of their major functions and aims, or perhaps there was an intention to publish it as part of C.E.W. Bean's *Official History* of the war then being written. It was never published (perhaps due to a number of 'vulgar' and confronting terms), but in 2001 I undertook some research on the manuscript, and put a version of both the original manuscript and an annotated edition online. Two draft manuscripts exist, the first dated April 1922, while the second is believed to have been produced in 1924.

Pretty's collection borrowed heavily from Downing's *Digger Dialects*, often providing some extra commentary or elaboration on Downing's entries. It is highly likely that Downing was the principal source (along with memory and personal experience), although not all of Downing's terms made it into Pretty's *Glossary*. Possibly terms were rejected because Pretty and fellow Museum staff members who assisted in the compilation, and who were veterans of the conflict, were not familiar with the terms. The *Glossary* does, however, contain a variety of other terms, including a number that were hand-written on the original 1922 typescript by A.W. Bazley, a staff member who assisted C.E.W. Bean in his *Official History* and who later became director of the Australian

War Memorial. John L. Treloar, the Museum's Director and a veteran of Gallipoli, also made contributions to the project.

Pretty's *Glossary*, like Downing's dictionary, is a valuable record of the language of the war as experienced by veterans of the conflict and compiled while the war was still a recent event. Its recording of a number of terms for which no other written evidence exists suggests the ephemeral nature of much wartime slang. It also makes the *Glossary* a record of the words and phrases that otherwise might have been lost. In particular, the willingness of both Downing and Pretty to include numerous 'vulgar' terms makes it an important historical document. Many of Pretty's collected terms have been mentioned throughout this book.

Internationally, the first significant dictionary of Great War slang was Edward Fraser and John Gibbons' *Soldier and Sailor Words and Phrases* published in 1925. In their preface, the editors note that the book was intended as a dictionary of war slang compiled at the direction of the Imperial War Museum. Public contributions were solicited in the making of the dictionary. The editors focused on many Service terms, a number of which pre-dated the war, and included words and phrases from Dominion and US military forces. Few Australianisms were included. Sidney Baker, Australian slang lexicographer, corresponded with the Imperial War Museum some years later, and confirmed that they had no knowledge of Downing's *Digger Dialects* when they compiled their collection. (*The Australian Language*, p. 160) Fraser and Gibbons' publication was widely reviewed, including in the Australian press, and was considered to be 'of the widest possible interest and of permanent value'. (*Cairns Post*, 2 July 1925, p. 8)

Brophy and Partridge and the 'war books boom'

The end of the 1920s and first years of the 1930s saw an outpouring of fiction, memoirs, and other writings about the Great War, a phenomenon which scholars have sometimes called the 'war books boom'. The war books boom produced a number of well-known accounts of the war that had lasting resonance in literary culture. They included Edmund Blunden's *Undertones of War* (1928), Robert Graves' *Goodbye to all That* (1929), Siegfried Sassoon's *Memoirs of an Infantry Officer* (1930), and Erich Maria Remarque's *All Quiet on the Western Front* (1929). Australian contributions to this genre included Leonard Mann's *Flesh in Armour*

(1932) and Frederic Manning's controversial book published anonymously under the title *The Middle Parts of Fortune* (1929) and in expurgated form as *Her Privates We* (1930).

Many of the books produced as a result of this small publication boom reflected on the war from the distance of some years, and many were critical of the war, and in particular military leadership. Some questioned the purpose of the war; others clearly were affected by social trends in the years following. Much of this critical literature was produced by those who had been officers and who were otherwise literary writers or poets.

One of the most significant of the Great War slang dictionaries was a collection compiled by two veterans of the war, and should be seen in the context of this literary output at the end of the 1920s. This was John Brophy and Eric Partridge's *Songs and Slang of the British Soldier: 1914–1918*. The first edition appeared in 1930.

Eric Partridge (1894–1979) would go on to be one of the twentieth century's foremost slang lexicographers. Born in New Zealand and educated in Australia and then Britain, Partridge credited the war as responsible for igniting his interest in language. He later argued that by enlisting as a private (he served both at Gallipoli and the Western Front), 'I learned more about Australian speech, about Australian English, than I could possibly have done as an officer'. (*Eric Partridge in His Own Words*, p. 47) He acknowledged that compiling *Songs and Slang* was a means of helping get the war 'out of my system', as was the writing of several other works, including a fictionalised memoir of the war and novels he wrote under the pseudonym Corrie Denison.

John Brophy (1899–1965) enlisted at the age of 14 and served on the Western Front as a private. After the war, he finished his education, and for a period, taught in Egypt. After returning to England, he took a job in advertising and then moved to writing. He published an autobiographical novel *The Bitter End* in 1928, and edited an anthology of soldiers' writings, *The Soldier's War*, in 1929; the latter contained a short glossary of military terms. Other publications followed, including his collaboration with Partridge.

Songs and Slang was published by Scholartis Press, Partridge's own imprint. In the preface to the first edition, the authors noted that if they had left the compilation of a book such as this one any longer, it would have been very difficult to collect the material. They argued that the glossary of words was to be 'not a mere dictionary-list, but a record-by-glimpses of the British soldiers' spirit and life in the years 1914–1918'.

(p. v) They acknowledged that the war had modified the English language considerably, and that the circumstances of the war had required a new vocabulary. (p. 186)

Two subsequent editions of *Songs and Slang* published by Scholartis—another in 1930 and one in 1931—added to the word-list of the first edition. With Partridge's growing interest in lexicography, a number of the etymologies for the slang terms were expanded or revised. The first edition, with many of the glosses to terms written by Brophy, reflected his pacifist leanings and bitterness towards the conflict. In many ways, the book echoed some of the themes presented in many of the more well-known literary productions of the period: fatalism, resentment of military hierarchy, and cynicism.

All of the dictionaries produced from the end of the Great War through to the 1930s were compiled by veterans of the conflict who drew on their personal experiences and memory (as well as those of their fellow veterans). All of these dictionaries serve as important cultural records. They were also important to their writers and editors: as Partridge suggested, this sort of work could be a form of catharsis, as well as a monument to their generation and fallen comrades.

Later war slang dictionaries

The Second World War and subsequent conflicts generated a variety of dictionaries and writings about the language of those conflicts. The Second World War led to a revived interest in the language produced by war, and included a glance back at the words generated by the previous conflict. One such collection was *The Soldiers' War Slang Dictionary: A List of Words & Phrases Used by British Soldiers in the Great War 1914–1918*, published in 1939 by T. Werner Laurie Ltd., and sold for sixpence. However, attention quickly turned to the new conflict, its new technologies, and a whole new vocabulary that was being generated. Eric Partridge turned his attention to the new words being produced by the events of the Second World War, which he wrote about in *Words at War, Words at Peace* (1948). Little new research was undertaken into the words of the earlier war. Sidney Baker produced the first edition of his influential *The Australian Language* in 1945, and asserted the importance of Australian words in helping to define Australian identity; the vocabulary of the Great War was briefly discussed, but he relied largely on Downing's *Digger Dialects*, and was more interested in the more recent Second World War.

Interest in the slang of the Great War waxed and waned in the decades following the end of the Second World War. In Britain, a revival of interest occurred in the 1960s, as a new generation rewrote the history of the conflict in a way that presented it as a futile, horrific, and pointless conflict in which a generation of young men were slaughtered due to the incompetence of the upper levels of the British military. The theatre and subsequent movie production of *Oh, What a Lovely War!* and popular histories such as Alan Clark's *The Donkeys* (1961) helped to promote this popular mythology.

In this context, a new edition of John Brophy and Eric Partridge's *Songs and Slang* appeared in 1965 under the title *The Long Trail: What the British Soldier Sang and Said in the Great War 1914–18*. Although Partridge by this stage was well known as Britain's foremost slang lexicographer, it was Brophy who did most of the work on the edition, which stripped back much of the commentary that had so distinguished the first edition. Brophy wrote a new preface, reflecting on how the generation who had fought the war were 'not the same people we were'. (p. 9) He presented his text as 'a document of social and military history', and wrote that the war was 'a war not only of physical endurance but of nervous and moral endurance'. (p. 13)

However, Brophy's pacifist and anti-war commentaries of the first edition were stripped out. This reflected the way in which many men of his age and generation, veterans of the conflict, reshaped their attitude towards the war. They didn't identify closely with the anti-war sentiments of the younger generation; rather, they identified with their veteran status and promoted their own knowledge and experience against what they saw as often inaccurate, popular portrayals. Many of the products of the 'war books boom' were rediscovered and reprinted, and unsurprisingly so was *Songs and Slang*. In addition, the book included many of the songs that appeared and were used in *Oh, What a Lovely War!* Brophy's new preface echoed the new emphasis by veterans on their ability to provide testimony and eye-witness evidence of the war.

In the 1990s an interest in the slang of the Great War again revived, reflecting the upsurge of interest that came with the last of the Great War veteran generation passing away. A new edition of Brophy and Partridge (the *Long Trail* version) was published in 2008, edited by Malcolm Brown and given the new title *The Daily Telegraph Dictionary of Tommies' Songs and Slang, 1914–18*. Brown, in his preface to this edition, regarded the book as 'a tribute to the indestructibility of the human spirit under the most demanding and challenging conditions'. It captured the 'forgotten voices of the First World War'. (p. vii) There were good things about the war, he argued, and 'this book is, among many other things, a notable memorial to them'. (p. xiv) Brown's preface reflected a new presentation of understanding of the war; it reflected the 'documentary' emphasis that the 1960s veterans emphasised, as well as reflecting the need to find 'forgotten voices', something that preoccupied a new generation of scholars studying the Great War. Brown saw the dictionary as a way into the demotic culture of the trenches, although he didn't mention the literary aspirations and milieu that influenced Brophy and Partridge in their original compilation.

The resurgence of interest in the Great War in the 1980s and 1990s included Australia, where no studies of the language of the war had appeared since Baker. Interest in Anzac revived, where it was reshaped to feed ideas of Australian nationalism. This happened alongside an interest in Australian English that resulted in the production of the *Australian National Dictionary* (1988), a dictionary of Australianisms. This created a context in which Australian soldier slang became a subject of considerable interest to lexicographers and historians. An edition of W.H. Downing's *Digger Dialects* was edited and annotated by J.M. Arthur and W.S. Ramson and published by Oxford University Press Australia in 1990. As mentioned in the discussion of Downing above, Arthur and Ramson were keen to demonstrate both the contribution made to Australian English by the Great War experience, and to make available what they considered to be 'a unique record of one of Australian English's most creative and crowded hours'.

Many of the more recent publications and collections looking at the slang of the Great War, which include my own work on the A.G. Pretty typescript and *Diggerspeak: The Language of Australians at War* (2005), along with overseas works such as Peter Doyle and Julian Walker's *Trench Talk: Words of the First World War* (2012), and Christopher Moore's *Roger, Sausage & Whippet: A Miscellany of Trench Lingo from the Great War* (2012), can be seen to be part of an ongoing interest in the cultural and social aspects of the war. They represent a continuing fascination with such a significant event in many nations' histories, boosted by the centenary anniversaries of the war.

BIBLIOGRAPHY

This bibliography includes all books referenced in the text. A guide to further reading on the Australian experience of the First World War and related topics can be found at the end of the Introduction.

Adam-Smith, Patsy, *The Anzacs*, Nelson, Melbourne, 1978.

The Anzac Book, Sun Books, South Melbourne, 1975.

Arthur, J.M. and W.S. Ramson, *W.H. Downing's Digger Dialects*, Oxford University Press, Melbourne, 1990.

Auchterlonie, Gloria (ed.), *Dad's War Stuff: The Diaries*, G. Auchterlonie, Morwell, 2001.

Baker, Sidney J., *The Australian Language*, Angus and Robertson, Sydney, 1945.

Baker, Sidney J., *The Australian Language*, Sun Books, Melbourne, 1981 [1966].

Barwick, Archie, *In Great Spirits: The WWI Diary of Archie Barwick*, Harper Collins, Sydney, 2013.

Bean, C.E.W., *Letters from France*, Cassell, London, 1917.

Bean, C.E.W., *The Story of Anzac: From 4 May, 1915 to the Evacuation of the Gallipoli Peninsula*, University of Queensland Press, St. Lucia, 1981.

Beeston, Joseph Lievesley, *Five Months at Anzac*, Angus and Robertson, Sydney, 1916.

Bell, A.D. (ed.), *An Anzac's War Diary: The Story of Sergeant Richardson*, Rigby, Adelaide, 1980.

Bloch, Henry Scharrer, *Diary of Henry Scharrer Bloch: Diary on Active Service No. 8496*, Carolyn Bloch and Beverly Threlfo, Sydney, 2010.

Brophy, John and Eric Partridge, *The Long Trail: What the British Soldier Sang and Said in the Great War of 1914–18*, Andre Deutsch, London, 1965.

Brophy, John and Eric Partridge, *Songs and Slang of the British Soldier: 1914–1918*, The Scholartis Press, London, 1931.

Campbell, Maurice and Graeme Hosken (eds), *Four Australians at War: Letters to Argyle, 1914–19*, Kangaroo Press, Kenthurst, 1996.

Coates, Albert E., *The Volunteer: The Diaries and Letters of A.E. Coates*, W. Graphics, Burwood, Vic., 1995.

Chandler, Mary J. (ed.), *'Dear Homefolk': Letters written by L.G. Chandler During the First World War*, M. Chandler, Redcliffe, Vic., 1988.

Christensen, Rachael (ed.), *To all my dear people: The Diary and Letters of Private Hubert P. Demasson 1916–1917*, Fremantle Arts Centre Press, Fremantle, 1988.

Crystal, David (ed.), *Eric Partridge in his Own Words*, Andre Deutsch, London, 1980.

Dinning, Hector, *By-ways on Service: Notes from an Australian Journal*, Constable, London, 1918.

Doyle, Peter and Julian Walker, *Trench Talk: Words of the First World War*, The History Press, Stroud, 2013.

Egan, Michael James, *The World War One Diary of Michael James Egan*, Self-published, Killarney Heights, 2011.

Falconer, John Harold, *On Active Service*, http://users.tpg.com.au/rnoakes/text/J%20Falconer%20WW%20I%20diary.htm

Fewster, Kevin (ed.), *Bean's Gallipoli: The Diaries of Australia's Official War Correspondent*, Allen and Unwin, St. Leonard's, 2007.

Fewster, Kevin (ed.), *Frontline Gallipoli: C.E.W. Bean, Diaries from the Trenches*, Allen and Unwin, St. Leonard's, 1983.

Fraser, Edward and John Gibbons, *Soldier and Sailor Words and Phrases*, George Routledge and Sons, London, 1925.

Gilding, Dorothy (ed.), *Letters from the Front*, Horizon Publishing Group, Sydney, 2012.

Goesch, Pamela (ed.), *Dear All: Letters from World War I—Bert Bishop*, Brynwood House, Sydney, 2010.

Granville, Wilfred, *A Dictionary of Sailors' Slang*, Andre Deutsch, London, 1962.

Green, Jonathon, *Green's Dictionary of Slang*, Chambers, London, 2010.

Harding, Edward, *Stanley Harding World War One Letters: Father—Soldier—Farmer, 1893–1968*, Harding family, Nathalia, 1995.

Hartt, Cecil, *Diggerettes: Digger Jokes and Stories*, A.C. Sandford, Sydney, 1919.

Hogue, Oliver, *Trooper Bluegum at the Dardanelles: Descriptive Narratives of the More Desperate Engagements on the Gallipoli Peninsula*, Andrew Melrose, London, 1916.

Howell, Arthur G., *Signaller at the Front: The War Diary of Gunner Arthur G. Howell*, Hesperian Press, Carlisle, WA, 2001.

Ingle, Judith (ed.), *From Duntroon to the Dardanelles: A Biography of Lieutenant William Dawkins*, J. Ingle, Canberra, 1995.

Kelshaw, Jean and Bruce Thornton, *Born to be a Soldier: War Diary of Lieutenant John G. Ridley M.C. World War I, 1914–1918*, Baptist Historical Society of New South Wales, Macquarie, 2010.

Knyvett, R. Hugh, *'Over There' with the Australians*, Charles Scribner's Sons, New York, 1918.

Laseron, Charles Francis, *From Australia to the Dardanelles: Being Some Odd Pages from the Diary of Charles Francis Laseron, Sergeant in the 13th Battalion, Australian Imperial Forces*, John Sands, Sydney, 1916.

Lay, Maxwell G. (ed.), *Edward Lay's First World War Diary*, Self-published, Bulleen, 2009.

Letters from Bert Smythe, www.smythe.id.au/letters/index.htm

Letters from Percy Smythe, www.smythe.id.au/letters/index.htm

Letters from Viv Smythe, www.smythe.id.au/letters/index.htm

Mant, G. (ed.), *Soldier Boy: The Letters of Gunner W.J. Duffell 1915–18*, Spa Books, Stevenage, 1992.

Mills, Frederick J., *Dinkum Oil: A Volume of Original Wit and Humour*, W.K. Thomas, Adelaide, 1917.

Moberley, Gertrude F., *Experiences of a 'Dinki Di' R.R.C. Nurse*, Australasian Medical Publishing Company, Glebe, 1933.

Moore, Christopher, *Roger, Sausage and Whippet: A Miscellany of Trench Lingo from the Great War*, Headline, London, 2012.

Nixon, Allan M. (ed.), *Somewhere in France: Letters to Home—the War Years of Sergeant Roy Whitelaw 1st AIF*, The Five Mile Press, Fitzroy, 1989.

Orchard, Arthur (ed.), *Diary of an Anzac: The Front Line Diaries and Stories of Albert Arthur 'Bert' Orchard*, Self-published, Tasmania, 2009.

Orsman, H.W. (ed.), *The Dictionary of New Zealand English: A Dictionary of New Zealandisms on Historical Principles*, Oxford University Press, Auckland, 1997.

Osborn, Jim, *The War Diaries of Sergeant Jim Osborn: The Great War 1914–18*, Jack Osborn and Julie Cattlin, Melbourne, 2010.

Oxford English Dictionary, online edition, www.oed.com

Papers of Lieutenant A.E. Sheppeard, 2DRL 10956, Australian War Memorial Collections.

Papers of Private Henry (Harry) Thomas Cadwallader, PR01199, Australian War Memorial Collections.

Partridge, Eric, *A Dictionary of RAF Slang*, Pavilion Books, London, 1990 [1945].

Partridge, Eric, *Words at War, Words at Peace*, Frederick Muller, London, 1948.

Partridge, Eric and Paul Beale, *A Dictionary of Slang and Unconventional English*, 8th edition, Routledge and Kegan Paul, London, 1984.

Paul, Winsome McDowell, *Blessed with a Cheerful Nature: A Reading of the Letters of Lieutenant George Stanley McDowell M.C. 13th Battalion AIF*, Bellevue Heights, South Australia, 2005.

Potter, Noel, *Not Theirs the Shame Who Fight: Edited Selections from the WWI Diaries, Poems, and Letters of 6080 Private R.C. (Cleve) Potter*, Ginninderra Press, Charnwood, 1999.

Pretty, A.G., *Glossary of Slang and Peculiar Terms used in the A.I.F.*, unpublished manuscript, available online at http://andc.anu.edu.au/australian-words/aif-slang

Ramson, W.S. (ed.), *The Australian National Dictionary: A Dictionary of Australianisms on Historical Principles*, Oxford University Press, Melbourne, 1988.

Skeyhill, Tom, *Soldier Songs from Anzac: Written in the Firing Line*, George Robertson, Melbourne, 1916.

Slater, Helen and David Widdowson (eds), *The War Diaries of William Slater*, Astrovisuals, Strathmore, 2000.

Smythe Family Letters, *World War I Letters from the Trenches*, www.smythe.id.au/letters/index.htm.

Treloar, J.L., *An Anzac Diary*, Cambridge Press, Newcastle NSW, 1993.

Whiteside, Thomas Clair, *A Valley in France*, E. Whiteside, Beaconsfield, 2002.

Wilmington, Margaret (ed.), *Alfred Robert Morison Stewart: Diaries of Unsung Hero*, Self-published, 1995.

Young, William Campbell, *Anderson Inlet Inverloch: World War I Diary of William Campbell Young*, Inverloch Historical Society, Inverloch, 1999.

Yule, Peter (ed.), *Gallipoli Diary of Sergeant Lawrence of the Australian Engineers, 1st AIF, 1915*, Melbourne University Press, Melbourne, 1981.

Yule, Peter (ed.), *Sergeant Lawrence Goes to France*, Melbourne University Press, Melbourne, 1987.

WORD LIST

Items in bold are words with their own entry; items in italics are slang terms otherwise referred to in the text.